Never give up
on a
Dream!

Linda Raker

Beyond the Journey

LINDA RAKOS

authorHOUSE®

AuthorHouse™
1663 Liberty Drive
Bloomington, IN 47403
www.authorhouse.com
Phone: 1 (800) 839-8640

Published by AuthorHouse   04/21/2016

ISBN: 978-1-5049-8310-5 (sc)
ISBN: 978-1-5049-8308-2 (hc)
ISBN: 978-1-5049-8309-9 (e)

Library of Congress Control Number: 2016903716

Print information available on the last page.

To Ron, Jamie, Kris

The best parts of my journey

Chapter One

The asphalt road snaked through hillsides colored in variable spring greens, from the deep green of the Douglas firs to the pale green of newly budding cottonwoods. The sense of stillness was broken by the wind in the trees, luminescent with green buds anxious to pop into leaf. Any day now the meadows would burst forth with an explosion of wild spring colors.

Austin Smith stopped on the ridge and gazed out over the rolling hills of grass and sagebrush. The distant mountains looked majestic and unyielding, so serene and undisturbed in their magnificence. The effect on Austin was powerful. He wanted no problems, no worries, and no memories. Just this moment, nothing more. Mesmerized, Austin continued to stare until the chilly wind made him shiver.

He turned away from the view and continued hitch-hiking. An approaching car slowed down as it drew near. Like the others it passed by, dashing Austin's hopes. He sighed heavily. One after another they all passed him by.

The sky had turned from a deep blue to a vivid pink as the sun dropped lower and lower behind the mountains. Austin was tired by the time the lingering sunset faded, too tired to see the enormous panorama of stars arched above, undimmed by city lights.

It was late by the time Austin wandered into the next town. He was fatigued and hunger pains were a constant reminder that he hadn't eaten all day. A neon sign flashing "Wild West Grill" caught his attention. Pushing the door open he looked for a place to sit. A waitress, wearing jeans and a denim shirt, stood at the cash register talking with a customer. Both looked up. The waitress nodded in his direction and grabbed a menu from beside the till. "Sit where you like. I'll be right with you," she called out pleasantly.

Eyeing an empty booth against the wall, he walked past local customers. Austin dropped heavily into the booth, turned to gaze out the window and saw a forlorn soul reflected in the glass. The lines on the face were deeply drawn. Weariness had taken its toll.

After the waitress took his order Austin sat back and checked out his surroundings. The western theme was apparent throughout. Austin surveyed the other late night patrons. His eyes lingered on a young girl sitting alone at the counter as she turned and looked his way. Obviously liking what she saw, she got up and meandered over. As she drew closer, Austin could see that life hadn't been kind to her. What had aged her was not a matter of years but of experience. He took in the black knee-high boots and the too tight, too short black skirt. She wore a black fringed leather jacket over a white blouse that was tied at the waist and had at least one too many buttons undone. Heavy make-up did nothing to enhance her features.

"Hi, I'm Mandy. No one likes to eat alone." Without hesitation, she squeezed into the seat across from him. A strong wave of cheap perfume drifted his way as she made herself comfortable. Mandy looked across the table and her appraisal of Austin remained cool and impersonal. Austin noted the hint of amusement in her expression as she recognized where he was coming from. Not the town, but the bitter place in life.

In a voice husky from too many cigarettes she asked, "What brings you here? I haven't seen you before." Leaning closer, she rested her arms on the table. Austin stared into cool green eyes fringed with long lashes and saw amusement, most certainly, and inquiry. She was definitely wondering about this good-looking young stranger.

Austin didn't really mind the intrusion although he was a little surprised by her directness. He introduced himself before responding to her question. "Just passing through." He knew his answer had piqued her interest but he offered no explanation.

Not to be put off, Mandy asked, "So, why you running away? Did you get your girlfriend pregnant so an angry daddy chased you out of town?"

Austin laughed in spite of himself. "You're certainly direct and personal, rather rude and you don't deserve an answer."

Undaunted, Mandy persisted, "Okay, that's not it. Why did you leave home?"

Austin leaned back and sighed deeply. Mentally he drifted back to the day he left home. Austin hated Mondays almost as much as he hated going to school and he had overslept again. After a hurried shower, he took a last look in his dresser mirror and ran a brush through his thick black hair. The shoulder length took nothing away from his masculinity. Austin shut off his stereo. Voices rose and lowered; he knew his parents were arguing. He braced himself before entering the kitchen. All conversation ceased and the air became thick with silence. Jordie, his twelve-year-old brother, and his six-year-old sister, Cassie, were sitting quietly at the kitchen table waiting for their mom to give them a ride to school. Even at their young age they were smart enough to leave their usual morning banter for another day. Jordie looked over and silently ran his finger across his throat, indicating to Austin that he was in trouble.

His mom glanced over at Austin. He hadn't failed to notice her concerned look before she spoke, "Good, you're ready." Mrs. Smith taught at the elementary school so the two younger children rode with her and most days Austin caught a ride.

Turning to the younger children she pleaded, "I told you to get your coats. Hurry up."

Both kids took off, thankful for the escape. The fight was about to begin.

Refusing to be daunted by his mom's abruptness, Austin went over and poured himself a glass of milk from the jug sitting on the counter. Mother and son exchanged a silent glance as he leaned back against the counter beside her.

A quick glimpse at his father indicated the source of the chill in the air. Richard Smith, a big man with a cold, hard look, was standing at the table. His thinning hair was noticeably streaked with gray as he bent over some papers in his briefcase. Richard held a prestigious and powerful position as a corporate lawyer. Always the professional, he was perfectly groomed and well-dressed in one of his dark tailored suits. The complete semblance made Richard Smith appear bigger than life.

Reacting to the emphatic snap of the briefcase being closed, Austin took a closer look at his dad's face. Harsh lines were visible at the corners of Richard's mouth. He was frowning at a letter he had removed from his briefcase.

As Austin made a small, involuntary movement, his dad's head raised. His gaze was exceptionally cold; more remote than usual. Austin steeled himself for 'Round One'.

His father broke the silence in a voice that held a hostile edge, "This is unacceptable. What's this all about?"

Allison hated the fights. "Leave him alone, Richard. Wait until tonight. If we don't get going we're all going to be late."

"No." Richard's voice rose emphatically, "We will deal with this right now." He waved the controversial piece of paper in the air. "It's all here in black and white," he bellowed. "Yet you don't have the decency to give us an explanation." His mouth curled with disgust.

The room filled with an oppressive silence that pounded as loudly as Austin's heart. He slipped his hands into his pockets as he shifted uncomfortably. After a pause, Austin said, rather defensively, "I haven't seen the letter. I don't know what you're talking about."

"Don't give me that crap. Even you have to be smart enough to figure out that the school won't tolerate students being late, let alone absences day after day," Richard yelled. With that, he proceeded to read from the letter. "As you know, Austin doesn't exactly have an exemplary attendance record. Absenteeism has been a common problem and the consequences for coming to class late have been well explained. Moreover, late is late. One minute or five, the line must be drawn somewhere and we choose to draw the line when the bell rings."

"Their rules suck," interrupted Austin.

"Don't get smart."

"I'm bored. Isn't it better if I'm not there disrupting the class?"

"Oh yeah, that's addressed as well." Richard continued reading, "By prolonging a discussion and challenging the teacher's authority, Austin undermines the tone of the class and monopolizes the teacher's time, thus inhibiting the teacher's ability to get on with the job of educating. This is not fair to others and will not be tolerated."

As Richard looked up and glared at his son his eyes narrowed. The fierceness of his expression and the hard edge of his voice made Austin flinch. His dad's face was stony as he gave a short, exasperated sigh and went on more forcefully, "Well, you're at the end of the line. You're on final notice. Any continuation of disrespect or absence from class without a reasonable explanation and you will be expelled."

Without a second's thought Austin grabbed the letter, tore it up and threw the pieces. His mouth and chin took on a set look. "They're being unfair," he cried out in anger.

Ignoring the outburst, Richard warned his son, "I don't want to hear from the school again. Do you hear me?"

Austin believed his dad's question neither deserved nor demanded a reply. He was wrong. His hesitation only made his dad madder. "No more chances, Austin. I've had it. You screw up again and it won't just be school that you're kicked out of."

Austin heard his mom gasp as she stared at her husband in disbelief.

Her husband was taken aback, but only for a moment. Richard wouldn't let up. Changing the topic, he continued yelling, "I should ground you. You were late again last night. No wonder you couldn't drag yourself out of bed this morning. You'd better get your act together because without an education you don't get far in life." With a final look of disgust, Richard looked down at the torn pieces of paper, then back to his son.

Cassie, who had returned to the kitchen, quickly went over and picked up the torn pieces. Frightened, she tucked them tightly in her little hand and went and stood by her mom.

Still irritated, Richard announced, "I'm not going to put up with this any longer. I'm tired of the school calling. I'm too busy to take needless calls."

Formidable as his dad was most of the time, today Austin threw caution to the wind. "I'm surprised they can get through to you. Usually you're 'unavailable at this time' or 'currently in a meeting'," he accused.

Austin was silenced for a moment by a forbidding stare from his mother. He shrugged his shoulders and turned away.

The gesture hadn't gone unnoticed by his dad. "You'd better change things real quick, starting with that attitude of yours."

"Why should I?" Austin challenged childishly. The boy's face was hard as he glared back at his dad. Resentment had taken hold.

Richard was visibly infuriated. His face was red, his breathing labored. "Your defiant behavior is going to get you in trouble just like your friend Ryan."

"I've been waiting for you to throw that in my face. It took longer than I thought it would." Austin's voice dripped with sarcasm.

"You're spending too much time with that Miller boy." Richard was always making disparaging remarks about Ryan. "I've told you to quit hanging around with him. He's trouble. You keep hanging out with the likes of Ryan and you're going to be nothing but a no good, worthless bum just like him and his old man."

Austin flinched at the harsh words and his eyes filled with hurt.

"Things better change and I mean right now," Richard's authoritative voice threatened.

Allison's voice was a biting command, "Let it go, Austin."

The control he was exerting for his mom's sake suddenly snapped. Austin shouted, "You want changes? You've got them. I'm out of here. I'm sick and tired of your attitude. You keep pushing and pushing. You never let up, never back off. I'm sick of everything. School. Arguing every single day. I don't need this." Austin pointed a finger in his dad's direction. "And I don't need you. You can't tell me what to do anymore."

The look of contempt still hadn't left his father's face. "Fine, be a failure," Richard bellowed in his condemning voice.

Nothing could mask the fiery burst of rage that sprang up in Austin's eyes. With a look of loathing he grabbed his jacket and slammed out the door.

Austin's tale of woe to Mandy had refueled his anger and resentment. He turned to look out the window but not before Mandy saw the torment in his eyes.

She attempted to change the subject, "You're lucky to have a brother and a sister. Mom and Dad just had me. They probably regret even having me. I was like a novelty purchase they couldn't return." She sat back. "I've always felt like I was in their way, an inconvenience. They had each other. I had nobody."

There was something sad in her eyes as she continued, "We kept moving all over the country. School became a nightmare. Everyone picks on the new kid. My parents said I should try harder. As if it was my fault that I couldn't make friends." Grief now replaced the sadness in her voice. "I never had a best friend to share my problems with. I hated school," she confessed dismally. "By junior high no one could hurt me. Before going to school I'd strap on my suit of armor; a black leather jacket and a tough attitude."

Austin wondered if Mandy was aware that she still wore her suit of armor.

Mandy sipped on coffee and smoked one cigarette after another while Austin ate his meal. Austin was glad of her constant chatter. "I kept looking for my Prince Charming. We'd run away and we'd live happily ever after. But life isn't a fairy tale," she declared sadly.

"Last time we moved I made different friends. They were older and wilder. When I was sixteen, Prince Charming moved into town. Danny was twenty and drove a black Camaro. All the girls dug him but he picked me to be his girl. Suddenly, they all wanted to be my friend. It was cool. I finally fit in."

Mandy lowered her voice and spoke softly, "I loved Danny." Mandy smiled as she remembered the first time they kissed. How could she not? It was the moment that she committed herself to something that was destined to go far beyond. She lowered her eyes. "Danny was so hot. I thought he was perfect."

She sighed. "One day Danny told me he was splitting and he asked me to go with him. My parents said Danny was useless, a drifter. They gave me the speech. You know the one; too young, puppy love. No way were they letting Danny take me off to some God forsaken place just to suit him. They refused to let me go. But when you're seventeen you don't listen to anyone. Life is an adventure and you go after what you want. If you don't take any risks, you're not really living so I ran away with Danny."

"You ran away, too?" Austin asked in surprise.

"Danny and I roamed from state to state." The tone of her voice changed as she confessed, "Six months later we ended up back in his home town. We lived in an apartment near the garage where Danny worked. I got a job cleaning rooms at the motel at the end of the street." After a brief pause, Mandy mumbled, "Things didn't work out the way I expected. I missed my parents and I wanted to go home."

"Did you?"

Defeat was in her voice as she shook her head sadly, "I did call them." Her voice cracked as she continued, "I'll never forget what they said. To them, I'd made my choice the day I ran away. They told me not to come back. My parents had disowned me."

"So you stayed?"

Mandy nodded her head reflectively, "I had nowhere else to go. I tried so hard in the beginning. Sex isn't love. Everything changed and things got worse. Danny was a jerk. He wouldn't grow up. It didn't take me long to figure things out. I was more mature than he'd ever be. Prince Charming had turned back into a toad."

Austin couldn't take his eyes off her; sadness was evident in her eyes as well as her voice.

"It wasn't long before Danny spent all of his time with the guys. He'd come home late or he didn't come home at all. When we'd fight Danny would yell, draw back his fist and threaten to hit me. I'd back down." She looked up, her face bleak. "I was trapped. There was no way out. I was scared and I had no one."

Austin remained silent. He didn't know what to say.

"It's not easy to be alone but you can live with someone and still be alone." Her voice became a whisper, "Sometimes even more so."

For a moment Austin thought he saw the sparkle of a tear, but if it was really there it was gone in an instant. It hurt to remember but Mandy was too worldly to let anyone see her cry.

Bitterness crept into her voice, "You think love can protect you from bad things, but it can't. I tried to live with misery and fear." Her chin lifted as she continued, "The last time we fought I refused to back down. Before I could stop him, Danny backhanded me across the mouth. It was the one and only time he hit me. I walked out the door and never looked back."

Her voice had registered her hurt and Austin flashed her a gentle, almost compassionate glance. No further explanation was necessary.

Mandy closed her eyes to shut out the pain.

Now Austin understood why those beautiful eyes looked so sad. He reached over and took her hand and spoke without thinking, "Why don't you go home?"

Mandy couldn't bear to feel the pity in Austin's touch. Her hand shook slightly as she tried to light another cigarette. The blue flame curled around the tip and Mandy inhaled deeply. She exhaled slowly, blowing a slow stream of smoke into the air. Her voice, husky with emotion, cried, "Home isn't always the best place to be, is it?" Her mouth was hard.

"Does he still scare you?" Austin asked with concern.

"He doesn't know where I am," she revealed. "Nobody does."

There was nothing Austin could say to ease the pain in the young girl's voice. Like her, he also had to find the courage to start over. This was more than Austin wanted to think about.

Silence fell between the two youth, broken at length by Mandy saying sadly, "Sometimes the quickest way to grow up is by making mistakes."

Austin nodded solemnly, "I think I'm growing up fast."

Mandy replied, "I think I'm very, very old." Only nineteen, she was already wise and well versed in pain. The pain of being alone.

Austin suddenly felt her withdraw. He sensed a reserve within her, not really wanting anyone to get too close. She was utterly unlike anyone he had ever known. She was incredibly direct, yet distant and aloof.

With more honesty than she intended to reveal, Mandy exclaimed, "You can do something in an instant that will give you heartache for life." The silence that followed had a still quality because Mandy was within a breath of the truth.

Exhausted, Austin stifled a yawn. "It's late. I should go."

"You can stay at my place if you like," Mandy replied, with an innocence that Austin didn't buy for a minute. The suggestive offer left little doubt to its implication, nor did the fact that Mandy deliberately moved her foot against his under the table. He could feel the warmth of her leg against his. Mandy had a query in her eyes; he could read her intentions clearly. She tried holding his gaze but Austin looked away.

Nervousness was tinting his earlobes and staining his cheeks. He was visibly embarrassed and checked to be certain that no one was paying attention to their conversation.

Mandy laughed at his reaction. "Come on, Austin, you know what I want," she teased, with a hint of amusement.

Staying at Mandy's would solve his problems for tonight so he was very tempted to say yes. Austin looked into her alluring green eyes and felt a compelling urge to stay but it would only complicate his life more. He sat back and tried to sort out his thoughts. After careful consideration a weary sigh escaped him.

Mandy's tone became serious, "You can stay, Austin. No strings."

His voice was pitched low and his dark eyes were anxious. "Thanks for the offer. I've enjoyed your company but I'll pass." Austin let his breath out.

Deeply disappointed, Mandy sighed, "Well, you can't blame a girl for trying. I was hoping 'Mr. Perfect' had just stepped into my life. I knew it was too good to be true. I don't have that kind of luck."

Austin knew he had hurt her by the pained expression in her eyes. Long lashes swept down to hide that knowledge from him, but not soon enough. In spite of himself, his conscience smote him. Austin wanted to reach out and erase the sad shadows he saw lurking in her eyes but he remained still. He was too tired to sort out new emotions.

This time it was Mandy who put her hand across the table to touch his. "What are you going to do? Where will you go?"

With a look of misery evident in his eyes, he shook his head, "I don't know but the further away from home the better."

Austin was relieved to be interrupted by the waitress as she brought his bill. Mandy gave Austin a quick smile as she rose. "Good luck, Austin." Then, without a backward glance, she went back to her stool at the counter and lit up another cigarette.

The air was brisk as Austin went outside. A gust of wind ruffled his hair. With a familiar gesture his fingers combed it back into place. He wandered aimlessly down the quiet street. As tempted as he was to return to Mandy, he knew it wouldn't be right. Not only was he physically and emotionally exhausted, he didn't need any complications in his life tonight. There were too many already.

Austin remembered passing an abandoned car in an alley. Figuring he was tired enough to sleep anywhere, his decision was quickly made. Turning on his heel, Austin retraced his steps, conscious of every hollow echo his shoes made on the sidewalk. He approached the vacant car sitting on its wheel hubs. Thankfully, the doors weren't locked when he tried the passenger side. Once inside, he made sure they were. Lying in the darkness, trying to get comfortable, his troubled memories leaped out from every corner. Austin had spent long nights in his bed planning what he would do with his life. He'd never expected it would come to this.

Through the window Austin heard the slam of a car door, voices, laughter, the chirp of crickets and the whisper of the wind in the night. All around him there was life. Yet he was all alone, vulnerable and isolated.

Austin felt far away and lost in his own uncomfortable world. Again he was haunted by lingering doubts. Unhappy about where his thoughts were taking him, he let out a deep sigh and shifted his position again. Austin shivered as an eternity of seconds ticked away in silence.

Chapter Two

It was early morning, the morning after a nearly sleepless, soul-searching night. There was coolness in the morning air as Austin headed out of town. He shoved his hands into the pockets of his jacket and hunched his shoulders in a momentary shiver. With a sigh, he glanced upward at the sky. The bright sun mocked him as storm clouds gathered. He gazed anxiously ahead because he knew it was only a matter of time before the storm would be upon him. He pulled his collar up and braced himself against the bite of the wind.

Storm clouds continued to build, towering up and up, growing bigger and bigger. They became intense: dark, brooding, full of rain. Aware that they were going to spill soon, Austin continued to look for shelter as he hurried along. Minutes later the skies opened. The storm that had been threatening all day released its fury. Rain poured down in torrents, drenching the earth. Within minutes the road was running with water. Cottonwood trees along the side of the road offered little protection as the buds on their branches waited, thankful for the rain that would nourish their growth. The storm swept through, drenching everything in its path before soaking quickly into the parched ground. As the rain beat on him, Austin impatiently brushed the drops from his face. The damp wind whipped at the legs of his pants, his runners were soaked through. Austin was wet and chilled to the bone as he trudged along.

Hours passed slowly as it rained off and on all day. Austin had had enough. Looking for some shelter, he almost failed to notice the brake lights of the semi that had splashed him as it slowed down and pulled over to the shoulder. He was almost afraid to get his hopes up. Was someone actually stopping to give him a ride? Relief was quickly replaced by apprehension. Instantly, Austin's chest tightened and all the horror stories about hitch-hiking flashed through his mind. He didn't know what to do. Reprimanding himself for being foolish, he drew a deep breath. Just then a clap of thunder boomed and Austin broke into a run toward the truck.

The door opened revealing the biggest man Austin had ever seen. Brawny arms extended beneath the rolled up sleeves of a T-shirt straining to cover a massive chest. Big hands with pudgy fingers wrapped themselves around the steering wheel. A huge shaved head sat directly on broad shoulders. If it weren't for the twinkle in the friendly blue eyes, Austin would have been terrified. He felt the disturbing grip of fear ease a little.

Austin ran his hands over his drenched hair and a stream of water ran down his face. He stood trying to catch his breath, his wet clothes clinging to his body.

"Sorry about splashing you. Climb in. Don't worry about the truck. I'm heading west."

"Thanks for stopping, Sir. West is fine." Austin's destination hadn't mattered when he left. It didn't matter now. "Not many will stop, especially in this kind of weather."

The driver let out a big booming laugh. "The name's Carl. Can't remember the last time anyone called me Sir."

Austin introduced himself and felt right at ease. He was relieved that Carl didn't ask him why he was hitch-hiking or where he was going. Mandy had asked enough questions that he didn't have the answers to.

Carl drove steadily and talked nonstop, first about his wife, then about his six children. He painted such vivid pictures of his family

Austin could almost visualize them. Before long Austin felt he knew more about Carl than he did about his best friend.

Austin sighed with a strange kind of contentment and thought about Ryan. They had a friendship bonded by childhood memories, teenage years, desperate fears and shared secrets. They were as close as brothers.

The Miller family had moved to town the summer that the boys went into grade three. The first week of school together they had to stand out in the hall for whispering in class. Over the years the hallway punishment was replaced by trips to the principal's office and long hours in detention. They became inseparable and what one didn't think of the other one did. Their adventures were endless. They were the best of friends.

When they were little it hadn't mattered that they came from dissimilar backgrounds, but as they grew older it became much more evident to both of them. As they advanced into their teens the bond between the boys grew stronger. Many found it odd that the two remained such close friends.

Ryan valued their friendship. "You never treat me different like some of the others do. They make me feel like I don't belong. You're a good friend, Austin."

To which Austin always replied, "Friends forever."

More and more often, Ryan compared the differences in their lifestyles. At times Ryan was embarrassed by his home life. Austin knew that Ryan's dad drank too much and that his mom worked too hard. Ryan's complaints were legitimate but Austin never realized how serious the problems were until Ryan confided in him one afternoon down by the river. They were in their early teens and had ridden their bikes to their favorite hangout.

Ryan had been withdrawn all day and Austin knew that something was bothering him. He also knew that Ryan would confide in him when he was ready. They shared everything. They were laying in the tall grass looking up at the clouds drifting by when Ryan blurted out, "My old man's a drunk."

"I know your dad drinks, you told me. So does mine."

"No, it's worse, my dad's a drunk," Ryan repeated emphatically. "That's why he never holds a job long. He got fired again yesterday. When he drinks he gets real mean. I hate the constant arguing and yelling, the underlying threats."

Their eyes met; Austin's questioning, Ryan's desperate.

"It isn't easy," confessed Ryan. Austin could see the pain on his friend's face. "He's more violent lately because the drinking never stops."

Ryan grew silent. Obviously, this was a painful subject for his friend and Austin didn't know what to say. The silence grew; awkward now. Suddenly, Ryan blurted out, "I hate being poor and having nothing. You don't know what that's like."

Austin felt a little ashamed because he knew he had everything and took it for granted.

Ryan continued to vent. "Do you know why I never try out for sports?" He didn't wait for a reply. "I can't afford to play. Life really sucks." Ryan paused, deep in thought. Then he pleaded, "Promise me you won't tell anyone."

Austin swore to remain silent. This was one more secret they shared that strengthened the friendship between them. Austin knew his friend would miss him even if his family didn't.

Carl shifted gears and began a steep climb, rapidly leaving the sagebrush behind. Tall evergreens seemed to close in making the twisting road seem even narrower. The engine purred and a train whistled off in the distance. Not having slept well the night before, Austin nestled down into the seat and fell asleep.

Carl glanced over, saw the boy shiver and turned up the heat. Shifting the wad of chewing tobacco to the other cheek, he began humming to the music.

When Austin awoke, cheeks red, Carl looked over. "You okay? You've been sound asleep for hours. Must not have slept too well last night."

Austin said he was fine but he couldn't quit shivering.

"This is my exit coming up, last stretch and I'm home. You sure you'll be okay?" At Austin's affirmative response he pulled over to the shoulder.

"Thanks again for the lift. It was good to get out of the rain," Austin said, as he lowered himself out of the cab. He turned up his collar, put his hands deep into his coat pockets, and continued to shiver as he pulled his damp jacket tighter. He watched as Carl pulled away. The prospect of the unknown filled him with a mixture of alarm and apprehension but it didn't stop him from moving on down the highway.

Night came quickly and there were no stars to light his way. The cloak of darkness held an eerie presence. It was like walking into a void, an unknown entity, just like his life. Austin believed his future loomed ahead, just as dark and empty, just as frightening. Again uneasiness crept over him. He heard a coyote howling in the foothills. The creatures of night were coming to life.

Austin was bitterly cold. Long gaps in traffic convinced him that no one else was about to pick up a stranger walking late at night. Disheartened and weary, he turned down a muddy dirt road lined with tall trees on both sides. Sooner or later, Austin told himself, the hilly, winding road would lead him to shelter.

Thankfully, the skies soon cleared and stars shone brightly guiding his way. The moon was his night-light, keeping the creatures that stalked in the darkness away. The rows of trees stood like sentinels silently protecting him. As the wind moaned through the trees, the rustle of the branches seemed intensified in the gloom of the night. The trees loomed larger than they were, their branches making grotesque shapes; though no more so than Austin's own fanciful imagination. Austin was trying desperately not to panic as he heard the quiet scurry and rustle of animals. He was completely out of his element here. In the distance he again heard the call of the wild and new fears came flooding in. Panic constricted his chest and he started to run. He thought the hounds of hell were snapping at his heels but it was only the mud grabbing at his shoes that was making it difficult to run.

"Please let me find a safe shelter, a warm place to sleep," Austin cried out to the universe. "I'm so cold and so tired." And frightened, he admitted silently to himself. His chest was rising and falling with deep, panicked breaths.

As Austin turned a bend, the moon illuminated the silhouette of a building sitting in an open field. Relief flooded through him. Crawling through a barbwire fence, he willed his numb body to move faster across the field. He suffered an unexpected wave of fatigue which dulled his brain and his responses. He stumbled, fell forward and banged his head on a large rock. For a moment Austin lay still, winded and bruised. His head throbbed and it was sticky to the touch. Groaning with pain, he pulled himself up and staggered forward until he reached the barn.

Austin pushed the door open and entered the shelter. Moonlight filtered through the wide cracks. Within seconds he was deep inside the shadowy interior. His legs were shaking so badly that he glanced around frantically for a place to sit. He spotted a bale of hay by a stall. When he reached the bale he collapsed. Folding his arms across his knees, he rested his head on them. He was cold and stiff and ached all over. Feeling nauseous, he became fully aware of the agony of his ordeal. But he was safe.

Once his eyes adjusted to the darkness, Austin took in his surroundings. Bales of hay were stacked against the wall. Some of them had tumbled over and had come undone, carpeting the floor with fragrant hay. Austin carefully eased in that direction. He pushed some hay together in the form of a pillow. It was such a relief to finally lie down.

Cold and alone, Austin curled into a ball. Within minutes his body shut down and his world became dark.

Chapter Three

Jake Hanson had lived on Echo Hill for the past twenty years. These days his only companion was his faithful dog. Although Sam had the strength and muscle of a farm dog, he also had the balanced temperament of a house pet. Sam was an excellent watch dog, not given to frivolous barking or unnecessary alarms. But this morning something had his attention in the barn. Was there an uninvited intruder on the other side of the door?

"What's up, Sam? Got yourself something cornered?" At the sound of his name the dog lifted his head and waited as his master walked over. Jake slowly slid the barn door open. As his eyes adjusted to the dark he noticed the shadow-darkened form lying on the straw. "So, this is what's got you excited."

Jake walked over, bent down and touched the still figure. It didn't move. With his index finger, Jake gently flipped a thick strand of damp hair aside and noticed the grazed wound on the boy's forehead. Dried mud and blood had left streaks down pale cheeks. Jake knew immediately by the heat radiating through the wet clothes that the boy wasn't well.

"We've got to get him up to the house and out of these damp clothes, Sam." Gathering the youth in his arms, he carried the unconscious boy to the house. Sam followed closely behind.

Laying him gently on top of the bed in his spare room, Jake stared at the pale figure. As Jake removed the wet clothing, his gaze was drawn to a long jagged scar across the boy's shoulder and he wondered what had caused such an ugly wound. Jake sponged the boy down, cleaned his head wound and dressed him in a pair of flannel pajamas. Having done that, Jake slid him gently between the sheets and covered him with the quilt.

Jake went over and bundled up the wet clothes. As he did, the boy's wallet fell to the floor. Feeling no guilt, Jake opened it up, looking for any kind of identification that would tell him something about his uninvited guest. "Well, Sam, I wonder what has brought Austin James Smith here." Jake turned and left the room while Sam went over and lay down beside the bed.

Throughout the day Jake looked in on his guest. The boy didn't stir even though the room was flooded with light. He was deeply asleep.

Jake's eyes passed over the black hair that fell rough and tangled across the boy's forehead and for a moment he studied the pale face.

The dog whined beside the bed. "He'll be okay, Sam," He patted the dog's head before turning and leaving the room. Sam lay back down.

Austin came to at hazy intervals. He didn't know where he was or what was happening to him. He couldn't seem to keep his eyes open and his mind was unintelligible chaos. There were times when his head ached so badly that he willingly slipped back into blissful oblivion. Austin's periods of semi-consciousness were brief. All he heard was the clock ticking in the silence, unaware that the hours had ticked away long into the night.

Somewhere, it seemed so far away, Austin heard the soft sound of a floor creaking and a dark shadow moved toward him. "Swallow this," he heard. A strangled moan broke from Austin's parched throat as he sipped. A low calming voice said, "You're safe, Austin. Lie down and go back to sleep."

Austin lay back down, confused. He rolled over on his side and pressed a hand against the dull ache in his head. He sighed wearily without knowing why and his eyes slipped shut. With a little moan, Austin buried his head in the pillow and went back to sleep.

Moonlight coming through the limbs of a pine tree cast shadows on the restless form and Jake wondered what dark shadows hid within.

Chapter Four

Austin awakened and slowly opened his eyes. Nothing was familiar as he took in his surroundings.

"Good morning, Austin."

Austin's eyes darted to the doorway. The unfamiliar voice came from darkened shadows. From the man's very stillness, Austin gained an impression of strength and control. Beside him sat his dog.

In answer to the questioning look the stranger replied, "I took a look in your wallet. I thought it only fair to know a little about my unexpected guest." The man had a quiet voice but it carried a note of authority. "It looks like it's been a tough couple of days for you. You had me wondering when you were going to come around. Feeling better I hope?"

When the man moved out of the shadows and stood where the light fully illuminated his features, Austin quickly took in the person behind the voice. The voice fit the man, strong and demanding. Here stood an intimidating figure, easily six-foot-three and every inch muscle. There was a quality of toughness in the lean, hard features. Time had etched lines around his eyes and mouth, suntanned skin was smooth over a sturdy jaw that showed strength and perhaps a bit of stubbornness. His brown, thick hair was just beginning to gray at the temples. Gray eyes, that were quiet and calm with quick flickers of light, were studying him openly.

"I'm Jake Hanson but you may call me Jake." He held out his hand.

Austin shook the hand that was extended to him as he met the man's gaze with the same frank curiosity. He quickly released it without saying anything in return.

"This is Sam. He's hardly left your side since I brought you in from the barn. You had us worried young man."

Austin glanced down at the dog.

Sam sat on his haunches, eyeing Austin with dark almond-shaped eyes. The dog's expression was gentle and friendly as he proceeded to wag his tail.

"Go and say hello," Jake spoke to the dog, which raised one ear at his master's command. Sam immediately rose and went over to the side of the bed. He offered his paw and wagged his tail. Austin extended his hand to the dog, the whole time letting the dog lick and sniff at him.

"The bathroom is down the hall. Have a quick shower and join me for breakfast. You'll find everything you need in the drawers. Come on Sam, let the boy get ready." Jake paused, his expression unreadable. "We'll talk after breakfast." With that the man turned, his obedient dog at his heels, and quietly closed the door behind him.

Cautiously, Austin slid his feet over the side of the bed. He stood for a moment waiting for the room to quit spinning. He noticed his freshly laundered clothes folded on the chair across the room. The mirror on the dresser reflected the pallor of his face. Austin examined his drawn features without pleasure. He looked pale and his deep-set eyes were shadowed by his thoughts. "What am I doing here?" he asked himself silently.

Austin moved to the window and looked out, not seeing anything but his own troubled visions and renewed anger intensified the throbbing in his temples. He closed his eyes. As he opened them, he lifted his chin, and steeling his nerves he left the bedroom. He reconciled himself to the fact that he'd be subjected to Jake's queries. It didn't matter because he'd leave right after breakfast.

The boy's steps echoed through the hallway as he walked to the kitchen where the smell of breakfast cooking made him realize how hungry he was. When Austin entered he inhaled the aroma of fresh coffee and frying bacon. Scrambled eggs and toast were already on the table.

The feeling of uncertainty hung in the air between the two strangers as they looked at each other.

"Have a seat. It'll be ready in a few minutes," commanded Jake.

There was a wary expression on Austin's face as he sat down. Sam immediately came to his side and rested his head on Austin's knee. Austin gently stroked the dog's ears. Enjoying the warmth of the morning sun, he let himself relax a little.

He let his gaze wander. The warmth of wood was welcoming throughout the rustic home. Oak floors and cupboards reflected the morning sun that streamed through the window behind him. From where Austin sat he appreciated the focal point of the living room. The far wall was dominated by a river rock fireplace centered between floor to ceiling windows. Hardwood floors were bare except for the sitting area by the fireplace. Centered between two deep chairs was an area rug. Next to one of the chairs was an end table with a table lamp and an open book laying face down. Facing the west window was a comfy, over-stuffed couch with a patchwork quilt draped over the back. The coffee table in front of it was bare of any knick- knacks. Austin didn't notice a television anywhere but the stereo system was very impressive.

Jake's voice interrupted his thoughts. "It'll be nice to have someone to share breakfast with besides Sam. Coffee?" he asked, as he poured a mug for himself.

Austin just nodded, still feeling a little uncomfortable and unsure of the situation.

Jake poured a second cup and set it in front of Austin. "Cream and sugar?"

"Just black, thanks."

Jake sat down across from Austin and looked into the dark watchful eyes. "It's a fine morning and the forecast is good for the rest of the week. Help yourself. I'm sure you're famished," he said, as he spooned a generous helping of eggs onto his own plate before handing them across to Austin.

Austin ate heartily and didn't refuse the last piece of toast when Jake offered it to him. Jake kept the conversation impersonal and light during the meal and Austin felt a measure of relief. Austin listened to Jake talk but his host revealed little about himself. The man never mentioned a family so Austin assumed he didn't have any.

Austin knew that as soon as breakfast was done the inevitable would happen.

As if his thoughts had been read, Jake spoke, "Tell me about Austin Smith and what brings you off the beaten track." Having spoken, Jake leaned back. His broad shoulders seemed to fill the chair. Balancing on the back two legs, he waited.

Conflicting emotions played across Austin's face as he was unable to stop the vivid memories. Eyes downcast, Austin twisted his cup between his hands. Although Austin kept his eyes averted, he knew he was being watched. This made him feel more uncomfortable.

As if sensing Austin's unease, Jake leaned across the table and put a hand on the boy's forearm. Oddly, it felt comforting.

Austin looked up and without further hesitation, he stated the obvious, "I've left home. I'm sure it won't surprise you that I had a fight with my parents." Too late, Austin realized that he'd opened the door for Jake to ask questions.

"Lots of kids fight with their parents but they don't leave home. What happened?"

In his mind, Austin relived every moment and his face darkened. He gave a censored version dealing with basic facts but accentuated by a lot of remaining anger. "They make me so mad, especially my dad. He's so arrogant and when he gets sarcastic I fight back. He's a lawyer so he's great at using words as weapons."

"Go on," Jake said encouragingly. He waited for the boy to continue.

Austin shook his head tensely, shunning a reply. The flickering glance Austin accorded Jake before lowering his eyes to his cup was hostile. He was struggling to keep his temper under control.

Austin forced a long sigh. "I don't want to talk about this anymore." There was enough snap in his voice to terminate the discussion but Jake ignored it. When Austin raised his eyes they were surprisingly direct and so was the remark that followed. "I'm a failure to my dad. He called me a loser, a no good worthless bum. He humiliated me, called me dumb and said I'd never amount to anything." How those words kept cropping up in his mind. "Do you know what it's like to hear your dad say that? That's why I left." The anger had been replaced by a cry of anguish. Austin hadn't intended to blurt out all the pain but he couldn't stop himself. Reliving everything, Austin felt a renewed sense of desolation.

Jake's gray eyes were scrutinizing Austin. Austin didn't like the fact that he had exposed his raw emotions to this stranger. But that's how he felt, raw and torn.

Austin held the cup of coffee in his hands. His whole body was tense. He wanted to be alone so he could shut out the bad memories, the grief, the pain and misery.

The man's next comment surprised Austin. "Look Austin, you're not completely recovered from your ordeal. Why don't you stay here for a day or two?" Recognizing the boys wariness, Jake interposed swiftly, "Don't worry, this won't interfere with your plans. Besides, you can leave whenever you want to."

Austin's face remained stony. He gave a short, exasperated shrug and declared more forcefully, "No thanks. It's time I moved on."

Jake smiled, but there was something sad in his smile. Something that spoke of times past, opportunities missed. "Time is the least of your problems at your age. Why is youth in such a hurry to go nowhere?"

Austin's lean frame revealed a trace of irritation and he avoided the piercing gray eyes.

Austin had been genuinely taken aback by Jake's offer. "You're willing to let me stay a couple of days without knowing anything about me." His voice remained guarded, "Why?"

Jake allowed the question to remain unanswered for a moment while he considered his response. "It'll be good to have company. One wearies, sometimes, for companionship. Besides that, the days are long and quiet. It'll give you time to think. There are a few things you should consider before you change your life."

"Life is about change," Austin said spiritedly.

The man's eyes were shrewd and worldly. "So, in anger, you're about to make a drastic life-changing decision. You leave home, quit school just months before graduating and begin your new life with just the clothes on your back and a few dollars in your pocket."

The hardening of the youth's jawbone caused Jake to sigh. "Anger is never a good emotion. It makes you unable to think clearly."

"What do you mean?" Austin asked, uneasiness invading his voice.

"Life on the road is hard and lonely. Think things out before you do something you can't change." Jake's tone held an underlying authority that Austin couldn't ignore.

Austin looked up, trying to read Jake's face. Jake looked perfectly serious and Austin found his persuasive tones very convincing. Was setting off into the unknown the answer? Yet going home meant facing his dad and the conflicting emotions his dad continuously evoked. He knew he didn't have the strength to do that. Neither option lifted his spirits. He could use a couple of days to sort out his thoughts. His earlier determination wavered.

As if sensing the boy's hesitation, Jake asked again, "Why not give it a couple of days?"

Grateful for the offer, Austin gave a nod of submission; relief immediately showing on his expressive face.

For a moment they were both silent. Jake slowly stood up and suggested in an off-hand way, "Why don't you go outside and take a look around while I clear away the dishes and tidy the kitchen. The fresh air will do you good."

Austin, who suddenly wanted to be alone, jumped at the suggestion. With a look of relief, he grabbed his jacket. Sam, who had been lying at the screen door, joined Austin as he stepped out into the morning brightness. For a moment, Austin stood on the front verandah taking in deep breaths of air, sweet with the scents of spring. He could smell the sweetness of the wet earth as the sun beat down on it.

Austin could see glimpses of the river that he'd heard from the guest room. The sunlight dancing on the water made the scene very inviting. Like a magnet, it drew him off the verandah. Sam led them along a well-worn path through the trees. When he found a puddle of water he lapped it almost dry, and then rolled in the cool mud. Austin had to laugh.

Down by the stream it was cool and peaceful. Birds swooped and landed, perching on boulders in the water or singing in the tree branches. Boy and dog followed the stream, the meadow rich and green beside them. The water rushed along, clear and cold. The air was pine scented; the sun rich and yellow.

Along the bank, Austin and Sam came across an old fallen log. Gratefully, he sat down, feeling the exertion from his physical exercise. Although Austin was physically fit, the last few days had taken a toll on him. Sam sat patiently by his side as Austin absently patted his head. Austin had always been naturally carefree but his recent ordeal had increased his despair. Everything was so mixed up and he didn't know what to do. For a long time he sat and stared at the crystal blue water, remembering his childhood and feeling the ache of nostalgia.

The small town where the Smith family lived held a great attraction for the local youths. Running through their town was a river and passing over the river was the railway bridge. With spring thaw came the rising of the water and hot summer days were quick to follow. The 'No Diving' signs posted on the bridge were no deterrent. There was as much of a thrill to jumping off the bridge into the river as there was to defying the law. Austin recalled it vividly. He could almost hear the children's voices; the dares to each other, loud cheers for those brave enough to jump. Austin always jumped. The adrenaline would rush through his veins making his heart hammer against his ribs. It lasted for only a moment and then his breath was taken away by the sudden shock of impact into the ice cold water. The feeling after jumping was immensely stimulating.

It had all been so good, so uncomplicated. A clawing surge of loneliness rose up. Austin sat still, a forlorn figure limp with unhappiness as he remained lost in the past.

A gentle nudge from Sam brought him back. The morning had passed unnoticed. Austin rose and stretched and started back the way they came. As Sam and Austin were climbing up the embankment, Austin recognized the sound of splitting wood. Following the noise, he came upon Jake chopping wood at the back of the barn. Austin surveyed the enormous pile of logs that lay scattered untidily around several huge chopping blocks.

Jake's shirt, half unbuttoned, revealed the bronzed color of his skin. His hair gleamed with rich brown tones, damp and curling slightly from perspiration. Corded muscles in his broad shoulders and long thighs contracted as he moved.

Jake stopped chopping when he heard them approach. He wiped the perspiration from his neck with a large handkerchief which he stuffed into his hip pocket. "Good timing, I need a break. There are sandwiches and iced tea in the fridge and glasses in the cupboard next to it. Why don't you bring them out to the front verandah? I'll join you as soon as I wash up."

Jake held the door for Austin while he carried the tray and set it down on the round table. He gestured to a nearby chair, "Sit down. It's such a peaceful day. The country has such lovely sounds; the river rambling along, the wind whispering through the trees." Just then a woodpecker began banging its beak against a tree trunk and Jake began to laugh. "Some sounds you like more than others," Jake confessed and chuckled again.

Austin took the chair indicated and leaned against the cushioned back, agreeing with Jake. It was a peaceful day. Both enjoyed the chirping of the birds in the nearby trees as they sat eating their lunch. Austin was more relaxed but he still looked tired and there were tell-tale signs of doubt in his face.

Although Jake often glanced over at him, Austin was again relieved that Jake endeavored to keep the conversation light. "It looks like your walk did you some good. That bump on your forehead has gone down a lot. How does your head feel? Any headache?"

Austin shook his head.

"It's never pleasant being caught in a spring storm."

"I'm fine. It was unpleasant but I know the rain was desperately needed."

Jake nodded in agreement. "That rain was a God send. Wyoming is facing drought conditions again this year. The streams and reservoirs are low, lower than normal. Without rainfall they won't support us for long. If we get into another dry year, we're going to be in trouble. Locals are struggling to survive. Many can't endure another drought."

Austin's interest was piqued.

Jake continued, "The other big concern is fire. Lightning causes most, but there are still too many sparked by careless people."

"Every summer it seems that the fire danger is extreme."

Jake nodded, "These dry conditions allow small fires to quickly spread out of control."

"It affects us all in different ways, doesn't it? We better smarten up and take care of our environment," Austin said, with a worried frown.

"You're so right. Benjamin Franklin is famous for saying 'When the well is dry, we know the worth of the water.' Our responsibility is to learn from the past, deal with the present, while preparing for the future."

"That's life in general, isn't it?" Austin declared solemnly.

Jake merely raised his eyebrow and didn't reply.

"Little things can tell a whole lot about something or someone if you look a little closer," Jake offered in idle conversation.

Austin didn't know what to make of Jake and didn't know what he meant. Was he stating a simple fact, or was he implying something? If he was implying something, what was it? Not wanting to look directly at Jake, he let his eyes wander, and then fixed them on the flag waving in the wind next to the drive.

"Take the flag up there, it tells a whole story, not just about Wyoming but also about the history of our land." With that Jake proceeded to share many historical facts about the state of Wyoming. Somewhat preoccupied, speaking almost to himself, Jake added, "We should be thankful that history is being taught in the schools. The more we know about our country, the more we learn to appreciate it. What we learn from the past and the decisions made now are what will impact the future of our land."

Obviously, Jake was moved by the spirit of the land and the spirit of the people. "This country was built on people's dreams. Their faith allowed them to move forward. Their courage was strong enough to take chances and face odds. It wasn't an easy life. The pioneers fought the elements, the wild animals and braved the unknown. They crossed mountain ranges and spanned great rivers. Working together in the wilderness these brave men cleared the land and survived the first winters without proper shelter. They made their dreams come true."

Austin was deeply interested in Jake's narration and was vastly reassured by the harmless way the time passed. They continued to discuss things less personal than Austin's troubled past.

Jake finished his iced tea and leaned back in his chair. "Beautiful countryside, isn't it? What do you see out there, Austin?"

Austin didn't like it when Jake turned the conversation back to him. He moved uneasily in his chair. Sometimes he felt uncomfortable around this man who asked too many questions. Jake's eyes were too penetrating, his perception too shrewd.

"A stillness that you don't see where I live. It's like the countryside is wakening after a long winter. Wide open spaces and endless sky. The adventure of the unknown on the other side of those mountains. Freedom."

"Oh, the privilege of youth. Definitely your age talking. You're too young to see the value of stability." Jake's voice was amused.

Austin wasn't.

Unfolding his tall form from the wicker rocker and rising to his feet, Jake was an imposing figure. "I'd better get that wood stacked. I keep the woodshed full. Winters can be harsh at the best of times and even our summer nights can be cold. Sam and I like to sit by the fire in the evenings." Sam, hearing his name, raised his head and wagged his tail lazily. Austin didn't hesitate when Jake said, "Come, you can carry some wood and kindling into the house."

When Austin had finished at the house, Jake was still carrying armloads of wood to the woodshed where it was stacked to season. As Austin turned to follow, Jake stated, "I think you've done enough for today. The last few days were hard on you."

"I'm fine," replied Austin. He was unaware of how pale his face had become. Jake turned and without comment led the way.

"Well, that job is done for a while," Jake said as he wiped his brow. "Thanks for the help. Now I better get back to my paying job."

Curious by nature, Austin asked, "What do you do?"

"I work independently as a contractor. I have to look over some blueprints and specifications that I've just received for a project my company is working on. Fortunately, I can do most of my work here at home. Would you like to come up to the loft and take a look? The view is spectacular." Jake turned from Austin to lead the way into the house.

Jake proceeded up the staircase to the floor above. The main area was fully set up for a home office. Austin's swift intelligent eyes took in the wall-to-wall bookshelves, each shelf lined with a variety of books. There were large inviting windows everywhere to capture breathtaking views from every vantage point.

"No wonder," Austin murmured, half to himself, "you choose to work up here."

"I'm glad you looked at the view and not the mess." Jake's rich mahogany desk was covered in papers and the wastebasket was spilling over with discarded paper. Jake had wandered over to the drafting table. He tucked a pencil behind his ear as he turned the pages of a roll of shop drawings. Austin noticed an empty plate and cup on the corner of the table.

"Lunches are usually eaten up here," Jake commented as he absently pushed them aside.

Austin felt a sense of relief. This enigma of a man was not as perfect as he appeared. It made Jake seem a little more human.

Austin went to look over his shoulder. "Hey, that's neat." Jake had flipped back to the front page revealing the architect's rendition of a school that Jake's company would be building.

Jake glanced sideways at him; his gray eyes alight with enthusiasm. "Thanks. I'm working with the architects on a new design. We're trying to optimize energy usage and improve the overall environmental performance of the school."

Austin interrupted, "That's not new. Energy conservation has been a concern for years."

"You're right. Now there are always new techniques to consider. It can begin at such simple levels like multi-level controls on conventional lighting or simply angling ceilings to reflect light into the rooms. Changes have been made to heating and cooling systems and there'll be more natural ventilation. Things are changing so quickly that it's getting harder to keep up." Jake started to grin. "What do the three 'R's' stand for?"

Austin replied without hesitation, "Reading, 'riting and 'rithmetic." He might as well have added, "The same as it did in your generation." There was an attempt to hide a smile.

Jake couldn't hide his. "Not anymore. Now it stands for reduce, re-use and recycle. There's a whole new public awareness to the importance of a health-conscious environment that uses resource-efficient practices and ecologically sound principles. Thus, the 'new' three R's."

Jake continued to point out various changes, which they discussed, and the two of them were completely at ease. Austin revealed a lot of hidden knowledge. Jake was impressed. "I bet you're a top student."

The recognition pleased Austin. "I'm brilliant," he admitted with a grin. He was one of the students in the running to be valedictorian of his graduating class.

"Are you now?" He looked at the boy with eyes that were appreciative of his intelligence and his ready humor.

"Mom and Dad have always encouraged us to do our best in whatever we do. Mom would be disappointed if we didn't. Dad would be dissatisfied." After a slight hesitation, Austin added, "Dad would never praise us. That was only to be expected." Young eyes hardened and the hint of a sneer appeared. "It's never been enough, any of it. School's always been easy. I get bored quick. So I skip, especially when spring is here," explained Austin.

"How do your parents feel about your skipping classes?"

"What do you think? We fight about it all the time. It's not like I start the day with the thought of skipping." Then he grinned. "Well, maybe occasionally. That was part of the fight the day I left," he confessed.

Although Jake didn't comment, Austin had the distinct feeling that the man stored the information away.

"Sometimes I think it's easier in school if you're just average. The slow kids have aides and less is expected of them. An average student is just glad that he can cope day to day."

"I don't think you really mean that Austin. The bigger the challenge, the bigger the rewards. School helps by preparing you to take on different challenges." At Austin's look of doubt Jake continued, "When they prepare you academically, they don't just teach you to read. They help you to comprehend what you read, something that you'll apply every day of your life. They teach you to formulate thoughts and to express yourself and communicate with others."

"I don't know why we have to take some of the subjects that we do," Austin put in, with a hint of disgust. "We'll never use it."

"You're right," Jake agreed. "Partly, it's to expand your mind. Part of the reason is discipline. School gives you the opportunity to develop skills and the knowledge to recognize the tools that will help you survive and compete in life."

Austin nodded thoughtfully. Jake had certainly given him a lot to think about.

On the wall behind the desk was a framed portrait of the most beautiful young woman Austin had ever seen. She was sitting in the meadow daydreaming amidst the wild flowers. With the sun glistening on her hair, it looked like golden wheat streaming down her back. She was wearing a sundress of vivid blue flowers against a backdrop of white. Sitting barefoot, the meadows lay at her feet stretching for miles in all directions. The heather tone of the flowers matched the unusual touch of lavender in her eyes. She appeared very delicate, small and pixie-like, adorable with a sprinkle of freckles across the bridge of her nose. Only the full, sensuous mouth belied the look of innocence. She sat there, smiling, her eyes shining, her face alive.

Austin was unaware of how long he had been staring at the picture and was somewhat startled when Jake spoke softly, "That's Katherine. She was my wife."

Austin picked up on the use of the past tense as Jake talked about Katherine, and he wondered what happened to her.

"I guess at your age you've never fallen head over heels in love?"

Austin shook his head. He'd had a few girlfriends but nothing serious.

"That's a shame," Jake sighed. "It happened to me the day I met her. I'd just received my Engineering Degree at the University of Wyoming. After graduating I was hired by an architectural firm based in Cheyenne. I decided that I wouldn't start working for them until October because I wanted one more spring and summer at my parent's homestead. Together, with my family, I helped with spring calving and branding. When we brand, it's a full day event that ends with a barbecue and barn dance. I was looking for my older brother, and drawn by the music from the barn, I wandered over to see if he was there."

A gentle look came over Jake's face and he smiled. "That's when I saw Katherine. She was with a group of friends. There was something about her beyond mere physical appearance that made her stand out." To which he added, with a quick grin, "Although she did look great in her tight-fitting jeans. In a room full of people she always stood out."

"Katherine looked up, our eyes met, and when she smiled her face lit up. Those violet eyes sparkled with calm self-assurance and she presented an understated air of sophisticated poise. At that very moment Katherine stole my heart. Without warning, she had knocked the daylights out of me. I didn't know what a powerful and positive impact this delicate creation would have on me." There was a hint of laughter in Jake's voice and tenderness, too. "I didn't know that there were people like her. Someone who changes your life just by being part of it.

Someone who makes you laugh until you can't stop. Two months after we met we became engaged and the next summer we were married."

Austin looked over at Jake, caught by the sincerity on his face and in his voice.

"It was a consulting job that first brought me here. Oliver Blackburn, an oil executive, had hired our company to design a home for him in the country. We were a successful, fast- growing company on the horizon of new ideas and I was one of the rising young architects. I did a lot of experimenting with new designs and materials." Without bragging, he confessed, "Mr. Blackburn wanted 'that brilliant young fellow' and I was given the project."

Jake looked over to the picture of Katherine as he continued. "It would've been easy to let such praise go to my head but Katherine kept me grounded. She always said I'd been given a gift and to remember to use it and never let it use me."

"The first few times Mr. Blackburn and I met at the office and I was quick to come up with a preliminary design. He was very excited. It was exactly what he was looking for in his house. Then I went to see his little 'piece of country' so I could work the design into the landscape. Katherine came with me and we fell in love with this hill. If I was going out to the site she'd pack a picnic lunch and we'd spend the whole day there. She'd wander off while I worked, sometimes she wouldn't return for hours."

Jake elaborated, "I went out often because I was having difficulty trying to fit his concept of a country home into what I believed should be built. I preferred to be given a free hand to use the ability that he was paying for."

Austin was having trouble understanding where Jake was coming from. He was unaware of how much he sounded like his dad as he spoke, "Why should it matter as long as your clients are happy and they're prepared to pay for it?"

Jake nodded, "That's what the firm thought. They said that every now and then we had to do a job we didn't like. The bottom line to remember, they said, was that the customer is always right. It's their money, not yours, that pays the bills. It was then that I promised myself that after this job I would no longer work for someone else."

"Katherine's belief in me was powerful and compelling. She taught me to believe in myself because she always believed in me. Together we started our company and although we kept it small it was successful and we had a reputation for quality work. Over the years I ventured more into the actual building instead of just the designing. Katherine became my Girl Friday and ran the office." After a moment he said "I'd rather take a job I want than compromise my beliefs to make more money."

Austin knew that to his dad success meant money and power. "My dad should meet you. Your idea of success is happiness, while my dad's idea of success is the almighty dollar."

Jake raised an eyebrow. "Actually, Austin, to me a person is successful when they realize what it is that they want in life and they make a positive move to get it. No one can be successful if they don't attempt to make the change needed to move forward. It's that simple."

Austin wandered over to the window. "The view is breathtaking. You can see forever." Austin's voice was filled with awe. He located the river winding its way through the countryside recently replenished by the runoff from the snow-crowned peaks. There was a natural terracing of the land as it descended toward the river. Bordering the scenic riverbanks, the meadows shimmered in the breeze. Thick forest fringed the lower slopes of the majestic mountain range. A person could enjoy the view of the meadows and the mountains from every window.

Jake had followed and was standing next to him. "There's no place like this. I like the unpolluted air. I like looking out of my window knowing that as far as I can see I have the right to wander. The land is so big and the mountains are so overpowering it puts everything into perspective. I look out at the infinity of space and I feel an incredible sense of freedom."

Freedom. There it was again, that word Austin so loved. Speechless with wonder, Austin looked out at the distant mountains and wondered what lay beyond.

They grew quiet, each lost in their own thoughts.

Returning to the present Austin asked, "How did you get this place?"

"Katherine," Jake replied simply. "She could transform her face into enticing witchery with a smile. Everyone fell under her spell. Mr. Oliver Blackburn never had a chance."

Jake had Austin's full attention as he continued, "Katherine never came with me if the owner would be on site. One day he came out while we were here. We didn't know he was coming but he had called my office and they told him where I was. I was having a conversation with Mr. Blackburn. Katherine stood alongside us as we were going over a few of the details on the drawings I had with me. I was having difficulty following his specifications because they didn't capture the beauty. I was struggling with some of the changes he was insisting on. A house, if it's designed right, should fit into the landscape like it grew there."

Jake smiled. "Mr. Blackburn wasn't getting it. Katherine walked over and looked him square in the eye. She told him to build the house around the panoramic view and have the finest quality of simplicity when surrounded by the peace and beauty of this natural paradise. She said each room should be spacious with large windows to let in natural light; not have crystal chandeliers hanging from ceilings that belong in estate homes."

"I gave Katherine several warning glances which she ignored. Her violet eyes radiated with wonder whenever she spoke of how wonderful the house would be and how much his family would enjoy it here. Her face glowed as she breathed in the pure air and took in the beauty surrounding her. Still avoiding my stares, she continued and it wasn't long before the look on my clients face changed and he was drawn in by Katherine, taking in every word. Her enthusiasm spilled out as she talked. More than once Katherine's laughter rang musically in the morning air. She was unaware that she was now referring to everything as 'our' as she took him by the hand and physically dragged him through our imaginary dream house as we'd done so many times before. I gave up and let my little whirlwind go," Jake said, with a generous smile.

"When Katherine was finished, a strange look came over Mr. Blackburn's face. He turned to me and said he was canceling our contract. I thought that Katherine had offended him and I began to apologize. He reassured me that it was just the opposite. 'Anyone who loves this place as much as the two of you do should live here.' He looked directly at Katherine and acknowledged, 'This land is more than a place you are fond of. It has become a part of you.'"

"Katherine grew wide-eyed and then quickly became shrouded in sadness. 'You're right Mr. Blackburn. This hill is like heaven to us but we can't afford this.' Her lips trembled and unshed tears glistened in her eyes."

"'No buts,' he insisted. Your husband and I will work out an acceptable agreement.' Hardly daring to breath, she asked, 'This can be ours. Really?' Her words were no more than a whisper."

"Mr. Blackburn grinned and nodded. Katherine shrieked with joy, jumped into his arms and kissed him smack on the cheek. Poor man, red faced and uncomfortable, gently patted her back. He looked over at me with soft eyes and said 'Be happy.'"

"After he left, I held Katherine and gazed out over what now was truly our land. As tears slide down her cheeks I asked her why she was crying. Wiping her eyes, she said she was too happy not to cry. My feelings echoed hers. It was then and there that we named this place Echo Hill."

Taking another look at the view, Austin understood why his host loved it here.

"This place holds a lot of memories. I could never live anywhere else." Jake's tone sounded a little wistful and momentarily he was lost in his memories. With a shake of his head, he was back in the present.

Jake glanced at his watch and moaned. "You know, Austin, I really must get some work done." He wandered back to the desk and flipped through a pile of papers.

Austin went over to the bookshelf and browsed through the books, once again impressed by the selection.

"Supper will be in a couple of hours. I have a casserole in the oven. I need to work while it's cooking."

Austin knew he was politely being dismissed. "I'll go for a walk."

"Take Sam with you. He could use a good run in the meadows. Even a good dog like Sam will misbehave if he doesn't get enough exercise."

Austin smiled in agreement and was off.

Chapter Five

Together, Austin and Sam spent a glorious afternoon frolicking through nature's playground. The hours passed unnoticed and for awhile life again was good.

When Austin returned, Jake was in the kitchen. Austin hesitated at the back porch. Jake glanced over, his gaze stopping first at Austin, then at Sam. Dried mud covered them both. Sensing his master's displeasure, Sam hung his head and went to lie at the back door.

Austin looked down, then over to Sam. With a slow grin he turned his gaze to Jake. "It's Sam's fault. There are hidden mud holes and Sam led me through every one of them." The smile broadened. "I left my shoes outside at the back door and my wet socks."

Jake couldn't help laughing. "Go and wash up. Grab a pair of dry socks out of my bottom drawer."

"Boy, it smells good in here. I'll hurry." True to his word, Austin was back in a flash. Jake was standing by the fridge with the door wide open. "It's almost ready. I just have the salad to do."

"Can I do something?" asked Austin.

Jake pointed, "There are plates in the cupboard over there. Knives and forks are in the drawer beneath it." While Austin set the table, Jake took a hot pad from another drawer and set the casserole dish on the table. Within minutes, they were ready to eat.

Jake served the casserole while Austin buttered a fresh bun.

"This is delicious," Austin admitted after a few mouthfuls. The surprise in his voice was evident and Jake smiled.

The evening meal was extremely enjoyable and not once did negative thoughts come into Austin's mind.

"Let's have our coffee by the fire," Jake said, refilling both mugs.

Before settling into his arm chair, Jake touched a match to the kindling in the fireplace. Within minutes the wood was crackling and the flames were leaping up the great stone chimney.

Jake went and sat in his chair. Sam went to lie beside Austin, his long tail brushing the coffee table as he passed by. Austin reached down to pat him.

Jake chuckled and said, "That's why I don't have anything on the table. Sam's tail is just the right height to knock everything off. You've certainly made a friend. Sam takes to most people but not like he has to you."

"You're a wonderful dog aren't you, Sam?" Austin said as he stroked the top of the dog's head and scratched him behind the ears.

A shadow passed over Austin's face. His lips were a thin line and his face had paled.

"Is something wrong?" Jake asked with concern. "You look so far away."

"Just thinking," Austin answered stoically. A vague kind of anger was apparent.

"About home?"

"That too," Austin said evasively.

"Tell me about home."

Austin hated the man's probing questions. His unease returned. Home. That had become a dark word with dark memories. "I'd rather not talk about home." Home was supposed to be a place of peace, of quiet. All that Austin had since he'd left were painful memories. He let out a long tired sigh as he stared pensively at the flames. He had to forget and move on.

"What's so terrible at home, Austin?" Jake suddenly asked.

"Lately, everything," Austin sighed grimly, still unwilling to elaborate.

Jake continued probing. "Suppose you tell me about your family. Do you have any brothers or sisters?"

Austin leaned forward to put his cup on the table. Jordie's image immediately came to mind and Austin smiled. "Jordie, my soon to be teenage brother, is actually a good kid. He has a great sense of humor and he loves to tease. Jordie doesn't get mad often but look out when he does. He's always asking questions."

"That's a good thing. How's he to find out anything if he doesn't ask questions?"

"Well, if he keeps it up, he'll know it all by the time he's thirteen," Austin laughed. "Mom says we're a lot alike and I guess in a lot of ways we are."

"Jordie loves to play sports and is a natural athlete. He's good at everything but he really excels at baseball. He has incredible control as a pitcher. Jordie can pitch strike after strike and he has more than one good pitch. He can really mix it up. But he lacked an important ingredient." A quick glance up told Austin that he had Jake's attention.

"Jordie knew that he was good but I knew how to make him better. His basic technique was already good. What he needed to do was work on attitude and I knew how to teach him that," Austin said cockily, folding his arms across his chest and smiling pleasantly.

"Our dad could never see beyond the technical part of the game which surprised me because I knew how good Dad was at playing mind games. Maybe he couldn't understand because it didn't relate to business. I started right back at the beginning, right at the very basics. I told Jordie to set himself a routine and do it the same every single time. The same way, over and over and over, until it became automatic.

Every pitch must start the same way. Enter the mound and approach the rubber from the same side. Right foot on the rubber, then the left foot on the rubber. Once you're set, look up and smile at the batter."

Here Austin had to chuckle out loud because Jake had the same expression on his face that Jordie did when Austin had told him. "More often than not it'll intimidate the batter. You want the batter to think that you're in control and that you know exactly what you're doing. It puts him at the disadvantage, creates doubt."

Turning sideways, Austin looked over at his host and produced a lopsided grin. "This is where the beginning of the mind game starts. Now it was time to teach Jordie the second most important point in the mind game. I asked him who controls the game. Of course he said the umpire." Austin looked over and Jake was nodding his head in agreement.

Austin shook his head, "Not really, it's the pitcher. The ump can yell 'batter up' but nothing's going to happen until the pitcher delivers the pitch."

Again that mischievous grin. "It gets even better. Let me give you an example. The batter approaches the plate. He has his routine too. He has to plant his feet just right, digging his front toe into the dirt and then planting his back foot just right. Then he wiggles his hips back and forth until he's set. What do you do?"

By now Austin had Jake's full attention. Jake shook his head, wondering where Austin was going with this.

"First pitch, you pitch him inside. His defensive reaction is to pull himself away from the plate. Now, when he goes back to his same routine with first one foot and than the other foot, the umpire isn't as patient and yells 'play ball.' This time the batter is uncomfortable standing at the plate and it's at this point that the pitcher has the advantage. It probably would be a good time to smile again. I taught him all the tricks," Austin bragged, looking confident.

At Austin's infectious smile, Jake couldn't help but grin. Austin was enjoying himself. "Go on," Jake begged.

"I went to all of his games and was Jordie's biggest supporter. I never interfered with the coach, but with eye contact I'd encourage Jordie and guide him. He kept getting better and better throughout the season. Last summer, Jordie's team made it to the state finals." There was an undercurrent of excitement in the boy's voice as he spoke. "The final game was the best. Jordie was pitching. We were up by one run, it was the last inning. All we needed were three more outs. The first two were easy but the next batter was their strongest hitter. With the right pitch, or in our case the wrong pitch, this kid would have no trouble hitting it right out of the park. Before Jordie made his approach he looked over at me, questioning from under the peak of his baseball cap. Meeting his gaze, I saw the determination written in his eyes and I nodded. I tried to look more confident than I felt as I stood on the sidelines. Jordie stepped onto the rubber like I'd seen him do hundreds of times. First the right foot at the corner of the rubber, than the left foot. The gaze he leveled at the batter was calm but determined. It was there in the unrelenting set of his jaw. Then his mouth curved into a smile. The grin spread slowly across his face. The first pitch, Jordie pitched him inside. At that moment I knew Jordie had him. The next pitch the batter popped up and we won," Austin declared smugly.

Austin remained lost in the memory. The awards banquet was held two weeks later. The treasured 'Most Valuable Player' golden statue came home with Jordie. It was immediately placed on the fireplace mantle, a glittering memento of his achievements.

"Well Jordan, you did yourself proud," his father said, with a pleased grin. "You deserved it."

"It's beautiful, Jordie." Cassie was not about to be left out.

Everyone was excited for Jordie, most of all Austin.

Later that night, Austin heard a gentle knock on his bedroom door. Austin opened the door to let a pajama-clad Jordie in. In his hand was the treasured trophy. Jordie went over and climbed on his brother's bed. Austin sat down next to him.

In a very serious voice, Jordie looked over at his brother and said, "If there was a 'Most Valuable Brother' award it would go to you, Austin."

True praise coming from a sibling and Austin felt honored.

Jordie continued, "You helped me. You made me practice, and practice, and practice."

Austin just nodded, not wanting to make light of the moment.

They talked for a long time, just the two of them. A strong bond had been woven even tighter between the two brothers. As Jordie was leaving the room he turned back and gave Austin a huge hug and said, "Thank you for being my big brother."

Looking back, Austin thought it was probably the single happiest time he and Jordie had shared together.

Austin was brought back to the present when Jake asked, "You mentioned Cassie."

Austin was unaware that his eyes softened when he started to tell Jake about Cassandra. "Our little sister, Cassie, is adorable. She has big blue eyes, dimples and black curly hair like my mom. She's spoiled, can be a brat and we all love her to pieces. She brings out the soft side of Dad. Heck, she brings it out in all of us," Austin declared truthfully. "I guess there are some people that everyone loves."

Jake's eyes glazed over and Austin knew where the man's thoughts had drifted to.

Austin, too, let his mind wander to one afternoon when Cassie was supposed to be practicing her piano lessons in the living room. Stopping at the door, he'd observed the tight-lipped child seated at the piano as his mother looked out the window. It appeared that this was to be a session of frustration for both teacher and student.

"I hate this," Cassie cried.

None too thrilled about it herself, Allison turned to study her favorite pupil gone sour. Cassie sat perched on the piano stool pouting. "You know that you have to play both pieces for your recital. I know the new one is harder but it'll get easier the more you play it. That's why you practice."

Cassandra was stubborn to a fault. As she was folding her arms in defiance, Austin sneaked up behind her, grabbed her hands and began playing chopsticks. Their mom came over and joined in, playing chopsticks faster and faster until all three were screaming with laughter. Cassie looked at her big brother in awe. Those darling dimples appeared as she smiled and her nose tilted up enchantingly. Austin leaned over and tweaked the tip, then left the room. As he walked down the hall, he could hear the practice notes coming once again from the living room.

Austin realized that one of the things he took for granted was the way his mom's laughter and love always filled the house. She was a wonderful mom and absolutely devoted to her family. "You'd like my mom," Austin said instantly. "She's the best."

Austin experienced a rush of homesickness as he talked about his family. A twinge of regret passed through Austin. It had hurt him to hear Cassie crying when he left.

Both brothers enjoyed teasing their little sister. They weren't always nice but it was fun. Austin remembered the time with the garter snake. "Don't be an idiot," Austin had cautioned. Jordie ignored him and there had been a mischievous glint in his eye as he approached his sister with his hands behind his back. The next thing Austin had heard was

Cassie screaming as she ran into the house. Both boys had stood there laughing, enjoying it immensely.

Throughout the evening many of Austin's stories revealed flashes of wit, and unknowingly a lot about himself, as he shared stories about his family and friends. Austin was very aware that he hadn't really talked about his dad and wondered if Jake had noticed.

"It sounds like you have a great family, Austin."

"They're okay."

Jake leaned forward as he looked at Austin. He challenged the boy by stating, "You've hardly mentioned your dad."

There was a momentary twist to Austin's lips. He took a deep breath before answering, "My father likes to be in control. He can be intimidating and mean. He's a genius at using words as weapons and he can make you feel very small and worthless when he directs his fury at you. He's a very smart man and he does have a good reputation as a lawyer. He has no room in life for anything but work. He lives, eats and sleeps work. Wonderful traits, right?" Austin questioned, his voice thick with sarcasm.

The bitterness remained in the youth's voice as he continued, "My dad's always positive that he's right. No one else's opinion counts. He always punishes us for what he thought we did, not for what we did do. He has no time to listen. There were times when he wasn't fair," Austin said, in disgust. "He never forgets, let alone forgives."

Jake continued to probe, "What do you think your leaving is doing to your family?"

Austin looked uncomfortable because he knew for sure that they would be worried about him. Instead he said, "I don't know. I'm sure Dad is mad as hell and of course Mom is hurt." He didn't know want to think about Jordie and Cassie. His homesick voice trailed off; his expression vulnerable, wistful, yearning.

They fell silent. Austin rose to his feet and crossed the room. A sigh escaped him as he poked at the fire. Sparks flew as the wood crackled and flames leaped up. His eyes were drawn to the mantle above the fireplace. At one corner was a single red rose in a crystal vase. On the other corner was a wedding picture of Jake and Katherine. It was a formal studio portrait. Katherine was a vision of loveliness in her floor-length antique white wedding dress, the very simplicity bespoke elegance. She wore her hair up with soft tendrils cascading over her ears, a spray of delicate flowers her crown. Her only accessories were a single strand of pearls around her slender neck and matching tear-drop earrings that dangled from the tiny lobes of her ears. Katherine looked like an angel. In her hands she held an exquisite bouquet of red roses and babies breath.

Jake stood poised beside Katherine wearing an expertly tailored black tuxedo. He appeared taller than ever standing next to his beautiful bride. Jake hadn't changed much. He was still handsome, but now with more rugged overtones. The softness of youth had been stamped out by the hard experiences of life. The lines in Jake's face now exhibited a harsh and unrelenting strength.

Jake's eyes, too, lingered on the photo. "We were married in a simple ceremony at a small church in the valley. It was filled with family and a few of our closest friends."

Austin returned the photo and looked at Jake. Austin was relieved when his host continued talking about himself.

"I could never have imagined a better wife or friend," Jake began tenderly. "She was soft-spoken and soft-hearted. Everyone loved her and most called her Kate but she was always Katherine to me. She was too much of a lady to be called anything else. Kate seemed too informal for her." Jake's light-hearted conversation soon dispelled the boy's dark mood.

The other item on the mantle was the single red rose. The fresh rose seemed so out of place that Austin had to ask Jake about it.

"The night of our honeymoon Katherine singled out a rose from her bouquet and pressed it between the pages of her parent's bible, the most treasured possession she had of theirs. She turned to me, tears shining in her eyes and said, 'This is an open admission of our love for each other and is symbolic of our lives together. This new bud offers us the hope of tomorrow.'"

"Katherine was an only child and her parents had adored her. They died in a car accident the year before we met. Katherine said it was a blessing that her parents died together because as much as they loved her, it would have been impossible for one to continue without the other. They were each other's best friend."

"That night in our room she said that her parents had always been an inspiration to her, a constant reminder of how beautiful love can really be. From that day, every Saturday I would bring her a single red rose. I still do. It helps me remember so many things that Katherine taught me and it keeps her alive in my heart."

"She was incredibly wise for someone so young. One particular Saturday I'd had rather an unpleasant meeting in town and I brought my bad mood home with me. I was still angry and told Katherine all about it. She thought I was being judgmental and too opinioned. She said I was being unfair. Katherine had an annoying habit of tilting her chin and looking me square in the eyes when we were in disagreement."

"The rose was still on the counter. She unwrapped it, held it in her delicate hand and asked me what I saw. I told her I saw my beautiful wife holding a perfect rose. She smiled, one of those infuriating smug smiles typical of women. The type of smile filled with secret wisdom and designed to make a man feel like an idiot."

"She smiled that annoying smile and told me to look only at the rose and tell her what I saw. She looked at me, her head slightly tipped to one side and waited. Adding insult to injury, she refused to explain. I knew that Katherine wouldn't give up so to appease her I played her game. I picked up the rose and started over. I told her that I saw a little flower bud. The leaves are wrapped tightly around it as it struggles to open. I said it would be much prettier in a couple of days when it opens up. Buds don't always open all the way but they sure are beautiful when they do. Then I grinned wickedly and added, just like my beautiful wife."

Jake shook his head, "I recognized the smile that curled her lips and it made me suspect that she had her own points to prove. She did. Her smile faded as she told me that I tended to be somewhat narrow minded at times. 'You only see what you want to see,' she stated in that quiet, direct manner of hers, as her fingers touched the velvet-soft petals. 'So soft. If you touch it too hard it can bruise, leaving a dark blemish. This delicate crimson bud is hiding behind the dark green leaves that embrace and protect it until it's ready to open. It enjoys the warmth of the sun on the tips of its petals, slowly unveiling its beauty to the eye of the beholder. It shares its fragrance now as a promise of what is to come. We don't know for sure what this bud will do. It may never open fully or it may open to be the most exquisite rose we've ever seen. Right now, we can only imagine the unexpected beauty it has to offer.'"

"My wife continued to make her point. 'Everyone and everything has its own time. This new bud offers us the hope of tomorrow. Part of the joy in life is watching something, or someone, grow and change. Two people can look at exactly the same thing and see something completely different. Who is right? Who is wrong? Our backgrounds or circumstances continually influence who we are and how we see things.'"

"I followed her over to the mantle. She placed the flower in the vase and picked up our wedding picture, continuing on. 'Look at my bouquet. Every rose is beautiful. Every flower is unique. When you look close, every flower is different, just like people. Under the petals, some may have hidden bruises. Some aren't as full as others. They haven't been as enriched by sunlight and water while growing. Sometimes it takes only a single bud to bring things into balance. Sounds a lot like people we meet in life, doesn't it?'"

Jake's voice became solemn, "Who are we to judge others, especially when we know nothing about them. So often we don't know anything about what they've had to endure in their lives." He turned, gathered the coffee mugs and carried them into the kitchen.

Austin watched Jake go, bewildered by the abruptness of his departure. He couldn't help but wonder about this man. As Austin stood watching the dancing flames, he repeated the conversation in his mind, trying to figure out all that Jake had said.

A wave of loneliness swept over Austin. Running his fingers through his thick black hair, Austin walked over to the window. He stared absently out at the black night. His hands slid partially into the pockets of his jeans as he leaned his head against the glass. Talking about his family had stirred many emotions and he felt more confused than ever. Austin was so deep in his thoughts that he didn't hear Jake approach.

Before Jake could say anything, Austin walked away from him. Suddenly Austin felt confined, almost trapped by this man's uncanny ability to know what he was thinking. Enough was enough for one day. Wanting to make his escape before any more awkward questions, Austin excused himself. "It's been a long day and I'm awfully tired. I think I'll go to bed." One hand was raised to his mouth, stifling a yawn.

"You're retiring early. Are you okay?" Jake asked anxiously.

"Just tired."

"Good night, then. Leave your clothes in the bathroom and I'll wash them along with mine. I don't know who found more mud today, you or Sam." Jake chuckled lowly. "I put some clean clothes for you to wear tomorrow on the chair in your room."

Jake returned to his easy chair, his face softened by the shadows, his long legs stretched out in front of him. He picked up his book as Austin retreated to his room.

To Austin, the guest room was the best room of all. It was nearest to the stream and when he opened the window he could hear the sound of running water. He took a deep breath. The clean air off the mountains seemed different here than any other place in the world. The breeze was light and caressing. Austin stared out into the night but the shadows of his thoughts were tangled so deeply that seeing anything was impossible. For a long time he stood there until he was too tired to wrestle with his emotions.

Closing the window, he turned and got into bed. As Austin lay there he pulled the blanket up over his shoulders. He listened, once again, to the sounds of the country at night and relaxed because tonight he was safe. The gentle rushing of the river outside lulled him to sleep.

Chapter Six

The next morning Austin awoke eager for the day. He had slept well. It had been a dreamless night, undisturbed, without the past rising up to confuse him. He felt good, wide awake almost at once and was conscious of a curious sense of happy anticipation. Not stopping to analyze the feeling, he threw back the covers.

As Austin stood hovering in the doorway, surveying the scene in the kitchen, Jake turned from the stove. "Good morning," he said cheerfully.

"Morning, Jake." Some of the lines had disappeared from Austin's face. He wasn't as pale as he had been yesterday. It was obvious that the boy had slept well.

Jake was dressed casually again in denim jeans and T-shirt and his manner matched his style of dress. Austin was dressed much the same, but it had a far different effect. The jeans Jake lent him were about four inches too long so Austin had double rolled up the bottoms and the T-shirt was two sizes too big. His unruly hair persisted in falling over his forehead.

Placing his hands into the pockets of the baggy jeans, Austin leaned against the cupboard. He sheepishly muttered, "Don't laugh. I look like a twelve-year-old waif."

"Yeah, you do," Jake said, with an irrepressible hint of laughter in his voice. As Austin grinned back, Jake laughed out loud. So did Austin. Shared humor cemented their relationship.

"Your clothes were still damp this morning. You can grab them out of the dryer after breakfast and fold them up. Keep them clean for when you leave."

Jake didn't say any more but Austin couldn't help but wonder if it was a hint.

Like the morning before, breakfast was waiting for him and he gulped down a glass of orange juice before starting in on the fluffy golden pancakes and link sausages. During breakfast, Austin listened while Jake discussed his plans for the day.

"I need to spend a few hours upstairs. I have a new client and the preliminary work has been a challenge. Depending on how it goes, I may have to run into town for a while to meet with him. I don't know what your plans are, so if I'm not here you know where I'll be."

Jake disappeared as soon as breakfast was over. Austin stepped outside and a refreshing breeze brushed his cheeks and ruffled his hair. Feeling restless, he whistled and Sam appeared at his side. They ventured off.

It was well past lunchtime when they returned. Austin was physically tired but mentally uplifted with a strange peace of mind. Austin patted Sam on the head. "I think we need something cool to drink." Sam stopped at his water dish, lapping so quickly that most of it splashed over the sides. Austin grabbed a glass from the cupboard and the jug of iced tea from the fridge. Leaning against the fridge door, he downed the tea and placed the empty glass in the dishwasher. He picked up Sam's water dish and refilled it for later.

"Knock, knock," Austin called from the doorway of the loft. "I've made some sandwiches. Do you want to eat up here or in the kitchen?"

"I thought you'd gone for a walk."

"I did. Aren't you hungry?" Austin asked good-naturedly.

Jake shook his head rather bemused, "What time is it?"

"Nearly one."

"It can't be."

"Want to bet?" Austin teased, a tiny smile lighting up his eyes.

Jake raked his fingers through his hair in a frustrated manner. "I'm sorry. Let's eat in the kitchen. I need a break." Jake automatically led the way downstairs.

Austin poured coffee and then joined Jake at the table. "How did the work go upstairs?"

"Not great. Projects like the new school are pretty basic. This one is a real challenge."

Austin's interest was piqued. "What are you working on today?"

"I'm doing a renovation and addition to a home built just after the turn of the century. This home is listed on the National Register of Historical Properties. Therefore, design restrictions have to be met before a building permit can be issued. The historical preservation must be maintained. The main limitations are to the exterior of the building but we try to replicate as much of the original both inside and out."

"How do you deal with that?"

Jake smiled. "We duplicate, as best we can, the design of the original. In this home the inside walls curve gently into the ceiling so my drywaller will duplicate both the design and texture of the original walls. Installation of new windows will match the existing ones. One of the difficulties that we know of is that the window trim throughout is a mixture of styles and, of course, none are available now."

"So what do you do?" Austin found Jake's work fascinating.

Jake continued, "In this case, the owner has agreed to copy one of the trim patterns and we'll replace the old trim where we have to. Obvious problems, like trim, are easy to deal with. While we're renovating, we'll replace the old and dangerous wiring and bring it up to code. There is much more to take into account on this kind of a project than if you build something new. Plus, with a renovation, you never know for sure what you're going to find behind some of the existing walls."

"You know, I'd give anything to talk to my dad like this. I often wonder what he's working on that takes all of his time. Maybe, if I understood his work better I'd understand him better." Austin was puzzled because he'd never really thought like this before.

Jake was surprised. It was the first positive thing Austin had said about his dad. "It's not too late to try to understand your dad a little better."

Feeling a heaviness inside, Austin looked directly at Jake and asked, "What should I do?"

Jake didn't know what to say because he was on foreign ground. He admitted honestly, "Wow. That's a complicated question. Let me think about it for a while because it deserves a fair answer and more time than I have right now." Jake placed a hand on Austin's shoulder, "Can we talk more about this tonight, Austin? I really need to do some more work upstairs."

Austin knew that Jake wasn't just putting him off like his dad would. Anytime his dad said later, it really meant the conversation was over.

Lunch seemed to have a reviving effect and Jake soon declared that it was time to get back to the drawing board.

Austin got up and started to remove the dishes. "I'll clean up." Handing Jake a fresh cup of steaming coffee, he ordered, "Now go back upstairs and get to work."

When Austin was finished, he strolled out onto the verandah. Sam, he noticed, was laying in the shade under an old apple tree. Over the last couple of days buds had popped open and flowers had bloomed. Austin went over and reclined next to the dog, resting his head on his cupped hands. The sun warmed Austin as it gleamed in shafts through the branches that creaked high over head. He let his mind wander. Time ticked by and he drifted into dreamland.

Jake shook Austin's shoulder. When Austin jumped Jake laughed pleasantly, "I didn't mean to startle you. I did call but you were sound asleep. I'm on my way into town. I've reached a road block and I have to meet with my client. I have no idea how long I'll be gone," Jake added apologetically.

"I'll be fine," Austin answered lazily, as he crossed his hands above his head and stretched his body to its full length. "Could I borrow a book from your library upstairs?" he asked casually.

"Go take a look. I have to run if I want to be on time for my appointment. See you later," Jake called over his shoulder as he headed over to the garage.

Austin remained where he was, closed his eyes and listened to Jake drive away. He drifted off again and it was late afternoon when he stirred. The sun was no longer as warm and cast long shadows on the lawn. The wind had sprung up, whistling through the trees and reshaping the clouds drifting above him.

Back in the house Austin found himself standing at the bottom of the stairs to the loft, reluctant to proceed. The loft was very much Jake's domain and Austin was hesitant to intrude. Boredom won out and up he went. Crossing over to the bookshelves, Austin went straight to the section that he remembered from his first visit. Inspired by Jake's talk about Wyoming, the book, 'Wyoming, the Early Years' drew his attention. Continuing to peruse other books, Austin glanced up and a thin volume titled 'Inspirational Quotes' caught his attention. When he removed it from the shelf, a yellowed piece of paper fell to the floor. As he knelt down to pick it up he noticed that it was written in the very feminine script of Katherine Hanson. Of course he should have put it right back but the temptation was too strong. Hoping to gain a little insight about this mystery lady, Austin sat down, leaned against the shelf and began to read.

"Where Fairies Dance"
I close my eyes, my soul takes flight,
I join the fairies in the still of the night;
While others sleep at the end of the day
I go to the meadows not far away
    Where fairies dance.
When flower petals open, I'm face to face
With fairies who emerge from their secret place;
Attired in dresses that sparkle and glow,
They slide down the stems to the ground below
    Where fairies dance.
Moonbeams shine on each delicate wing
As they romp and play, dance and sing;
Mystical music fills the air,
This I know, for I've been there
    Where fairies dance.
Sprinkled with magic from the stars above,
I'm happy with them in a world of love;
Escape with me to this wondrous sight,
To magical meadows in my dreams at night
    Where fairies dance.

Austin replaced the book and he felt that he had invaded Jake's private life. Even though Jake had given him permission to be up here, Austin now felt uncomfortable. As he was leaving he was drawn to the window. Before him lay the meadows leading to where? To the freedom which he longed for? Would there be fairies dancing in the meadows tonight? More distant still, the mountains. As light from the sunset filtered through the west windows, Austin remained drawn by the mountains and their rugged grandeur. The view continued to hold him captive as the mountains moved perceptibly nearer. The meadows and the tops of the gently swaying trees glowed in the final rays of the day. All too soon, the view was gone. The evening curtain had come down and taken it away.

Austin turned, walked along the landing, and descended the stairs to the main level, the silence broken only by his footsteps on the wooden floorboards. He found he was looking forward to Jake's return. Austin didn't always care for where some of the conversations took them but it was a change to talk to an adult who really listened to what he said.

Returning to the living room, Austin became aware of how the house had cooled. He flicked on the wall switch. A warm glow filled the room and only the corners hid in shadows. He went to the wood box and selected some kindling. It quickly caught a steady fire and its reddish glow colored the room as the scent of wood smoke filled the air. Slowly, Austin added sticks of firewood, stacking it as Jake had done the evening before.

Austin left the fire and dropped into one of the easy chairs. His fingers trailed absently down Sam's head, for the dog had trotted over to sit quietly at his side. Austin stretched out his long legs and gazed at the dancing flames leaping up the chimney while he listened to the ticking of the clock on the wall. How many minutes would have to tick away before Jake returned?

Austin picked up the book he'd brought down to read. It wasn't long before he was totally absorbed, discovering interesting facts about the state of Wyoming. It had the lowest population of all fifty states. It was the first state to allow women to vote. The license plate features a man on a bucking bronco. The name of the horse on the license plate is Old

Steamboat, named after a bronco that couldn't be ridden. He continued reading, turning page after page. The time passed unnoticed.

Once again the room had chilled. The big log that had blazed so friendly earlier was now a bed of red hot ashes. He pulled himself up, poked at the coals in the fireplace and put on another log. Hearing the back door open, Austin turned.

Jake strolled into the kitchen carrying two boxes. The smell drifting through the air gave away the surprise as Jake proudly declared that he had brought pizza from town. Sam flew at Jake, clambering up his long frame.

"Down boy." Then he laughed his hearty laugh. "It's been a while since there was pizza in this house. I didn't know what to get so I got us a Meat Lovers and a House Special that's loaded with everything. Is that okay?"

"Perfect." Austin got plates from the cupboard and Jake grabbed a couple of sodas.

"This is good," Jake said, speaking with his mouth full. He went back to attacking his pizza with gusto. Between them, they had no trouble devouring both pizzas. "Have you had enough or would you like something else?"

"I'm stuffed." Austin leaned back with a contented sigh.

They quickly cleaned up the kitchen and retired to the living room with their coffee. Jake stoked the coals, added more wood and within minutes the fire was ablaze. Sam looked up at his master, wagged his tail, and rolled over onto his back. Jake laughed but it was Austin who leaned forward and gave the dog the belly rub he was looking for.

"We had a dog once, a black cocker spaniel. Jordie was always bringing home stray cats and starving dogs. Dad wouldn't allow us to keep any. One day Jordie brought home a stray pup. He begged Dad to let him keep it. Dad's response was the same as usual. 'You better find a home for it or it'll be going to the pound'. Mom noticed the tears that sprang to Jordie's eyes and with a lift of her chin announced, 'We already have. Go find a box for your dog. I'll find an old blanket to put inside.'"

Austin's tone took on a hint of pride. "Mom didn't stand up to Dad very often. I think they were both shocked. Mom gave a nervous giggle and then we all burst out laughing. Dad was furious and went to his den slamming the door behind him. Jordie actually hugged Cassie. Jordie picked up his dog and said, 'Hey, lucky boy, isn't Mom the best?' and from that moment on Lucky was christened. Jordie carried that puppy around the house like royalty."

"Lucky's new bed and bowls for water and food were put in the back porch. Jordie wanted Lucky to stay in his room but Mom put her foot down to that. Well, Lucky may have started out sleeping in the porch but it wasn't long before he was sleeping at the end of Jordie's bed. Lucky was definitely Jordie's dog and he loved that dog more than anything. Lucky and Jordie were inseparable from that very first day."

There was a pause as Austin took a long drink from his cup and then set it on the table. He pulled himself out of his chair and went over to stir the embers with the poker. Sparks flew. The wood crackled and flames leapt forward. Austin determinedly breathed in deeply to gain control. Dropping his head in an attempt to hide the grief in his eyes, Austin continued.

Trying to keep his voice level, he recounted, "No one knows who left the gate open. It doesn't matter. Before anyone could stop him, Lucky ran out as Dad was pulling into our driveway. Dad didn't see Lucky and he hit him. By the time Dad was out of the car we'd all run out to where Lucky's still body lay. Jordie sat hunched over his dog, tears running down his cheeks. He tried to wipe his face with his shoulder. The tears just kept coming and Jordie screamed at Dad for killing his dog. Dad said it wouldn't have happened if we hadn't kept the dog. It was horrible."

The memory still caused Austin pain. Their mom said they could bury Lucky in the back yard. Instead, Austin and Jordie took Lucky down to their favorite place by the river and buried him under a tree. The two brothers looked at each other as they said good-bye and the tears in Jordie's eyes were reflected in Austin's. For timeless moments they clung to each other with wordless tears, mingled grief. With a blink, Austin returned to the present.

Austin turned and faced Jake. A muscle twitched in his jaw, indicating underlying anger that wasn't fully under control, despite the evenness of his voice. "After Lucky, Jordie never brought another stray home again. I hated Dad for that, too."

A heavy silence fell. Austin moved to the window and stared sightlessly out. Jake got up and went into the kitchen. Austin appreciated Jake's thoughtfulness. He needed a few minutes alone to get control of himself. Austin stood silently looking out at the night as he rested his back against the sill. His face was in shadows when Jake returned but the anguish was still evident on the boy's face as the memory lingered. Gradually, Austin managed to bring his thoughts back to the present. He felt Jake move behind him and glared at him. "Why don't parents admit it when they're wrong? Why didn't he say he was sorry?"

Jake couldn't answer.

The heavy silence was broken by the settling of the burned logs into the powdery ashes. Jake said hastily, "The room's getting chilly. I'd better put on another log. I'm sure glad that spring is here. It was a long winter." He sat back down in his familiar chair.

Austin moved from the window and went and sat down on the couch. They continued talking over their cups of coffee. Conversation had strengthened the friendship between them.

Jake's face had taken on a faraway look and Austin guessed that he was thinking about Katherine. "There were winters when we'd be closed in for days but the house was always cozy and warm. Katherine and I would sit by the fire dreaming of the coming of spring. I often read aloud as Katherine stitched. Books are wonderful. They can take you anywhere."

Austin nodded his head. His mom had taught all of her children to love literature.

"Katherine and I had many discussions about what we read and our views weren't always the same." Grinning like a mischievous child, Jake continued, "That only made it more interesting. Katherine may have had an angelic face but she could be a real spitfire when championing someone and I'd intentionally play devil's advocate. There were times that we argued fiercely but that never affected what we felt for one another deep down." Jake's voice softened, "I'd rather have had those few years with Katherine than a lifetime with someone else."

Austin, feeling more comfortable, began to open up. "Ever since I was little I loved poetry and literature," he admitted. "Dad can't understand but Mom and I love to read. I've always enjoyed historical novels, especially ancient history. Jordie, Cassie and I love to role play and Mom encourages us. We have our costume trunk. Each one of us becomes a character and we dress up. Mom's fun. Lots of times she'd join in."

Austin smiled at his memories. "Many rainy days were spent in medieval England. Cassie's always the fair maiden, Angelica. I'm her knight in shining armor and Mom's role is usually the evil Queen. Jordie loves being Merlin the Magician. Dad, unknowingly, is always the Duke of Doom. Sometimes we'd get carried away and Dad would yell at us to keep it down. Merlin would wave his magic wand and cast his spell on the evil Duke. Dad has no idea how many times he became a frog."

Jake's eyes sparkled. "That's a shame. Your dad missed a lot. He might have enjoyed being a frog."

Austin burst out laughing; his dark eyes alight with amusement at the very idea. Richard Smith was the last person who would appreciate such an adventure.

"Jordie's favorite was when we were pirates. Probably mine, too."

Before Austin knew what was happening, Jake leaped to his feet and placed his hand over his eyes as if viewing off into the distance. "Aye matie, do ya see what I see? That would be the Black Queen and its thievin' crew closing in on us." Letting his imagination soar, Jake cried out, "Sound the alarm and wake the lads. They'll not be getting our treasures this day."

Caught by the humorous glint in Jake's eyes, Austin jumped to his feet. Together, they waved their invisible swords in the air, warding off the invading pirates as they tried to board their ship. Having thwarted the enemy until another day, they fell back onto the couch. "Well, you can be one of us anytime," Austin said generously.

Austin sobered first. "Mom calls me her dreamer, someone with lots of imagination. She says I need to believe more in myself. That's hard to do when your dad keeps putting you down. He's always so critical. He makes me feel that I'm not smart enough even though I should be valedictorian of my graduating class. He says I should do better in sports even though I have 'MVP' trophies and first place ribbons. No matter what I do, it's never good enough."

Austin knew that over the last couple of days he'd allowed his host glimpses of some of his very private and personal grief. He couldn't help it. It was always there under his skin eating away at him. Austin got up and placed another log on the fire.

Jake straightened the quilt that had been pulled down while they were fooling around and laid it gently across the back of the couch. "Katherine made this quilt. She said it would be like looking through a photo album, each square would have a story of its own. She was right. The yellow gingham square up in the corner is from the first curtains we had in our kitchen. She sewed them herself and when she was done she cut this square from a piece of remnant and the beginning of our memory quilt was created." Jake smiled at the memory.

"Over time the patchwork quilt took form. Many evenings were spent reliving special times again and again. A lot of our conversations began with 'Do you remember when?' Together, we were never lonely here." Jake sighed. "That came later."

Next to the mentioned square, Austin recognized a piece from the sundress Katherine had worn in the portrait. Jake touched a square, enjoying the feel of the soft velvet. "Katherine had a floor-length cloak with a hood that was trimmed in white fur. She loved to walk outdoors after a snow storm. The air was always so fresh and the snow-covered countryside looked like a Christmas card. The air was so still, for a few moments the world was at peace."

Jake drew Austin's attention to a shiny red square. "This was from her favorite dress. Red was her favorite color." Jake was drawn back in time. "Katherine loved everyone but especially babies. They'd nuzzle into her arms as she'd cuddle them." His voice broke, "We both wanted children of our own." It was a revealing remark with so much left unsaid. Jake turned and left the room.

It was evident that both Jake and Austin were reluctant to reveal too much to the other.

Chapter Seven

Austin slouched into a more comfortable position and rested his head on the back of the couch. He sat lost in thought. For a moment he was taken back home. He recalled the time Jordie had gone to his first dance. How excited and nervous Jordie had been. He stood stoically, accepting his mom's comments while she adjusted his tie. Jordie shifted from foot to foot and his eyes flashed with impatience until she finally folded down the shirt collar.

Even though Austin felt sorry for his brother, he couldn't resist teasing him. But after his mom had instructed Jordie on the proper etiquette, Austin grabbed Jordie. Putting aside the teasing, Austin coached him. By the time Jordie left he was swaggering with confidence. When he came home he had a whole new attitude going on. Jordie had discovered how to charm the girls with his ready smile and they were all impressed with the boy who could dance.

Happy thoughts of home once again turned to angry ones. Emotions, too, changed quickly from one to another. Austin sat up slowly when Jake returned from the kitchen. With eyes sad, Austin suddenly asked Jake another profound question, "If your son had a special event, and I do mean special, would you be there for him?"

"Of course," Jake replied immediately. "Who wouldn't?"

"Richard Smith, that's who," Austin responded acidly.

Just then the phone rang and Jake excused himself to answer it. While Austin waited for Jake to return he relived the days leading up to his special event. Austin never understood why he'd been selected as the local citizen to carry the Olympic torch past their small town. However, he did understand the privilege accorded to him and he was honored.

The day Austin received the call he'd waited like an over-wound toy for his parents to get home from work so he could share his news. They'd been just as excited. Even his dad seemed proud of the honor that had been bestowed on his son. This was one of the rare occasions that Austin could actually remember his dad verbally declaring pride in him.

The anticipation of the run had built to a frenzied high. Finally, it was the day before his leg of the run. Ready for school much earlier than usual, he'd joined the family at the breakfast table. That morning the conversation was all about Austin.

Jordie couldn't refrain from teasing his older brother, "What if the flame goes out while you're carrying it?"

Austin, so caught up in the event, took Jordie's comment seriously. "That can't happen. It can withstand any weather conditions including heavy wind and snow. It has enough fuel to burn for at least half an hour. My leg of the run should take only twelve minutes, fifteen max."

"Is it heavy?" Cassie wanted to know.

"No. It weights about three pounds."

"Do you get to keep it?" she continued.

"I get to keep the uniform but you have to buy the torch."

"What if you slip on some ice and fall?" Jordie taunted.

Austin gave Jordie a dirty look and Jordie laughed.

"Jordie, that's enough," their mom chided.

Changing the subject, Richard made a gloomy comment about the headlines in the morning paper. Employees at one of the local companies were threatening an illegal walkout and there had been talk of striking for weeks. Things were getting more and more heated.

Richard shook his head, "Hell, I'd just fire them all and hire new. There are lots of people looking for work."

"They have rights and their unions would protect them," Austin reminded him. "I'm sure some of those workers have been there for years. Doesn't that matter?"

"Unions are too powerful," Richard declared quickly. "If I were the boss I'd show them a thing or two. You've got a lot to learn, Austin. It's always best to be the boss. You get to make the decisions and you don't have to answer to anyone. Of course you leave people behind but it isn't up to you to help them along."

Austin recognized his dad for who he was. "You're a hard man, Dad."

Taking his son's comment as a compliment, which was not the intention, Richard replied smugly, "You have to be. You don't get anywhere unless you are. You've got to be harder, quicker and stronger than the next guy or he's going to step on you as he goes up the ladder. Never let anyone get the upper hand if you want to be successful."

Austin had to admit that his dad was successful by his own definition. When it came to business, his dad could drive a forcible bargain. He knew what worked and used it well.

Just before leaving the house, Richard had hesitated at the door, turned to his wife and said, "Remember to pick up the dry cleaning before you come home tonight. I want to take my navy suit with me when I fly to Philadelphia tomorrow morning. Coldwell Steel wants me at an emergency board meeting." Richard Smith was a shrewd lawyer; he was a recognized expert in his field. Richard was a schemer and very calculating and knew when to execute his final blow.

"A major deal is threatening to blow up in their faces and their contract is starting to unravel. We'll be lucky if we can salvage it. What a cutthroat business." Despite the magnitude of the situation, his voice held a hint of excitement. Richard Smith would be up to the challenge.

Austin looked up from the kitchen table, taking in the unspoken message his father had just delivered. Anger, tempered with self-pity, seethed just below the surface as Austin realized that his dad wouldn't be there to see him carrying the Olympic torch. With an abrupt movement, Austin pushed over his chair and got to his feet. "You can't do that." He jammed his tightly clenched fists on the table. "You said you'd be there to see me run. It isn't fair."

"Life isn't fair," deemed Richard. He glanced away from his son as if struggling to control his feelings. "Unfortunately, life is unpredictable and irrational. With everything else that's happening right now, I can't Austin." His dad sighed, "I just can't."

Although his sigh accentuated the lines of strain in his face, they evoked no sympathy from his son. Inwardly, Austin was boiling with rage and resentment. His voice rose as indignation took hold. "All you think about is business. I'm your son. I deserve some of your time. You said you'd be there. You promised." Bitterness crept into Austin's voice. "Just like you've promised a hundred times before. I believed you. Stupid me. I should've known by now that your work will always come first."

"For God's sake, Austin, spare the drama. Listen to reason. I have a business to think of. This is a multi-million dollar deal. I didn't just dream up this crisis to avoid you."

Austin's eye's narrowed and his mouth tightened. His look of savage cynicism turned the room cold, despite the warmth of the morning sun filling the window. "Who cares anyway? I don't need you there," Austin declared fiercely.

"Damn your insolence." Stern eyes looked at his son. A mask of control slipped over Richard's features and he walked out, firmly closing the door.

Austin stood glaring after him.

Allison, who had remained silent during the angry exchange, turned to her son. She murmured apologetically, trying to ease the pain, "If your dad could've sent one of his senior associates he would have. They demanded your dad because of the urgency of the situation."

"Believe what you want, Mom, but Dad's work will always come first. He doesn't have time for any of us." Defeat was reflected in his voice as well as his eyes.

"You're being pretty hard on your dad. He may not fit the father image you want but, unfortunately, he is the way he is." Her voice softened, "In his own way, he loves you."

Austin shook his head. "You're wrong. The only thing he loves is his work. None of us matter to him anymore." His rebellious mood brought a worried frown to his mother's face. At the back of his mind he knew that his dad was hard and callous, selfish and uncaring.

"You're not making it easy," Allison said, sending her son a cross glance of her own.

"When has he ever made my life easy?" Austin asked coldly. He looked at his mom again. She stared down at his tightly fisted hands. Austin didn't argue any further. What was the use? Austin clenched his teeth, feeling his jaw muscles tense.

Allison went over and placed an encouraging hand on his shoulder as he picked up the overturned chair. A worried frown creased Allison's face. "I hate this constant fighting between you and your dad. You like hurting him and that's wrong. We all have the right to be angry, but we don't have the right to be cruel."

A muscle jumped in his jaw. "Tell that to Dad," cried Austin, with an indignation that struck her as pure Richard.

"You and your dad are very good at cutting remarks and it's getting worse. Neither of you think how wounding they can be," Allison stated quietly. "Austin, you're responsible for what you do and what you say no matter how you feel. Being angry doesn't excuse it. One of these days you're going to go too far."

While his mom was talking Austin shrugged his shoulders and moved toward the door. She put a restraining hand on her son's arm but Austin pulled away.

That night at dinner it seemed that there had been a mutual, if silent, agreement between father and son to suspend hostilities, if only for the course of the evening.

After dinner Austin was alone with his mom as she was clearing the table. "You know you can't leave things the way they were this morning. Your dad deserves an apology."

Austin tossed the idea aside. "Why should I?" Austin demanded, forcing his mother to look at him. "He's the one who let me down."

Allison was insistent. "You were rude and insulting. Your behavior was inexcusable."

"So was Dad's," exclaimed Austin. To which he quickly added, "He's supposed to set the example. Fine example."

"Don't talk like that." Allison's voice was low-pitched and deeply injured. "Your dad and I aren't the enemy."

His temper quickly subsided and he was ashamed. It was his dad who he was mad at but it was his mom he was taking his anger out on. Austin squared his shoulders as he spoke, "I know. He makes me so mad. I really wanted Dad there. You know how special this is."

"I know, son."

"I feel that he's let me down, again," Austin said. In a small voice, he added, "I'm sorry if I hurt you but I'm not sorry for what I said." Austin was stubborn, not insensitive.

Allison changed her tactics. "He has a lot on his mind."

"Who doesn't?" Austin said, with a worried frown. "I received another scholarship offer from one of the 'acceptable' colleges Dad wants me to go to. Why can't he accept that I want to go to college here? I can always transfer later if I need to."

"Talk to your dad," she urged.

Controlling his temper with effort, Austin said, "What's the use, Mom? He just listens to what he wants to. As soon as Dad hears something he doesn't like he changes the subject, or worse, he becomes almighty. So what's the point of telling him again?"

Unable to deny what her son had just said, she nodded. "Don't give up. I've been talking to him. You might find him a little more open-minded. Give it a try. Make him understand how important this is to you." She smiled encouragingly. Austin didn't smile back so Allison coaxed him, "Go ahead. It won't be so bad."

Reluctantly, he allowed himself to be persuaded to her point of view and having done so felt a measure of relief. Austin gave his mom a rare hug.

Allison put an arm around his shoulders and held him tight. "I love you. You're forgiven for your earlier behavior. Now, what about your dad? Doesn't he deserve the same?"

Austin's head jerked up. He met her eyes and got a mocking little smile. He knew his mom was right. "Okay."

She gave her son a gentle shove, "Now go talk to your dad. He's in the den."

Raking a hand through his hair, Austin stood facing the closed door to the den. In truth, Austin didn't relish another confrontation with his dad. Taking a deep breath, he knocked quickly before he could change his mind. At his dad's "Enter" he opened the door.

Richard's jacket was off, revealing broad shoulders and an expanding waistline. His tie had been removed and the top button on his shirt was undone. Richard looked up from behind the desk, an open file in his hand. He looked tired and put out.

Shifting uncomfortably, Austin spoke, "You okay, Dad? Worried about tomorrow?"

"There are always problems," Richard said abruptly, "but nothing to be too concerned about. We'll have to be real tough but I haven't found any loop holes in their contract."

"That's good, Dad. I hope they appreciate your commitment and the sacrifice you've had to make to be there tomorrow."

If his dad caught the cynicism in his son's comment, he chose to ignore it. "If they try to back out of this contract, legally, we can sue their asses off." He looked up at his son, sighed, and raked a hand through his thinning hair.

Austin lapsed into silence. His whole body was tense now. Why had he allowed his mom to talk him into this?

Richard ruffled the papers on his desk. "Look, Austin, I still have a lot to do in preparation for my meeting tomorrow." He motioned for his son to take a seat.

Austin hesitated for a second before going to sit in the leather chair across from his dad.

"What's on your mind, Austin?" asked Richard. "What's the matter now?"

"Nothing's the matter. I just wanted to tell you that I was sorry for what happened this morning. I was rude." Reacting to the skeptical look from his dad, Austin added, "Okay, I was ruder than usual and I said some things I shouldn't have but I was hurt and disappointed."

Conversation proceeded on casually for a few minutes until Richard demanded impatiently, "What really brought you in here?"

"Does it matter?" asked Austin, becoming defensive immediately.

"Austin, get to the point. I'm busy."

"Actually, there was something else," Austin admitted. He paused and drew a deep breath, "If you're too busy it can wait. I don't want to set you off again."

"Austin, out with it. Now."

"Okay. I'm not quite sure how to tell you." It was difficult to swallow. "Dad, I'm not going away to school." Unexpectedly, his words burst out in a flood. "I'm going to register in a two-year program here that can be transferred to most four-year colleges." He continued quickly before his dad could interrupt, "You can't deny that they have a good reputation."

For a moment his dad was perfectly still. "I thought I made this quite apparent to you. Your mother and I decided that was a bad idea."

"You mean you decided." Austin's voice was sharp.

Richard leaned in angrily. "I thought we were clear on this. The bottom line is that you've been offered full academic scholarships from all of the elite colleges out there. That's going to make a big difference when you transfer to law."

Austin interrupted before his dad could go any further. He'd come too far to let it go now. "I'm not going into law." Austin's eyes held a challenge.

There was complete silence in the room after he uttered the words. Austin took a deep breath and then exhaled slowly. He was relieved for having told his dad at last.

Richard placed his elbows on the desk, finger tips together, eyes gone cold. He continued to stare at his son without saying a word.

Austin had seen that expression on more than one occasion. His dad was mentally shifting roles and the lawyer was about to take over.

A cynical smile curled Richard's lips but his jaw was set. He pushed his chair back and stood up to gain the advantage. His dad stepped around the desk, looming over Austin, staring down at him with cold, calculating eyes. "Why not?" demanded Richard.

"I'd be bored," Austin answered automatically. Even to his ears, it sounded lame but he wasn't prepared to be cross-examined. Austin hated that his dad could make him feel like this.

"I'm not bored. Does this look like I'm bored?" Richard asked, as he touched the stack of files on his desk.

"I'm not you. I can't see myself wearing a suit every day and working in an office from eight in the morning until five at night and then working at home for hours."

Richard remained silent, unable to deny what Austin was saying.

"I want to do other things. I want to travel and see the world," Austin informed him.

"So look into international law. It's a growing field. You'd be able to travel while you work," his dad interrupted.

"Dad, you're not listening. I'm not going into law. I am capable of making a decision on my own. I'll go to school where I choose and take what I want."

Before Austin could go any further, his dad interrupted. He resumed his cross- examination. In the same forceful voice that he used in court he asked, "You think that's enough to get you by in this world?" It really wasn't a question. It was more of a verbal sign of the contempt he obviously felt for his son's opinions.

It made Austin all the more determined. He quickly retaliated, "I don't know but I'm going to try." Austin sat stone-still and waited, fully aware of his dad's calmness.

As Richard glared at his son, his lips compressed so hard that a muscle twitched in his cheek. Finally, he spoke. "You don't know anything. Life is tough and you need every advantage you can get. As your parents, that's what we've done for you. And, as your parents, I think we know what's best for you."

Austin knew his dad was determined to beat him down. He wished that just once in his life that his father's primary concern would be his son's happiness and that he'd quit demanding more than he could give. Was that asking too much? "You obviously don't care what I think," Austin accused ungraciously, giving him a distinctly hostile stare.

"Not when you're not thinking straight," agreed Richard.

Austin glared back in dismay, "You like everything your own way."

Richard offered no denial.

Austin sighed heavily, "It doesn't matter that I want something different?"

The silence descended again, thick and unhappy. Austin looked at his dad hopefully. "Dad, doesn't it matter what I want?" His eyes pleaded as he stared unhappily at his father.

Richard tried to interrupt but Austin stopped him, determined to be heard. "I'm almost eighteen. I should be able to decide what to do with my life."

"Not while you're under my roof and I'm paying the bills. It's not your life until you're eighteen or out on your own. Then you can make all kinds of decisions. Like where your next dollar is coming from because it won't be coming from me."

Austin sighed, "So, if I don't do what you want there's no money?" He took a deep breath. "Enjoy your power trip with someone else, not with me. I'll decide what I want to do with my life."

Richard was visibly angry but his voice remained controlled. "Look, you're wasting your time and mine. I told you, I still have work to do. There's nothing further to discuss, is there?"

Austin got the message loud and clear. He knew he'd been dismissed. Austin stood up, his eyes almost level with his dad's. Their gaze locked briefly before Austin turned and left, slamming the door behind him. Father and son had come to a stalemate.

The memory continued to flow. The eventful day had finally arrived and Austin was filled with nervous excitement. Even though it was bitterly cold, both sides of the road were lined with people, many waving flags. For a moment he was overwhelmed. Austin stood proud and tall and the cheers became louder the closer the torch bearer came. Austin shivered as he waited for the torch runner to light his torch. Suddenly, Austin's torch accepted the flame. He turned and ran. Austin heard everyone cheering loudly. He recalled passing friends and classmates and his family was all there except for his dad. Austin refused to allow his tide of bitterness dampen the experience. When he saw his mom, she was waving like crazy and he could see the tears in her eyes. He figured that would happen. His mom cried at the oddest times. He knew that the Olympics meant a lot to her. She said they represented friendship, loyalty and a lot of hard work. All of those things make an athlete and her son was representing all of them by being a torch runner. Austin was so proud and he carried the torch high.

In the distance Austin could see the next torch bearer. He was about the same age as Austin but of native descent. As Austin ran closer he could see the other boy's large brown eyes dancing with excitement. Austin understood. They greeted each other with a smile of friendship and understanding. This was a time of honor and pride as well as good will. Their torches touched, transferring the flame that had traveled all the way from Greece. Wow! They held their torches together for a few more seconds to savor the moment. Both boys had tears in their eyes and it was okay.

A feeling of allegiance passed through Austin as he saw the torch being carried off into the distance. Runners crossing the land while holding the torch high. This truly symbolized the Olympic ideal of peace and understanding through friendly competition. Now he really knew what the Olympics were all about.

Austin was jolted back to the present by Jake's voice, "Sorry about that, Austin. Care to explain that last comment?"

"I was privileged to carry the Olympic Torch for the winter Olympics. My dad couldn't be there to see me run because, like usual, business came first. A meeting was more important than his own son." The boy's voice filled with loathing, "Is it any wonder I hate my dad?"

"Don't say that."

"Why not?" Austin challenged defiantly.

"You don't really hate your dad."

Austin sat there stubbornly.

Jake sighed. "I think you two definitely rub each other the wrong way," chided Jake.

"I don't think so," Austin said, getting annoyed immediately.

"Don't get so defensive. This morning you wanted to know what I think."

Austin shrugged, "I believe I asked you what I should do."

Jake ignored the rudeness. "We've spent a lot of time talking, Austin. Unknowingly, and more often unwillingly, you have revealed a lot about your relationship between you and your dad."

Austin refused to comment.

Jake persisted, "You're prejudiced. I don't know why but I can see it in your attitude toward your father. You have blinders on when it comes to your dad. I think you've pigeon- holed him as the enemy and he can't do anything right by you."

Austin's temper flared. "How can you say that after all I've told you about my dad? Believe me, I know my father inside and out."

"Don't misunderstand, Austin. You've painted a very clear picture of your dad and I recognize him for what he is; strong, opinionated, controlling. Need I go on?" Getting no reply, Jake continued. "Regardless of his character flaws, I think that the two of you have reached a point in your life where you're no longer communicating."

Noticing Austin's look of defiance, Jake continued before he could speak. "Don't interrupt. What I'm saying is that you're not communicating. You're talking, or more often yelling, but neither of you are listening to each other. It has become more a battle of wills than anything and if something doesn't change you'll never have a good relationship with your dad."

"I don't care," Austin cried, but he knew he was lying.

So did Jake. "Of course you care, or you wouldn't be angry." Jake waited a minute before asking, "Who are you really mad at?"

"I'm not even sure anymore," Austin said truthfully, as he stared straight ahead.

"Forget the anger. Forget the insults. Austin, tell me how you feel, deep inside."

Austin deliberately evaded Jake's question. How could he confide his feelings to anyone when he was having trouble admitting them to himself?

"I've spent a lot of the day thinking about your question earlier. What do you really want to do? I don't mean with a career. I mean tomorrow."

Austin shifted his position. "To me they're intertwined. If I go home am I giving in and my dad plans my future. Or does the fighting continue until he kicks me out or until I get to this point again and I leave?" Austin's voice suddenly regressed to its anxious pitch, "If it's the last scenario, I'd say I'm ahead of the game."

Jake wasn't about to quit now. "But?"

"No but."

"I heard a 'but' in your voice," Jake insisted.

"But, this isn't what I want." Austin looked up at Jake hoping for understanding. When he saw it there, he continued. "How did you decide what to do with your life? Did you follow in your father's footsteps or did you get to chase your own dream?"

"I knew that I'd be a builder ever since I was little. At first, I built with blocks and Lego. My first real project built from my own design was a tree house that Dad let my brother and me build. Over time childhood dreams became reality." Jake's eyes lit up as he continued, "I love watching those bulldozers pushing huge mounds of dirt around, changing the shape of the land."

"I know." Austin was excited. Here was someone who understood. "Something that only you can see and then those thoughts are transformed into something real. For people like you it's with sticks and stones. For some it's with words on paper. For others it's paint on canvas or musical notes on a keyboard." The words were tumbling over themselves in an amusing burst of jubilant excitement. "It's the realization of the inner you coming to life," Austin added, recalling the shop drawings that Jake was working on up in the loft. Austin grinned at Jake and said in reverence, "It's a long way from Lego land."

To which Jake threw back his head and laughed.

"Your parents will understand too, Austin."

Austin shook his head, "You're jumping to conclusions. You're assuming that my dad is a reasonable man."

Jake leaned forward, "Can't you compromise?"

"How can you even ask that when just yesterday up in the loft you talked about starting your own company so that you wouldn't have to compromise?"

Jake looked more closely at the young man in front of him. "You're right, wrong choice of words," he replied calmly. "It might not be possible to please everyone but you can come to an agreement." With that, Jake simply stood there, regarding Austin through eyes that missed very little.

"My dad's rules never change," Austin replied, "and I'm tired of playing his games. I can't win and my dad never could tolerate a failure." After a few seconds of silence, Austin continued, his anger quickly gone only to be replaced by bitterness. "It's not like I'm going to ruin my life if I do what I want based on my decisions. At least they could give me a chance to show them that I'm not totally inadequate."

"Well, you know you're far from being totally inadequate but you're definitely argumentative and defensive. I think you're being shortsighted and right now you're still allowing anger to cloud your decisions. Do you really want to determine your future based on anger?"

There was no response.

"Well?" Jake asked.

Austin's mind flashed back to Mandy who was lonesome and scared. Did he want to live the same kind of life as her, alone and desperate for companionship from strangers because she no longer had a relationship with her family? Austin still said nothing.

"Well?" Jake said, again.

Austin resented the way Jake was making him feel so antagonistic. "You're wrong." Austin's voice was cold. "You know it's not just anger."

"Maybe not, but it's still the driving force. You haven't let go of your anger and until you do you can't think clearly. Let it go, Austin."

"I'm trying to," came back the unconvincing response.

"The point is."

"I know what the point is," Austin interrupted, before Jake could continue. "I know that if I don't finish high school, I eliminate a lot of possibilities for my future. I know that, but why can't my dad let me make my own choices?"

Ignoring the youth's interruption, Jake continued, "The point is that graduation from high school is not the end but the beginning of a new chapter of your life. It's not the end of a journey but a step toward a long journey that has just begun."

Austin shrugged indifferently.

"If you don't care where you end up any road will do. But if you have a destination in mind, I suggest that you begin to chart your course."

His logic was irrefutable but Jake didn't know his dad. Austin shook his head sadly, understanding what Jake meant, at least in principal. How did he explain to this overpowering man that it wasn't that simple? It made Austin angrier. "Right now, my dad's in the driver's seat. Things can only be done his way. He has this ideal vision of the man I'm supposed to grow into. It's his vision, not mine. I'm not going to let my dad do this to me. He's trying to ruin my life. Why can't he see that?" Austin's voice shook as he argued his case.

"Why do you feel your dad's trying to ruin your life? I think both your mom and dad want what's best for you," Jake surmised.

"Take their side," Austin declared defiantly. "Why should I have any say? After all it's only my life," he continued, in that insolent tone he frequently used with his parents.

"We are older," Jake said simply. When Austin shot him another look, Jake added, "Don't you think we've learned anything? Learn from our mistakes, not yours. Parents."

Before Jake could finish, Austin interrupted, his anger having taken hold. "And you're experienced in the art of parenting?"

Jake's own temper surfaced, a sudden glint appeared in his eye. "No, but I see that you're gifted in the art of rudeness." With that, he walked out of the house, mumbling something about needing more firewood even though Austin had filled the bin earlier in the day.

Austin hung his head in shame. As soon as he'd said it he realized his mom was right. No matter what people may say or do, they're always responsible for their actions. Austin was embarrassed by his. He'd been cruel to this man who had extended nothing but kindness to him.

It wasn't long before Jake returned. He looked slightly more composed but his silence and his drawn brow forced an apology from the boy.

"I'm sorry, Jake. I didn't mean it. I was angry. You sounded so much like my dad."

Jake accepted the apology with a shrug. "What did I tell you about anger?"

"It doesn't get you anywhere," Austin conceded.

The silence between them was unnerving.

Jake sighed, his face grave, "You're looking at all of this only from your point of view. Try it the other way around. Remember our conversation about the rose?"

A thread of anger remained. "This conversation seems rather pointless," Austin muttered under his breath as he turned to walk away.

Jake shook his head. "No conversation is pointless if it brings understanding," Jake replied quietly. "Although some of us seem more able to understand than others."

"Meaning what?" Austin demanded. "I'm not understanding because I won't comply with my dad's demands."

"So you're just going to quit? Then what?"

Austin seemed momentarily absent, lost in his thoughts. Why did Jake persist in making it tough for him to think clearly? When he came back to the present he confessed, "I don't know. I haven't thought that far ahead."

"Well, Austin, I feel that you've reached a crisis point in your life and you're too intelligent to simply drift aimlessly. If you can learn to let go of your anger, you're going to have a happier life."

Austin shook his head.

Jake looked at the boy sadly. "Be a man. Stop running the minute life gets too difficult." He couldn't miss the look of defeat in the boy's eyes. In a softer voice, Jake added, "Going home doesn't mean that you've given up. You talked about your choices earlier. I hope that you've realized that not one of them is an easy choice. Tough reality."

Jake paused before continuing, "Maybe you need to do some thinking about all of them. Ahead of you lay the challenges of the world. Every one of us has to face life's challenges our own way, but they must be faced. Obstacles must be faced with hope. Fear must be faced with courage."

Austin knew he was right but remained silent.

"It's been a long day. Go to bed and get some rest. Nothing can be settled tonight. Tomorrow will be soon enough." Jake pulled himself up and walked out to the kitchen.

Austin stared at the empty room. Had an ultimatum just been given? Did he have to make his decision even if he hadn't made up his mind?

Austin went to his room in a wave of tiredness and closed the door. He wished it was that easy to close his mind. Austin lay awake for a long time reflecting on many things that Jake had said over the last few days. That night Austin slept poorly for his dreams were troubled.

Chapter Eight

Birds chattered and fussed in the trees outside his window as Austin woke. It was early and the house was still as he passed through it on his way to the kitchen. Sam, who was lying at the back door, lifted his head for a familiar caress. Austin reached down to pat him, then quietly opened the door and stepped out onto the verandah. Sam, as usual, rose and faithfully joined him at his side. Since his arrival, wherever Austin went the dog followed.

The air was crisp with a gentle breeze. Morning dew still sparkled on the lawn. Austin strolled across the yard and down to the corrals. He climbed up and sat on the top rail and gazed out across the meadows fenced with barbed wire. He was soon hypnotized by the way the dawn sky lightened to lilac; then transformed from a brilliant red to orange to yellow and finally to blue. It was a beautiful, clear morning. So perfect, it should have made him feel wonderful, but there were nagging darts of doubt pricking at his conscience. Over the past few days his thoughts had turned more and more to home, bittersweet memories lingering in his mind.

Austin knew that he couldn't rely on Jake's hospitality indefinitely but he felt he wasn't ready to leave. His gaze turned inward. Solitude was what he needed right now. He needed time to digest a lot of what Jake had said and think things out for himself. Although Austin had let go of some of his anger, he needed more time to gather his thoughts. He still felt lost and without purpose.

Hopping off the fence, Austin stretched his legs. Working the stiff muscles made him aware of how long he'd sat there contemplating his life.

From a distance the house snuggled down into the stand of cottonwoods, their huge limbs sheltering the lawn from the intense heat of the day. He quickly ran back across the lawn, Sam nipping at his heels. The dew was gone, having evaporated into the warm morning air.

Jake sat on the verandah, his body sprawled in the wicker chair. He watched Austin and Sam approach over the rim of his coffee cup. Austin's face had a great deal more color today and his energy had returned.

"Getting up earlier all the time," Jake called out to the boy.

"Good morning," Austin answered back brightly as he reached the steps. "Sorry, the time kind of got away from me."

Jake reached for his Stetson and placed it firmly on his head. "I ate breakfast while you were gone. I didn't want a late start. What are you going to do while I'm gone?"

Jake had mentioned that he always went into town Saturday mornings to do his errands but Austin had lost track of the days. A smile warmed Austin's face. "Don't worry about us. We'll keep ourselves busy, won't we Sam?"

Jake smiled, too. There was a difference in Austin's voice today. The resentful tone had been replaced by a happier pitch. Also, the frown lines between his brows had disappeared and his shoulders had sprung back, as if released from an invisible load.

"I probably won't be back until late afternoon," Jake reminded him. "Are you sure you don't want to change your mind and come along?"

Austin shook his head, so Jake took his leave. The sound of Jake's footsteps echoed down the walk. Austin heard the truck door shut and the motor start. Jake reversed out of the drive and then thrust the engine into forward gear. He lifted his hand in farewell and accelerated away, leaving a cloud of dust hanging in the air behind him. Austin stood, his thumbs hooked into the pockets of the faded jeans, watching until the dust had settled. With Jake's departure, however, Austin experienced an intense feeling of depression. The realization of a lonely life ahead overwhelmed him. It didn't take long for solitude to end and for loneliness to begin. Just then the sun passed behind a cloud and the whole world seemed, momentarily, to grow darker.

It was a warm coatless day, certainly not the kind of day one wanted to spend indoors. "Want to go on a picnic?" Austin asked his constant companion. The dog wagged his tail back and forth in agreement.

Together they entered the kitchen. Austin went over to the counter, peeled a banana and ate it while making sandwiches for lunch. He grabbed a few dog biscuits from the cupboard, tossing one to Sam before putting the rest into the lunch bag. Throwing them into a bigger paper bag along with an apple, he was ready. He grabbed the bagged lunch and the thermos he had filled with water. With a slam of the porch door they were off. What a glorious day.

Austin and Sam romped through the meadows investigating the lay of the land. Taking a deep breath, Austin drew in the perfume of the flowers that had opened to greet the rays of the sun. For a moment in time he was as carefree as the birds flitting around him. There was a spring in his step as he ambled across the meadow and headed up the valley where it narrowed behind the homestead. As the hot sun broiled down out of a cloudless sky, the hills called to him with their cool green pines. As they walked, Austin would throw a stick and Sam would fetch it; boy and dog in harmony with nature. Enjoying the tranquility of the day, they meandered at a leisurely pace toward the woods.

The air was invigorating and the physical exertion felt good. Together, Austin and Sam tromped through the pine trees where the footing beneath them was cushioned with a carpet of needles. The terrain unfolded quite suddenly into an open glade. There, in the shade of a willow tree, stood two granite markers in the grass. Austin walked across the clearing as the wind in the pines whispered secrets of the past. Even before Sam went to lie beside the headstone, Austin knew Katherine lay beneath the carpet of grass. He felt her very essence and knew instinctively that she wouldn't mind him staying. Austin wondered who lay beside her but he felt it would be an intrusion to venture further and he'd already intruded on Katherine once before.

Here, in the secluded clearing, Austin sat on the cool grass to have lunch. Sam left Katherine and came over and flopped down at his feet. Opening the thermos, Austin tipped back his head and drank deeply. He wiped his mouth with the back of his hand and then poured some water into the lid. He held it beneath Sam's nose. Sam lapped noisily. Laughing, Austin repeated the process. "Feel better?" he asked, as he replaced the lid and patted the dog lovingly. The big dog flopped back down, let out a long sigh and shut his eyes.

Sitting quietly, munching his sandwich, Austin watched the bright-winged birds. The vivid green of the land contrasted with the sharp blue of the sky, a combination of colors only nature could make. Out of the corner of his eye he noticed the chipmunk. He quietly watched as it approached. First a quick rush, a frozen pause, another sudden rush. It bravely worked its way closer to gather food. Smiling, Austin tore a corner off his sandwich and tossed it over. With a rush, squeak and flip of its tail, the chipmunk snatched it and was gone.

Feeling the warmth of the afternoon sun, Austin took his shirt off, brushing his hand against the familiar scar on his shoulder. Terrible memories flooded through him. He closed his eyes a moment, his heart pounding. Austin took several deep breaths and let the memory flow.

Several months had passed since that fateful afternoon and Austin could remember every detail as if it was yesterday.

Austin had been worried about his friend Ryan. He knew it was time to have a talk with his buddy. They'd always shared everything but lately Ryan had become withdrawn, his manner remote and sometimes unfriendly.

"Ryan," he'd called to his friend when he had spied him down the hall between classes. Seizing the moment, Austin walked with determination to his friend's locker. A group of teenage boys scattered as he approached. Austin recognized a couple of them as part of a gang that had gotten into some trouble the summer before.

Ryan shot him a guarded look, quickly declaring, "I'm in a hurry. What do you want?"

Austin looked at his friend closely. Ryan looked a little gray and drawn. "What's with you? You avoiding me? What's your big hurry, anyway?" Austin gave Ryan a questioning look that Ryan was oddly reluctant to meet. What was the matter with him?

"Why are you hanging with those guys?" Austin questioned his friend. "They're trouble. Stay away from them."

Ryan lifted his shoulders in a defiant shrug. "Don't tell me what to do." There was a white line around his mouth. "Nothing's going on." Ryan's eyes were wide and candid but something flickered in their depths and Austin knew his friend was lying.

"Like hell there isn't. They're always up to no good."

Ryan looked extremely uncomfortable. "You don't know what you're talking about," was all he said. Not willing to open up to his friend, he remained evasive and sullen. "This has nothing to do with you."

"I'm warning you, Ryan. You'll end up in trouble if you keep hanging with them."

"You're just like everyone else. Something bad happens in this town and right away kids like us are blamed. It isn't us," Ryan cried out defensively. While Austin wanted to believe Ryan, his friend made a mistake. He said those revealing words. "You haven't any proof."

Austin looked at Ryan with disapproving eyes.

About to leave, Ryan halted and then yelled miserably, "Leave me alone."

Austin continued to watch his friend. Before Austin could utter another word, Ryan turned away and quickly flew down the hall, escaping further questioning.

Austin would have gone after him but the bell rang for his next class and he couldn't afford to skip another class. As he hurried down the hallway, he decided he'd just have to track Ryan down after school. Too much had been left unsaid.

At the end of the day, Ryan was nowhere in sight. Instead of going home, Austin headed straight for his friend's house. The altercation earlier had left Austin with the distinct impression that his suspicions about his friend were right.

Austin never really felt comfortable in Ryan's neighborhood. Like too many trailer parks it was one of concentrated poverty. There were no white picket fences or flower gardens here. Weeds had taken over most of the yards. It was with a sense of relief that Austin climbed up the steps and knocked loudly on the door.

Ryan's mom came to the screen door, drying her hands on her apron before opening it.

"Hello Mrs. Miller. Is Ryan home?"

She shook her head. "He didn't come home after school."

Austin frowned. "I need to talk to him. I'm worried about him."

"I know. He lives in his room and when I ask him what's wrong he says nothing." Her voice broke as she spoke. Mrs. Miller suddenly became very interested in a hole in the screen. She said, after a minute, "I know kids hang out but I don't like the guys Ryan's hanging around with. He's off with them all the time. They have a control over Ryan that scares me."

Austin sighed heavily.

"They're boys from our neighborhood, not yours. They're not like you. You're different than us. Ryan's different when he's with you, Austin. He's less angry. You're his best friend. You've been friends ever since you were little. I'm afraid he might be in trouble. Go find him," she pleaded.

Austin looked at Ryan's mom with level eyes. He saw her tears and there was a brief silence. Finally, he asked, "Do you know where Ryan might be?"

She thought for a minute before answering. "The abandoned barn close to town. Do you know where it is?"

Austin nodded. Kids partied there all the time. He turned and walked down the uneven steps. As he walked home, Austin tried to push the troublesome thoughts away but his mind wouldn't let him. Austin was convinced that Mrs. Miller's fears for her son were justified. His gut was telling him that his friend was in trouble. Ryan needed him.

When Austin got home there was no one around. Without a second thought, he grabbed the extra set of keys for his mom's car and left.

Deep in thought, Austin scowled as he headed out of town. When he turned into the farmyard his heart began to race. There were a few vehicles parked outside. He pulled over and killed the engine but he remained behind the wheel waiting for his breathing to slow down. He didn't know what to expect but he anticipated the worst.

Once out of the car, Austin walked decisively to the closed door of the old barn. As he approached, he could see flickers of light through the windows. Once inside, Austin scanned the room looking for his friend. The room smelled of drugs and liquor. He perceived everything at a glance as he stood looking around in open curiosity. Most of the boys standing around were like Ryan, normal teenagers who were rather awkward and certainly uncomfortable.

A familiar voice rang out from a dark corner. Ryan was sitting at a table with another boy. Austin walked directly toward his friend. Ryan was talking in a dead even voice while he stared at nothing. It didn't even register that it was Austin who sat down beside him. Austin tried getting his attention but Ryan didn't seem to hear him.

Ryan took another drink of beer and then wiped his mouth carelessly on the back of his hand. He laughed to himself and Austin shuddered.

Austin tried talking to him again. This time Ryan turned to face him. He blinked as he realized who was sitting there. He blinked again and for the first time Ryan looked at Austin with focused eyes.

Ryan touched his forehead in confusion. "Austin? What are you doing here?"

"Looking for you," Austin answered accusingly.

Close set eyes narrowed contemptuously as Ryan watched him. His straight mouth compressed. "You alone?"

"Yeah."

"How did you know I was here?" There was an unpleasant curl to Ryan's mouth and he didn't wait for an answer, "Get out." He waved his hand in the air. "You don't belong here."

Austin's eyes narrowed at the barb.

"I do 'cause I'm one of them." He tapped his fingers nervously on the tabletop and his eyes kept darting to the door. "Get lost, Austin. If Blade sees you here there's gonna' be trouble, sure as hell," Ryan's voice cracked, reflecting the fear building within.

Austin stayed where he was.

Irritated, Ryan rose and strode across the room, weaving dangerously.

Austin didn't follow immediately but he watched his friend closely. Ryan walked around the room before he came to rest in the corner farthest from Austin. He leaned against the wall staring into space as he shifted his body uncomfortably. Austin wasn't used to seeing his friend like this. He got up, went over and grabbed Ryan by the shoulders.

Ryan looked at him blankly but Austin firmly stood his ground. Then Ryan's face stiffened again. "I told you to leave."

"Not without you," Austin answered slowly. Forcing himself to speak quietly and calmly helped Austin feel that he was at least in control of himself, if not in control of the situation. "Friends look out for one another."

Before he could finish, Ryan interrupted, "Don't you get it? I don't want to hang out with you anymore. These are my friends now."

Austin stared at Ryan in horror as he let the words sink in. He compressed his lips and glared back at Ryan. Austin's tightly clenched fist was the only sign of his deep hurt and growing anger. "They're using you." Austin's other hand tightened on his friend's arm.

Ryan replied sadly, "You don't understand. I fit in here."

"What the hell does that mean?" demanded Austin, no longer attempting to hold his temper. "You fit in because you drink and do drugs?" Austin asked, unable to hide the disgust he felt. "This isn't where you belong."

"Think again, Austin. We're different," Ryan said bitterly.

"Not that different."

Ryan kept on as if he hadn't heard, "I tried being like you. I feel like the outsider with your other friends."

Austin digested this without comment but he wasn't willing to give up.

As they were talking, the door banged open. Ryan immediately pressed against the wall. His face drained of color. Austin detected a flicker of fear in his friend's eyes.

The entire atmosphere changed instantly. A hush fell over the room. Austin turned and stared at the newcomer. There was something eerie about him, something scary. Austin knew immediately that this was the leader. He was a year or two older than the others; surer of himself, with an arrogance born of experience. He presented an aura of toughness that was very intimidating. Physically, he was overpowering; tall, wide shouldered and strong.

Everyone knew him as Blade, a name well deserved because he carried a switch blade at all times and he didn't hesitate to use it. Austin had never liked the brooding youth who terrified others with his stormy moods.

A sense of apprehension shivered down Austin's spine at the look in the leader's intense black eyes. The look was cold and direct. Blade was not happy seeing an intruder in their midst. Austin's eyes moved hurriedly away, trying to hide his own reaction. He looked at Ryan who was refusing to meet his gaze.

Fear began rising within. He knew he had to get Ryan to go with him. Austin put a warning hand on Ryan's forearm. "Look, I understand but you don't need to fit in here."

Some of the fear left Ryan's face, only to be replaced by anger. Ryan denied the statement with a quick shake of his head. "No, Austin, people like you don't know. We're outcasts because of how and where we live. Poor kids grow up branded," he added bitterly. "You don't know what it's like to be poor. Really poor. Not enough food, second-hand clothes, shoes that you've outgrown and my old man couldn't care less. Take the last of the money for booze and damn the fact that we're freezing our asses off 'cause there's no heat. I hate him," Ryan said frankly.

Ryan's eyes reflected his inner feelings. Fear, torment, disgust. Feeling them all, Ryan turned more fully into the wall, withdrawing further from life.

The anger Austin had been feeling drained from him as he accepted the cold, hard facts. He couldn't change any of this for his friend but he wouldn't give up on him either.

Austin thought for a moment, and then placed his arms on both sides of Ryan, caging him against the wall. "I told your mom I'd bring you home."

At the mention of his mom there was a hint of remorse, "She's too good for us. My old man beats the hell out of her." Anguish pronounced every word as Ryan's eyes filled with tears. Shocked as he was, Austin let Ryan continue without interruption. Ryan kicked at a crack in the flooring. The one-sided conversation continued. "I've had to listen to my parents fight my whole life. Once Dad beat my mom so bad she missed work for days."

The volume of his friend's voice had increased with his anger. The only thing that kept Ryan from blindly lashing out was Austin. Austin's steady, steely gaze held firm, deflecting the stares from the curious and the cruel. By his very presence, Austin protected his friend. Austin didn't like the situation, but his calm exterior went a long way toward convincing Ryan that everything would be all right. The intensity of fear slackened briefly.

The troublesome memories brought a break to Ryan's voice, "He's a real mean son of a bitch. I never saw him hit her but there were always bruises. She said they weren't from Dad. She's lying. I ever catch him hitting her he's dead."

Austin jumped at the opportunity that Ryan had just given him. "Your mom needs you now, that's why I'm here. I'll take you home. Let's go," Austin pleaded.

Ryan looked up, tense, but listening. Austin was relieved to see the fight drain from Ryan's eyes. He'd pierced Ryan's brittle wall of self-defense. As stone after stone fell, the color returned to Ryan's face. Even though Austin expected Ryan to come with him, he just stood there watching Austin intently.

Once or twice Austin caught Blade looking at them. Austin was well aware that those fierce eyes held distaste and distrust. Nor did he miss the signals and silent nods that passed between the gang members who'd become a lot braver since their leader had arrived. He could feel the disgust and hatred that now radiated from the defiant youths.

Austin caught his breath and lowered his voice, "Ryan, never mind Blade. He doesn't matter. It's you and me, remember. Just like it's always been."

"Your dad hates me, doesn't he? He thinks I'm not good enough to be your friend."

Unable to deny it, Austin tried changing the subject, but today Ryan wouldn't let it go. "Wouldn't he be pissed off if he knew you were here with me?" Ryan sneered. The mockery in his voice was harsh.

Austin refused to react.

Blade, who was within hearing, laughed without amusement. Eyeing them sullenly, the dark eyes had an electrically-charged rage in them that made Austin feel weak and hopeless.

Austin moistened his dry lips with the tip of his tongue and tried to swallow the lump of fear in his throat. He was determined to get his friend to leave. "Don't be an idiot, Ryan. You're smarter than this."

Life had conditioned Ryan to expect the worst. "My old man thinks I'm stupid. He thinks I should quit school and get a job. He just wants the money." Ryan laughed resentfully. "He says people like us never make it out."

"Then prove him wrong," Austin challenged.

"I don't have to prove anything to him," Ryan said contemptuously.

"Then prove it to yourself," Austin came back. Austin persisted, "Is this really what you want? Come with me before it's too late. Don't stay."

Trying to show more confidence than he felt, Austin took his friend by the shoulders, needing him to accept the truth. "Listen to me, Ryan. I'm trying to protect you." The words were ripped hoarsely from his throat. Austin was desperate. He needed to get Ryan out. Now.

The whole time that Austin had been talking to Ryan he'd been listening for approaching footsteps and watching for any sudden movement.

Ryan looked up to make an angry protest, "I don't need you to protect me." For a few seconds their eyes warred in angry silence. Ryan was the first to look away.

Keeping his voice steady with difficulty, Austin continued, "Don't be a loser like your dad. You're better than that, Ryan."

Ryan stood there, his hands clenched into fists. After a long silence, he ran his hand shakily through his fine hair. "It doesn't matter."

"It does matter," Austin hastened to assure him, his eyes probing his friend's pale face.

Then some instinctive force, deep within, alerted Austin to sudden danger. As he turned, Blade was directly behind him. Beside him were two other youths.

"What's up?" Blade asked. "You bothering my boy, Ryan?" Blade spoke slowly and low pitched to lull Ryan into a sense of false security.

"He ain't bothering me, Blade. He came to give me a ride home. My mom needs me."

Blade appeared to be giving the matter intense consideration but his eyes narrowed and he stepped between the two friends. His stare rested on Austin. "It's time you were leaving. My boys here can give you a hand out." It was an unveiled threat that brought laughter from fellow members. A chill ran down Austin's spine but he held his ground.

Behind Blade's intense dark eyes was a hard, calculating mind. His voice was so controlled, so lacking in emotion as he spoke with authority, "Ryan will be staying. We have things to discuss, don't we Ryan?" He put his arm around Ryan as he spoke, laying claim to him. Ryan was agitated and upset, which pleased Blade immensely. The cruel tightness of his fingers intensified as he spoke.

This terrified Austin. He realized how Ryan felt as he saw his friend's eyes widen in fear. Ryan's face was stark white; his eyes enormous as he watched several more youths closing in, slowly making a circle around the outsider. They stood there, watching and listening.

Looking at Ryan, Austin saw the tension as Ryan felt trapped. The most disturbing part of the situation was that they were both trapped.

Goaded by Blade's arrogance, anger raced in Austin's veins. He never knew that it was possible to feel such rage, such fury as this. To have this moron order him around and take control over his friend. "Stay away from Ryan," Austin grated in a low tone. "When I leave, so does Ryan." The challenge was clear and harsh.

Blade's smirk immediately changed to something meaner.

Speaking through closed lips, his voice barely audible, Austin turned back to his friend. His look never wavered, nor did his voice. "Let's go." Austin managed to force a smile.

Ryan's resistance collapsed as he moved toward his friend.

Blade's reaction was immediate. "Ryan's not going anywhere." The dark eyes filled with hatred.

Before Austin could utter another word, Blade threw a punch, knocking him to the floor. Austin felt the pain and then a blinding rage. Picking himself up, Austin knew he had only one chance. With blood streaming from his nose, he doubled up his fist and struck Blade with every ounce of strength he possessed. As Blade stumbled, Austin quickly grabbed Ryan and pulled him toward the door.

Mesmerized with fear, Ryan glanced back. The familiar click of a released blade tore a scream from Ryan. He tried to warn his friend, "Austin, look out."

Austin knew he couldn't stop Blade. Defenseless, he raised his arms to protect himself. Not quick enough, Austin felt the intense burning sensation as the blade slashed his body. As he fell to the ground someone began kicking him. He held his body rigid as he received blow after blow. The last thing Austin heard before he passed out was the departure of running feet.

As Austin slowly regained consciousness, he lay motionless, paralyzed in pain. When he was able to, Austin slowly raised his head and looked around. At first, he thought he was alone. It was the sound of crying that drew his glance over and he noticed a form huddled in the corner. His friend had stayed. With tremendous effort, Austin gradually dragged himself over to Ryan. Pulling himself up to a sitting position, he leaned against the wall. Holding his shoulder, Austin felt the warm stickiness as blood seeped through his fingers. Austin gently nudged his friend with his elbow.

Ryan turned his head and leaned into his friend. In the stillness around them, they sat huddled together. Was it just moments, minutes, or a whole lifetime that they sat there holding each other? It was when the quiet of the night was broken by the sound of sirens that both boys were drawn back to reality.

"Your dad always said I'd get you into trouble. He was right."

Austin thought the same thing but he quickly pushed it from his mind.

"What do we do, Austin?" Ryan trembled as he spoke. "I can't go back home. My dad'll kill me."

Not for a moment did Austin doubt him.

The sirens grew louder.

Austin looked over at his friend who sat there white-faced and shaking.

"I'm scared," Ryan muttered. Fatigue had set in but it didn't quell his bitterness. "I got us into a real mess this time."

Austin let out a haggard breath. "I'm scared, too," he confessed.

"Austin, I'm sorry." Austin knew he was. "Are you mad at me?" Ryan needed to know.

"Mad as hell," Austin conceded. Then he smiled reassuringly. "We're in this together and I'm here for you like always."

Ryan sniffled and swallowed and presented a brave, pale face stained by tears. Ryan swiped a sleeved arm across his eyes. Then he said heroically, "Let me help you up."

Once they were both up Austin draped his good arm around Ryan's shoulder and together they walked out the door.

The emergency room was overcrowded. Ryan sat with Austin while he waited for his turn. Commotion down the hall drew their attention and without even looking Austin knew it was his parents. The triage nurse was busy at the main desk so his parents strode past her. Austin hung his head and waited.

Allison Smith was shocked to see Austin's blood-stained shirt. She broke into tears and sat down in the empty chair next to her son. Austin took his mom's hand to comfort her and whispered, "It's not as bad as it looks." He was glad he'd been able to wash the dried blood from his face and hands.

Meanwhile, his dad, true to form, started yelling. "Get away from my son you no good punk. You're nothing but trouble."

Austin's indignation surfaced. "Ryan's my friend and he's staying."

"Some friend."

"He didn't do this," Austin retaliated.

"Semantics. Fine, he's the reason this happened. I said he'd get you into trouble."

Ryan's body tensed and he moved restlessly. Austin held him back as he attempted to leave, trying to escape the wrath hurling his way.

"The cop's waving me over." Lifting his chin, Ryan continued, "I better go."

"Damn right." Richard said in a voice that indicated he had drawn his own conclusions.

Ryan hesitated, glancing back at Austin. "I'll look for you when I'm done."

"Stay away from my son." Austin's dad wouldn't let it go. "Low-life's like you are ruining this town." Richard turned back to Austin. "I suppose you're involved, too?" he asked, glaring at his son.

Trying to control his resentment, Austin subsided into silence. His dad goaded, "Come on, you and he are best buddies. How long have you been hanging around with those thugs?"

"Why the third degree? You've already found me guilty," Austin replied, face bleak.

"Okay, smart boy. Why don't you set me straight?"

"There's no need for sarcasm, Richard." Allison turned to her son. "We need to know the truth. Tell us what happened," she pleaded.

"Ryan was in trouble. He needed my help." Austin hesitated a moment before continuing, "He had no one else, Mom. Things got out of hand real fast and sometimes you have to fight to protect yourself."

"You can be so stupid, Austin. You charge in without thinking and no one can stop you. Do you always have to learn the hard way?" The admonishment came from his mother.

A smile reluctantly curved Austin's lips. So that's what he was doing now, having a learning experience. He winced with pain. Tough lesson. Fact was he was totally shaken by what had happened.

His dad misread the smile. "So you find this funny. Do you have any idea what kind of trouble you're in? Your so called friend just drags you down lower and lower. I don't know why you trust a dangerous kid like that."

At the sound of their arguing, the nurse at the station looked up.

Austin lowered his voice, "Ryan is no more dangerous than I am." He knew he would never be able to convince his dad that he was wrong about his friend. It would be hard enough convincing him that he was wrong about his own son.

An orderly approached. "We can take you in now and stitch you up." The condemning frown was still evident on his father's face. "Why don't you wait here Mr. and Mrs. Smith? It won't take long." There was a flicker of relief on Austin's face as he followed the orderly.

Everything happened quickly, the x-rays and the stitches. It really didn't take long. Austin wished it had so he wouldn't have to face his father right away. He was buttoning up his shirt when he heard a familiar voice calling from the other side of the curtain. Before he could answer a thin pale face poked through.

"They'll find me in a minute but I needed to see you before they took me away. How many stitches?"

"Thirteen, plus two cracked ribs. The doctor said it was a clean cut and should heal quickly." Austin gave his friend an encouraging smile.

"I was scared as hell back there," Ryan admitted solemnly. Tears glistened in Ryan's eyes. "I thought you were dead." Blinking back his tears, Ryan said seriously, "Nobody else would've done what you did."

Ryan informed Austin, "The cops want to talk to you, too. I told them what you did for me," he added quickly. Ryan paused, and then continued, "I can't go home, and I can't go back to school. They're taking me straight to a rehab center. I guess it's better than jail. I'm scared, Austin."

"I know. You'll get through it," Austin said with confidence.

Ryan gave him a doubtful glance. "What if I can't?"

"You can." He knew this was his friend's only chance. "You are okay, aren't you?"

Ryan nodded. "Will you come see me?"

"I'll come," Austin vowed.

"You've given me your word and you never break it."

"Not for anything in the world," Austin promised.

Ryan couldn't contain the tremendous relief he felt. "I couldn't have a better friend. I'll never forget what you did," he said huskily. He extended his hand and Austin shook it.

Austin winced in pain and tried to keep his voice light, "Friends forever."

Once Ryan was gone, Austin returned to the general waiting room and sat down next to his mom. His dad glared at him. Austin kept his eyes down, struggling for control. He was fighting to keep back the words of wounded protest that he knew his dad would never believe. Besides, there was no point in saying anything? His dad wasn't going to listen.

"You'll have nothing more to do with that felon," barked his dad.

"You can't stop me." The words were spoken with chilling indifference. They were a statement of fact, no more. Austin would always be there for Ryan. He had given him his word.

"He's no good, Austin," Richard said flatly. "I mean it. Stay away from him from now on. I'm going to talk to the police to see what you've been charged with. Am I in for any other unwelcoming surprises?"

The question wasn't worthy of an answer. Austin obstinately stayed silent, aware of the gaze but refusing to meet it.

"This isn't over." Richard turned on his heel and walked across the room. How his dad loved to have the last word.

"You had us so worried. Taking my car without permission," his mom cried. "Then to get a call from the police. Thank God you're all right." Tears fell softly onto her cheeks.

Allison wiped the tears away as she put a loving hand on her son's shoulder.

Austin turned to his mom. "I did what I thought was right. I tried talking to Ryan at school. I demanded to know what he was doing hanging around with that gang. I called him on it and he didn't deny it. He just walked away. I looked for him again after school. When I couldn't find him there, I went to his house. Mrs. Miller was home but Ryan wasn't. She and I talked for a while. She started to cry, Mom."

Austin took a deep breath and let it out slowly, "At first I didn't know what to do. Then I knew what I had to do. I promised her I would bring Ryan home."

Allison didn't interrupt, knowing her son needed to talk.

"I couldn't leave him there. It would've meant that I'd given up on him. Friends don't do that." That simple statement said it all and his mom understood. Austin came to a confused stop before continuing, "Dad doesn't understand our friendship. He doesn't know Ryan. He just yells and screams and says that Ryan is no good just like his dad. He isn't."

"Isn't he?" Allison questioned. She continued before Austin could defend his friend, "They both have problems with substance abuse. Your friend needs help before it's too late. He has a chance with the right help. It'll be hard but this may be the best thing that has happened to him. Experienced people will be able to help Ryan more than we can right now." She kissed Austin on the forehead and held her son close. She bit her lip to keep from crying again.

After a few minutes, Richard returned. His face was harsh.

Austin wanted to say he was sorry but he wouldn't. It would be a sign of weakness to his dad. Richard despised weakness of any sort. All the same Austin was sorry. He would tell his mom later.

"They have the one who knifed you in custody. They'll overlook the trespassing since you haven't been in trouble before so we're done here. They'll call if they have any more questions." He glared at his son with contempt. "Don't think this ends here. I will not condone this behavior. You know the rules. You'll take the consequences."

Allison rose and stood in front of her husband. She flashed him an angry look. "Yes, Richard, he broke the rules." In the next breath she lowered her voice. "There'll be no more discussion tonight. It's late. We're all upset. Tomorrow is soon enough. Let's just thank God no one was hurt any worse and we can take our son home tonight." With that she turned to Austin and said, "Come on son, let's go home."

Two friends would share the memory of that night for the rest of their lives.

Austin had kept his promise and visited Ryan at least once a week while he was in rehab. At first Ryan was so desperate for encouragement. "You know I'd never have made it without you."

Austin shook his head, "Give yourself the credit, not me. No one can do it for you."

"I guess." Ryan felt a warm glow inside.

Once Ryan started to open up, he revealed a lot to Austin. It may have been Ryan who was going through the therapy but there were many times Austin had to reflect on his own life, especially during the times they talked about their shared past.

Ryan confided, "It was easier when we were kids and it was always you and me. We can't go back and we aren't kids any more. Life changes and so do we." His profile was grave.

"Things really changed once you had a girlfriend." Ryan's voice was condemning, "I didn't know what to do. All of a sudden you were busy with Janice and it wasn't the same anymore." Before Austin could defend himself, Ryan continued. "Oh, you still always invited me along but I could tell there were times that you were glad I said no." Ryan hung his head in shame. Quietly, he confessed, "I hated you and I really hated Janice for taking away my best friend." The words were tumbling over themselves. "That's when I began hanging out with Blade and his gang. In my confused mind it was all your fault. It was easy to blame you and you didn't even know." Unshed tears glistened in his pale blue eyes. "How's that for honesty?"

During the months that followed Austin could see the return of his old friend. Austin knew he had his friend back for good when they were sitting together on his back steps and Ryan said, "I've always envied you. You have a brother and a sister, even if they are a pain lots of times. Your family is well off. Your family has it all while mine struggles just to make ends meet. Sometimes I'd feel like a failure whether I was or not. I couldn't help feeling that way. A guy needs to know that he fits in even though sometimes it's the wrong choice. You're lucky, Austin. You're always so sure of yourself."

Ryan had spoken evenly, "I owe you a lot. Like I told you before, I never thought much about my future. Thanks to you, I have a lot to look forward to. Somehow, I'll make it out of here." He said it carefully, his eyes never leaving his friend's face. Gone was the inferiority complex of the boy from the wrong side of town.

The gap in their friendship had closed. They argued heatedly about this or that and then laughed when it was over. They again shared their ups and downs, their secrets, their dreams.

As Austin sat quietly in the sun, he sighed, hoping his friend wouldn't think that he'd let him down along with everyone else. The burdens of his thoughts were creating more problems than they solved. He understood a little better how Ryan must have felt so many times.

Austin's thoughts made him uncomfortable as he sat there in the meadow, his hands gripping his bent knees. He closed his eyes and dropped his head. It was the feel of something rough, warm and wet on his arm that forced his attention away from his misery. Austin opened his eyes and found Sam staring at him with limpid brown eyes. Austin gazed into those mesmerizing eyes and could have sworn Sam understood his torment and unhappiness. Without thinking he grabbed the dog by the neck, buried his face in the shaggy coat and wept.

Tears came bursting from behind the dam he'd built up over time. The sound of release tore from his throat. The tears washed away the pain and let out the buried feelings of hostility and fear and along with that went a lot of pent up anger. Hollowness remained where all that anger, regret and sorrow had been.

Austin didn't know how long he held Sam. When Austin lifted his head, Sam stared at him. Two brown dots over his eyes twitched, his tongue hung out one side of his mouth, and his shaggy tail thumped against the ground. Cocking his head, Sam gave Austin a quizzical look. Austin hugged him tight and then patted his head. Surprisingly, Austin felt much better. He sighed with a strange kind of contentment.

With lithe grace, Austin stood up and dusted off his jeans. "Let's go for a swim."

Together, with his comrade, they began running across the meadow, back through the trees and down the hill to the river below. Sam stayed close to Austin's legs, keeping pace beside him. Austin laughed a rich joyous sound that came from deep within.

Once they got down to the river, Austin took off his runners and socks and rolled up his pant legs. He dangled his feet in the rushing water, gritting his teeth at the cold. Sam jumped in, splashing Austin, who laughed at the sheer joy of the moment. Eyes half closed against the afternoon sun, he raised his face and soaked in the rays. What a way to spend the afternoon.

A doe had come to drink at the stream several feet from Austin, light-footed and graceful, head lifted. Fearing he would startle her, Austin didn't move and barely dared to breathe. Sam was sleeping quietly at his side. Austin became absorbed with the deer, watching her bend her neck and touch her nose to the water, bracing herself on the rocks with her tiny hooves. Her ears twitched and once or twice she seemed to look directly at Austin. He remained motionless, his breath caught in his throat. When had he ever seen anything as free and wild as this?

Jake's voice broke into his thoughts. "She's a beauty, isn't she?"

With the babbling of the stream, Austin hadn't heard Jake's approach and with a start, he jumped. The doe fled.

Sam took off after the doe, splashing through the water and up onto the other bank, unconcerned that he'd never catch her.

Jake stood as quiet as the mountains. "I didn't mean to startle you," he apologized.

"I was watching the deer."

"They come here through the meadows. They've figured out there are no hunters here."

Within minutes, Sam came bounding out of the stream and jumped up, catching Austin off guard and throwing him to the ground. Austin's startled face peered up at Jake. Sam shook his long shaggy coat until it was almost dry and then set off running back through the stream. Jake's grin changed to a deep chuckle and then he erupted into laughter. The sound was rich, mellow and contagious. Austin burst out laughing, too. Once again, the sound of laughter echoed through the hills.

Jake lowered himself and sat down next to Austin while pushing his worn hat back on his head. The older man sighed as he assumed a more comfortable position.

Austin waited, knowing Jake was watching him. After a few moments of silence, Austin sat up. He turned his head to look directly at Jake.

Jake spoke first, "What's bothering you?"

Austin had grown used to Jake's directness over the last couple of days. Without hesitation, he answered, "Everything."

Austin glanced over and studied Jake through narrow eyes. He had the feeling that Jake was choosing his words.

Jake drew a slow breath and rubbed his jaw before speaking. "Beyond the horizon are the dreams; beyond the dreams, the reality. This means, in today's lingo, that you can wiggle and evade the issue and run away as much as you like. In the end, you are forced to face the truth even if you don't like it. We need to have a serious talk, Austin."

Austin declared, softly, "I wish things were different. Do you think I like fighting with my parents?"

"Wishing won't make it go away," declared Jake, before the boy could continue.

Austin shook his head. "You wouldn't understand. Forget it."

Jake couldn't. "I realize that this is a hard time for you but do you really think running away is going to make the pain any easier? I'm sure your dad regrets the pain he caused."

"Regret?" As Austin turned toward Jake the question hung in the air. "You think Richard Smith ever feels regret?"

"Of course he does. Any man would."

"The only regret he has is that I'm a failure and it reflects on him," Austin cried in exasperation.

"Austin, your continued antagonism toward your dad concerns me. How am I going to make you understand? When you're angry everything around you is wrong. Nothing's right. The problem with most people is that they lose control of their emotions. It's the emotions that control the behavior of the human, not the human that controls the emotions. When control is lost we say things we don't mean and we do things that we don't want to do. Like leaving home," Jake added quietly. "That's not the answer to your problems. The big problem is really between you and your dad. You better break down that barrier before it's too late. You two need to talk and resolve this issue about school."

Austin's tightened voice declared, "With my dad, talking doesn't change a damn thing."

"When do you talk to him? When you're both so angry that you're incapable of communicating? That's the problem. You aren't thinking as clearly as you and I are right now. You let anger cloud the issues," Jake said carefully.

"So does he," snapped Austin. Every muscle rippled with the tension of the moment.

Jake controlled a flare of annoyance. "You're right. Does it make you feel better?"

Austin hung his head. "No."

"Good." Jake persisted, "What's really continuing to make you angry? Say it out loud so you can deal with it. Don't keep it locked inside."

Austin gave Jake a curious look. "You already know. I told you it's my dad."

By now, Jake knew Austin well enough to know that there was more to it than this. "Don't be afraid to open up. Let it all out." Jake paused for a moment before he decided to push further. "Are you afraid of what other people will think of you? Are you afraid of your dad's feelings towards you? Or, do you hate what this is doing to you. Therefore, you hate your father because you think it's all his fault."

"Okay, I am afraid, but not of that," Austin cried out.

Jake didn't let up, "What are you really afraid of, Austin?" It was a probing remark designed to get Austin to open up and be completely honest with himself.

Austin waited for a long moment and then sighed. With a look of pain in his eyes he answered, "I'm afraid I'll grow up to be like my dad and I don't like who he is." The words were torn from his soul. It was a heavy confession for Austin to make. "We're a lot alike. I can be bull-headed and stubborn. I get mad fast. I'm self-centered just like him. I'm getting to be more and more like him." A lot of anguish was channeled inward.

"Listen to me. From what I can see you're nothing like your father. He can be mean- spirited and a bully. He has to have control. That's not like you, Austin. How can you even think that you're remotely like him? Sure, you get angry and you even lose your temper. We all do. You can be stubborn but you're not insensitive. You care about others. I hear it when you talk about Jordie and Cassie. You're aware of people's feelings. You're loving and caring."

Noting the look of scorn on Austin's face, Jake stated, "That is not a weakness, it's a gift." Jake's eyes were square on Austin. "Stop it," Jake said sternly. "Weakness makes a man human, Austin, and human beings are the toughest, most admirable creatures in existence."

Austin had to wonder how two men could see weakness so differently.

Jake leaned forward a little, his hands clasped between his knees, and the sun shone through the trees onto the tawny color of his hair. "You may not know what you want to do with your life, but I believe deep down you know who you really are. I also believe you have the courage to move forward and find the answers."

Looking out, Austin saw a bald eagle perched on a cottonwood limb. Jake, always observant, noticed as well. "They like it along the rivers in winter. In summer they head for the high country. To many, the eagle represents freedom. What does freedom mean to you?"

"I don't know, but it's out there, somewhere." Austin's gaze returned to the mountains.

"It's here, Austin," Jake said, as he touched his heart. "True freedom has to do with the human spirit. It's the freedom to be who we really are and express ourselves. Therefore, you must believe in yourself. You were right when you told your parents that it was your life. No one else can give your life direction. We can only tell you what has worked for us. What you make of your life depends on you. You're the one who must make your decisions. However, your father was also right. You control your attitude or it controls you. Ultimately, you are responsible for every choice you make. For things to change, you must change."

Jake continued seriously, "You need to chart your course and set your goals. They're your road map to success. So many people just wander through life without setting goals because they're afraid they'll fail. To do nothing is worse than failing. Sometimes things don't turn out the way we want but you can always reset your course based on what you've learned. That's one of the things that make life so exciting. Knowing that you have the potential to do whatever you want to. Sometimes we ask for so many things that they're actually in direct conflict with one another but at the time we're unaware of it. So when things don't turn out the way you want them to, trust that maybe it wasn't meant to be at this time."

Austin turned his head slightly and found himself looking directly into Jake's eyes. His expression was so different from anything he'd expected. Jake's steadfast eyes looked at Austin as an equal.

The two of them looked at one another and they both smiled. For a long time there was silence between them while they sat enjoying the tranquility of their surroundings, feeling the sun on their faces, the breeze lifting their hair.

Jake put a hand on Austin's shoulder. "It's getting late. I don't know about you but I'm hungry. Let's go home and we'll barbecue up some hamburgers."

Austin nodded in agreement and the three of them were off.

Jake slapped a couple of burgers on the grill. "Here." He handed the job over to Austin. "You watch them while I go in and get the fixings ready." Given no choice, Austin took over.

Within minutes, Jake was back. "Everything's ready. How are those burgers doing?"

"They're done to perfection," Austin said proudly. Jake held out the plate while Austin removed them from the grill.

Austin followed Jake into the house. Once seated, both quickly assembled their buns with lettuce, tomato, onion and everything else that Jake had laid out. Placing the top of the bun on his creation Jake grinned at Austin. "Let's eat." Jake bit into his hamburger with great gusto.

Once supper was done Jake rose, gathered the empty plates and began loading the dishwasher. Austin pitched in and within minutes the evening meal had been cleared.

"Coffee by the fire?" Jake asked.

Austin felt restless. "I need some air," Austin said abruptly. "Sam, want to come?" His voice softened as he spoke to the dog. What he really needed was to be alone for awhile.

"Oh, don't mind me," Jake said. "I'll be content with my book that I borrowed from the library in town today." He reached over and picked up the book sitting next to him. Austin was close enough to see what he was reading and had to grin. What answers was Jake looking for in 'For Parents, Managing and Coping with Anger'?

Austin picked up his jacket from the chair and slipped it on as he walked through the house to the verandah. "Hope he doesn't try any new ideas on me," he murmured to Sam as he closed the door behind them.

Jake, who overheard, chuckled to himself and began reading.

Austin sat down on the top step of the verandah and stared out at nothing, unaware of the ever-changing scene around him. Clouds were piling up in the sky as they did most evenings. The sun was falling behind the mountains and the tall cottonwoods stood dramatically silhouetted against them.

The conversation with Jake this afternoon by the river had made an impression on Austin but he needed time to think it through. The wheels of his mind went round and round. Austin, looking for answers, cried out to the night, "What should I do?" Startled, an owl flapped away and disappeared over the treetops.

Austin sat in the growing darkness for a long time, unconcerned that the air was chilling as the sun descended. So long did he remain fixed in thought, waiting for answers, that the owl returned to perch in the top of a nearby tree and hooted his return.

"What are you telling me?" Austin asked, hoping the wise old owl had the answers. No great voice of wisdom answered his question.

Austin stared out at the night sky, deeply conscious of the great universe beyond him. The clouds drifted and blocked the moon and in the darkness it seemed to Austin that he could be at the end of the world. It was a big world and he didn't want to live in it alone. That knowledge went thorough him with such force it took his breath away. A deep longing crept out of hiding and at that moment Austin wished he were home.

He stood up and walked back into the house leaving the night behind, closing it out with the shutting of the door. The house was warm and inviting. Jake had touched a match to the log in the hearth and the fire had already begun to burn brightly.

Jake looked up from reading and smiled at his guest. Closing his book, Jake laid it on the table next to him. "Come, let's talk."

"So you can spend the rest of the evening counseling me?" Austin asked with a grin and Jake knew the boy was okay.

Austin walked over and settled himself comfortably in the chair next to Jake. Austin swallowed his pride. In a voice that was more man than boy he confessed, "I feel like I'm in a maze and I can't find my way out. Tell me what I should do, Jake?"

"Think of the position that would put me in, Austin. I'll help where I can but the final decision can only be yours," Jake said carefully.

Austin knew Jake was right again.

Jake smiled encouragingly, "The time has come for you to make that decision. I'll give you one more day. If you decide to go home I'll rearrange my schedule and drive you. Or I can take you into town and get you a bus ticket home. Or I can let you walk out that door and take whatever path you choose."

A slow smile quirked about Austin's lips. "You've made your point, Jake. I know there will always be important decisions to make but this one is the biggest. I need to chart my own course. You see, I have been listening to what you've been saying. Thanks for tomorrow. I really appreciate you letting me stay here this long."

Austin acknowledged seriously, "I know this ongoing conflict isn't all my parent's fault. I've been blaming everything on them, especially my dad." Austin looked over and smiled. "How's that for honesty?"

Jake looked impressed. "So maybe your dad deserves another chance?"

"Maybe we both do," Austin conceded.

"It's not a crime to be human, Austin. As humans, none of us are perfect. We all have our flaws and you have to love him in spite of his," Jake added.

"Mom says there are always three sides to everything. My side, your side, and the truth that falls somewhere in between. The good part of me comes from Mom," Austin declared, as he flashed Jake one of his wicked grins.

Jake leaned back with a contented sigh.

Austin, too, too felt a sense of contentment. It was amazing what one day could bring. He was looking forward to tomorrow.

Chapter Nine

Over a late breakfast, Jake discussed their plans for the day. "If you help me throw something together for supper tonight, I'll give you a tour of the place. I try to take Sundays off so we have the whole day if you like," Jake said, with a conspiratorial smile.

"That would be terrific," Austin said, face eager. While Austin busied himself peeling potatoes, Jake cleaned carrots and onions. Fifteen minutes later the kitchen was tidy, there was a pot roast and vegetables in the oven with the timer set and the three of them were off.

Rather than crossing the side lawn that sloped into the woods, they went around the back toward the barn and corrals.

Jake took a deep breath of the fresh morning air and exhaled slowly, "It's good to get out of the house. As you know, I can get caught up in my work and the day is gone before I know it. If I didn't enjoy my work so much I'd be ranching."

"Do you have horses or cattle of your own?" Austin inquired as they passed the barn where he had spent his first night. Austin was accustomed to the sudden cloud that flitted across Jake's eyes as old memories came to haunt him. He knew it would pass quickly.

"Katherine and I always had horses. I keep them down in the lower pasture. It seems I don't have time to ride as often as I like anymore. A few years ago I took the other livestock to our homestead south of Medicine Bow. My family has ranched in the County of Laramie for generations and our land runs along the Medicine Bow River."

Austin was familiar with city names like Cheyenne and Laramie but not Medicine Bow. Jake turned to the boy with a smile. Austin met his gaze with frank curiosity so Jake continued, "The name 'Medicine Bow' is legendary in these parts. Its origin is from the Indian tribes that settled here, mainly the Arapaho and Cheyenne."

"Along the banks of the river, the Indians found excellent material for making their bows. To them, anything they found that had a purpose was called 'good medicine'. So they named the river Medicine Bow River and the mountains they called Medicine Bow Mountains."

Then the architect in Jake took over. "The land is shaped by the winds and the shapes can be very striking and awesome at times. It's amazing how the wind can create wonderful structures that look like castles rising from the hills."

Austin couldn't help teasing, "And you call me the dreamer."

Jake smiled. "Most of this area is covered in grass and sagebrush which supports a huge livestock industry. It's also a sportsman's paradise. The fishing is great."

Jake laughed again. "I do get somewhat off topic. My dad's forefathers were original settlers along the Medicine Bow River. The homestead has stayed in our family and over the years we've bought up adjacent land. My older brother Matt lives in the main house with his wife Gail. Their eldest son Glen lives on the next ranch and together they have a large ranching operation. I often go down and help them when time allows. It's always good to go home."

Austin didn't say anything but got the message.

"It'll always be home even though my mom and dad retired into town. Sadly, Dad passed away five years ago but Mom is still well and keeps herself busy."

"Is that your whole family, then?" Austin asked. It was the first time Jake had opened up about anyone other than Katherine.

"Matt and I were the only children but Matt has another son as well." Jake chuckled. "Their younger son, Billy, well that's a whole new story."

Recognition clicked immediately. "Billy, as in Billy Hanson, the steer wrestler?"

"You've heard of him?"

"Who hasn't? He's awesome. I hear he's going pro this year."

"Right you are. Billy never does anything by halves, always taking the bull by the horns and devil be damned." Both laughed as soon as they realized what Jake had said. "Billy's introduction to the pro circuit will be at Cheyenne's Frontier Days. It's definitely a favorite rodeo for competitors and rodeo fans."

"Billy should do well. He really is incredible and a real crowd pleaser. I saw him in a local high school rodeo a few years ago. Man he's fast."

Jake had to agree. "Billy's been a powerhouse since he was little. As soon as he could walk he was chasing the newborn calves. An unknown steer wrestler was born the first time Billy actually caught one and threw it to the ground instead of the other way around. He loves what he's doing but his parents think he's nuts. They wish he'd quit and find a real job," Jake exclaimed, in dismay.

"Parents. What do they know?" A comment Austin had often shared with Ryan.

Suddenly, and quite unexpectedly, Jake threw back his head and laughed. Jake continued, "Even though they aren't crazy about his career choice they're very supportive."

Austin sensed that Jake was proud of his nephew.

"A good steer wrestler needs more than brute strength to be successful. A good hazer can make all the difference."

"What's a hazer?" Austin asked.

124

"A hazer is the rider that keeps the steer in line so it can't suddenly veer away. Many hazers use their own horses but Billy and his hazer Clint Davis use Hanson horses. In the off season, they train at the ranch and work for Matt. To them rodeo life is more than a sport, it's a lifestyle. But rodeo life is pretty tough. Lots of broken bones before fame and fortune."

"At least he's doing what he likes." For a change there was no bitterness when Austin spoke. The boy had come a long way over the last few days.

Moving off the footpath, they ascended through the trees. Their climb was a bit rough but well worth it when they reached the top. Austin hadn't ventured this far and the view spreading below and far into the distance was of immense beauty and splendor. Jake pointed. "Over there you can see all the way to the river valley. It's a pretty spot, don't you think?"

Austin could only stand and stare. The scene must have changed little in the last hundred years. His eyes scanned the landscape of valleys and hills with their patchwork-like fields. The river sparkled and whipped its way through ageless rock formations. The greenery seemed to grow right out of the massive rocks. Downstream the river was high and turbulent with spring runoff. There were mature pine trees here, twisted by the wind. They had defied the cold of winters and the heat of summers. Somehow they endured. Their fragrance scented the air. The mountains were powerful against the horizon. Every sense and nerve was alert to the silence and vastness of his surroundings. Austin found himself drawing deep, long breaths.

A long silence fell between them before Jake broke it. "Like my ancestors, I want to save the land. I want to keep things the way they used to be. Ranching has changed. Rich people are buying the ranches. They hire some cowboys to oversee and they only show up at their places a few times a year to ride horses and have a barbecue." He shook his head. "That's not ranching."

As Jake began descending the hill, Austin hurried to catch up. Wandering over the tree scattered hills they emerged into a familiar meadow and Austin knew they were going to see Katherine. The explosion of springtime flowers accented the dark green meadow with an array of colors ranging from the brilliant yellow of the goldenrod to the vibrant hues of the native Indian Paintbrush. Their delicate fragrances filled the air. As they strolled leisurely through the meadow, Jake picked a variety of wild flowers. Austin followed, sticking close beside him, the way he did with his dad when he was a kid. "Katherine loved flowers. This was her favorite time of the year. For her, it was the rebirth of the land, the promise again of life to come."

Listening, instead of looking where he was going, Austin tripped and nearly fell. He murmured nostalgically, "My mom always teases me when I trip. She says I must have grown during the night and haven't adjusted to my longer legs. Jordie does the same thing. I bet he ends up taller than me before he's done." A wave of homesickness washed over Austin as he talked about his family and he longed to be home again.

Jake knelt beside the grave and laid the bouquet of fresh flowers along the headstone. "Other than the house, this was Katherine's favorite place. Sometimes I think I hear her, especially here, laughing in the meadow."

Austin sat with his elbows on his knees beside him. "Where she danced with the fairies," Austin declared. A bright red tinge immediately flushed the boy's cheeks. Embarrassed, Austin hurried to explain. "On Friday I was up in the loft. You gave me permission, remember? While I was browsing I came across a book of quotes. When I opened it a piece of paper fell out. I didn't mean to pry but I couldn't stop myself from reading it. I just wanted to know Katherine better," Austin stammered, with the look of someone who wished that he hadn't spoken.

"Oh, that's all right." After a thoughtful pause Jake said, "Katherine was such an interesting mixture, so transparent in some ways, so puzzling in others. She was open and honest and spoke her mind yet so many of her friends would seek her out for advice. She understood, without passing judgment, and that's a rare human quality. Life interested her in all its aspects. She had a mind that never stopped questioning and an insatiable craving for things of the spirit. The spirits are pretty friendly up here," Jake teased. "If you come with the right attitude." His eyebrows lifted in mock earnestness.

Jake's face softened as it always did when he talked of her. "Katherine isn't really gone. She lives within me because she's the sunshine, the gentle morning rain." He paused and looked directly at Austin before continuing, "The rose on the mantle."

They lapsed into a companionable silence, sitting side by side in the meadow, both distracted by their own thoughts. Jake's in the past, Austin's in the future. Austin hoped that he would find a 'Katherine' one day. He thought of his own parents. Their marriage worked. They shared the same morals and beliefs. They didn't argue about mundane issues like the house or money. His dad was definitely the boss; strong, opinionated and controlling. And his mom quietly softened the hard edges. He looked at them differently now and wondered at the depth of their love for each other.

Jake made himself more comfortable, as if he were in no hurry to leave. "I couldn't live anywhere else." Austin knew it was because he couldn't leave Katherine.

Austin looked over at Jake and smiled. How fortunate he was to have been guided here that night. A shiver ran down his spine as a butterfly came to rest on his arm.

Jake spoke with calm deliberation, although his eyes were gentle. "There's a reason our paths have crossed, that you found your way here that stormy night. 'God's master plan', Katherine would say. He weaves people into our lives but we don't always know why or for how long."

Austin shivered again and the butterfly flew away.

Jake smiled faintly as he reached over and caressed Katherine's name on her headstone.

"We don't tell ourselves how good it is to be alive." His tone became very serious. "We knew Katherine had a heart condition. Katherine was very accepting of her delicacy. To her, this was simply what God gave her to deal with. She believed that a person's life should be devoted to growth. Growth doesn't just come from happiness. Just as often, it can be the result of sadness. Being miserable or depressed doesn't change anything. She said none of us know how long we'll live. If we knew we would just sit and wait for it. She believed every day to be a gift and regarded idleness as a waste of the greatness of life. Her enthusiasm for life was contagious. I knew she was right and I became more accepting of circumstances."

"Although her ailment certainly affected her physically, it had a very positive effect on her overall. I believe her condition gave her a profound understanding of how frail a human is. I don't just mean physically. It transformed her to someone with extraordinary compassion. She was more open to love and living. She had an unmistakable ability to enjoy each moment."

"We were happy but having a baby was constantly on her mind and once the house was done she told me she wanted to start a family. I knew how much she wanted to be a mother. When we spoke to her specialist he reassured us that as long as Katherine didn't over exert herself, there was no reason not to have a baby. To avoid the stress of labor, she'd be scheduled for a Cesarean section. Katherine persuaded me to let her have the baby she longed for and just after our fifth anniversary Katherine became pregnant. We were thrilled."

"Katherine was fine during her whole pregnancy. In fact, she glowed. Being pregnant suited her. She was even more beautiful. We were happy. We had it all." Jake's voice trailed off for a moment as he remembered.

A look of sadness darkened Jake's face. "She was in her seventh month and had an appointment for her monthly check-up. We usually went together and made it a full day outing. I'd been working on a major project and we were into the final changes. I had a deadline to meet. Katherine said she'd be fine. It was still six weeks before the baby was due. She said she'd visit a friend of hers who was also pregnant. They would go out for lunch and really 'baby' talk. I patted her round little belly and kissed her good-bye. Katherine smiled and walked out the door."

"I lost track of time after she left. Before I knew it, it was late afternoon and Katherine wasn't back. I figured she and her friend got caught up in visiting but I was surprised Katherine hadn't called. When it started to get dark and I still hadn't heard from her I started imagining the worst. I tried calling her friend but there was no answer. That's when I decided to go find her."

Austin sensed Jake watching him closely. "It's the not knowing that's the worst," declared Jake and for a brief instant Austin felt intense guilt thinking what his parents must be going through.

"As I stepped outside I saw headlights coming up the drive. I was so relieved, believing it to be Katherine. As the lights drew closer I realized it was my brother. Katherine had called him. She had gone into premature labor and was taken by air ambulance to Cheyenne. Matt had come to drive me to the hospital. I was so grateful. I was terrified and in no condition to drive."

Not knowing what to say, Austin remained silent.

Jake's mouth tightened, "I couldn't understand. She was fine when she left. It seemed to take forever to get there. I kept praying over and over that the doctors would know what to do, but over and over the same thought kept repeating in my mind. Katherine's never coming home." Jake stopped and a spasm of pain washed over his face.

Jake's voice was thick with emotion, "The doctor told me the worst. Katherine didn't have much time left. The delivery had been too much for her. They weren't sure if they could save the baby either. I opened the door to her room. As I walked in, her eyes opened. Katherine knew she was dying and I knew she'd been waiting for me. Every breath was labored as she told me to name our son Michael Conrad. Conrad was her maiden name."

Jake confided the worst to Austin, "Her voice grew weaker and weaker as her life slipped away. She closed her eyes, a tear ran out the corner and I gently wiped it away. Katherine opened her eyes one last time. Her words were barely audible as she said 'I love you'. I thought my heart was going to break. I knew I'd never hear Katherine say those words again. As I kissed her tears away, I whispered to Katherine that I'd love her forever. I sat by her side and held her hand. My wife died that night," Jake said huskily.

Recovering his composure, Jake continued to tell the rest of her story. "A real tribute was paid to Katherine. Funerals are for the living. They give us an occasion to say good-bye in our own way and to celebrate a person's life. The support from our friends really helped me as I tried to face the reality of her death. You see, true friends share the good times and the bad."

"I'm sorry about Katherine," Austin said compassionately.

Jake was quiet for a minute and then in a solemn voice he continued, "Katherine was my best friend. We shared everything. The joys, the pain, the loss of loved ones, successes and failures. Life has it all and we got through everything together. Now Katherine is gone and there's only this aching void where she was. I'm sure that feeling of loss may be especially strong when a death comes too soon."

"Aren't you lonely up here by yourself?"

"Everyone is a little lonely," was as much as Jake would admit to before tilting his head back proudly to show it didn't matter. A cool mask stole over his face. "Life doesn't always work out the way you plan but my life is of my own making."

Jake became quiet once again. Austin waited for Jake to go on, but he seemed to be lost in his thoughts. Jake's face showed the anguish these painful memories brought back. He was remembering the pain of losing Katherine. Jake let out a jaded sigh and with a ragged voice he continued, "Your life can be changed in a matter of hours. I've learned that the people you care about the most in life can be taken from you too soon."

As ashamed as he was over the parenting remark of Friday night, Austin dared to ask, "What happened to your son?"

Jake's eyes were intense as he glanced over at the headstone next to Katherine's. A look of despair was evident and his voice was edged with an unexpected sharpness when presently he spoke, "My son died a few days after he was born. He wasn't strong enough to survive. He would've been almost your age if he'd lived."

"I had a difficult time when they died. For a long time I blamed myself. I thought it might not have happened if I'd gone with her but it wouldn't have made any difference. I even blamed my son, but blaming doesn't change anything."

Another wave of guilt passed over Austin.

"I learned a lot about death and the meaning of life. We live by loving and losing and letting go. We must all come to know loss because death is also a growing experience. Changes will occur in our lives whether we want them or not. The only choice we have is to decide how we will react to them. I've accepted being alone but there are times when I miss them terribly and often times, like now, when I wish they were still here."

Jake wasn't bitter about life, but Austin recognized Jake's pain. Austin wished that Jake and Katherine and their son Michael had been able to spend their lives together.

"Nothing can protect people from bad things. Maybe love is what makes the bad bearable. We all have burdens, unique sources of pain, sometimes despair. Great aching hurts that we would choose to forget but never will." Jake reached over and put his large hand on the boy's shoulder. "Each of us has the gift of compassion, understanding and forgiveness. Don't you understand that you have to learn to forgive?"

"I want to, but it isn't easy." Austin's voice trailed off in a barely audible whisper.

Jake's look had a hint of challenge. "Forgiveness allows you to move forward."

When Austin stared back uncomfortably, Jake said, "Destiny took my family. Don't let pride take yours."

Austin was quiet, gazing in the direction of the mountains. They had an influence on Austin. Their silent power had calmed some of the anger and disappointment within. Yet they still remained his symbol of freedom.

Jake's voice became somber. "Sometimes our problems seem as big as mountains. When we look real close, we can see the different ways to solve them and get to the other side. Sometimes you have no choice but to go over the top. Other times you can go through the pass because others have gone on before you. Or you might want to blaze your own trail. There's never just one way. Only you can decide which way will be the best for you."

Feeling a great heaviness inside, Austin asked, "What do you suggest I do?"

"Consider your options and know why you want to get to the other side in the first place. Then make your plans," Jake advised. "Always remember that you can go back and change direction if you find that you've gotten off course."

Over the last few days it had become quite natural for this man to ask questions and for Austin to confide in him. Austin didn't resent his advice; he didn't even wonder at it any more. Jake knew about the reality of life and of death. Just as there are different kinds of love, there are different kinds of happiness. With Jake's help, Austin had come to the realization that there are consequences in life, in choices, in actions, in all aspects of life.

Austin got up and began to walk back across the meadow and down the grassy hill. When Jake caught up with Austin, he swung into step and put his hand on the boy's shoulder. Austin felt Jake's hand tighten. It brought comfort. Jake let him have his silence as they walked back to the house.

Jake led the way into the kitchen. "Sure smells good in here." Jake grabbed a dish towel and opened the oven door, releasing a new wave of cooking smells. As Jake lifted the lid off the roaster, Austin couldn't resist taking a quick peak.

Both of them quickly washed up. While Jake sliced the roast and made gravy, Austin grabbed plates and cutlery from the cupboards and set the table. It was fun working together and within minutes they were sitting down. Austin picked up his knife and fork and began to eat, no longer surprised at how flavorful the food was.

"It's delicious," Austin said and then realized he'd started eating before Jake and was embarrassed. Where were his manners? "Sorry. I should've waited."

Jake grinned and shook his head. "It's good to see someone enjoying my cooking."

When he finished eating, Jake moved his plate forward so that he could lay his folded arms on the edge of the table.

Austin shoved his empty plate aside, too. "You're an excellent cook, Jake." He had proven it every day. "I'll clean up tonight," Austin offered.

"Let's do it together," Jake said. "It'll only take a few minutes."

Austin rinsed the last of the dishes and added them to the nearly full dishwasher. Jake switched on the machine and they stood looking at each other. Jake handed Austin a tea towel, and grumbling good naturedly, Austin started to dry the pots and pans. When the dishes were done Austin asked, "What else do you want me to do?"

There was no hesitation as Jake said, "Phone your parents. They have no idea if you're even okay. Do you think that's fair?"

As though he hadn't heard, Austin moved into the living room. Jake poured two cups of coffee and joined the boy. Before he sat down he turned on the stereo; rich musical notes from one of his favorite composers played quietly in the background.

Jake sat listening to the music but Austin knew he was waiting for him to acknowledge his last comment in the kitchen. Austin remained silent as continuous doubt infiltrated his thoughts. Finally Austin spoke, "Jake, what am I going to say to my dad?" He searched the older man's eyes for answers.

"Speak from your heart and the words will come," Jake said gently.

"I hope they'll forgive me," Austin sighed deeply.

"Sometimes you have to forgive yourself first." Jake chose his words with care. "We all make mistakes. The key to our character is whether we learn from them. Be honest with him. Explain to him why you said the things you did, how you feel, what you want. Believe me; both your parents love you. They only want the best for you. Won't you let them try? Have faith in yourself and don't give up on your parents just yet."

Half turned, listening, Austin nodded.

"Recognize that there'll be difficult adjustments to make."

"I said some awful things." Austin lowered his eyes and his lips trembled. "It's gotten worse lately. We seem to fight about everything, especially Dad and I. With him, a little disagreement can quickly erupt into a ferocious fight. We both say things we can't take back and I hate what comes out of my mouth." Austin didn't want to think of the terrible names he had called his dad. "I know it's no excuse but I want to hurt him as much as he hurts me."

"I know," Jake said kindly. "It's human nature to want to hurt back." Jake had wisdom only experience could give. "Regrets are a waste of time, Austin. We can't change the past. We can't make up for the hurt we've done to each other. We can only try not to hurt each other in the future."

Austin lowered his head and didn't say anything; his strong mouth was a hard line.

Jake gently raised the boy's head. "It's over. Don't punish yourself any longer."

Tears of self-pity stung Austin's eyes. He suddenly felt so sorry for himself and for the mess he had made of his life.

"What you do now, no matter how hard it is, reflects who you really are." Jake looked at the boy squarely. "Sometimes you have to take a risk to make things better. When you finally do, it's not as bad as you thought it might be."

Austin spoke with gratitude, "Thanks for not telling me how stupid I've been. I've had a lot of time to think." Nothing remained of the haunted, slightly vengeful boy who had first come to Echo Hill a week ago. All the bitterness was gone and only sadness was in its place.

"Considering how your outlook has changed, I think you're ready to go home." Jake sighed, "The company has been nice and I'll miss you."

Austin raised his cup and savored the aroma of the coffee. He took a sip. The warmth felt good going down. He'd miss Jake, too.

As if Sam could sense the mood of the moment, he went over and laid his head on Austin's lap. Austin stroked the gentle dog's ears.

"I was tough on you a few times but I was doing it for your own good."

A deep chuckle rumbled from Austin's chest. "You sound just like my parents." This time there was no sarcasm. At that moment Austin knew he needed to go home.

"I'll take that as a compliment," Jake said sincerely. He was deeply moved.

Austin had found talking with Jake a new experience. He could be open and honest without being prejudged by the past. There was no history between them, good or bad, and Austin found he could just be himself. It had been nice for a change not to be somebody's son or somebody's brother. With Jake, he wore no labels. There were no expectations. Jake had given him time to get a sense of who he really was. Jake made him aware of strengths and weaknesses and helped give him the underlying courage to recognize both. How did he know that not using a strength became a weakness?

"I've learned a lot about myself and what is important to me." With that, Austin held out his hand and offered it to Jake. Jake's eyes darkened with admiration. Jake took Austin's outstretched hand in a warm firm clasp, then pulled the boy close and hugged him long and hard. As Austin pulled away, with a husky voice he declared, "I'm going outside for awhile."

"I'm going to call it a night. See you in the morning. Good night, son."

Austin wondered if Jake was aware of what he had called him. He managed a husky good night. Turning away, Austin left the room, banging the front door behind him.

Austin stepped out into the cool of the night, Sam right behind him. He stood with his hands on the verandah post for a brief moment before deciding that a solitary walk down by the river was just what he needed. The moon was high and bright and he was now familiar with the worn path. He wasn't going to let any of his concerns intrude on the beauty of the evening. Austin paused at the edge of the river, and closing his eyes, he listened to the sounds around him. Crickets sang out their shrill songs, drowned out now and again by the distant scream of a screech owl. A breeze tickled the tops of the trees. A cascade of stars adorned the sky while the moonlight cast silvery shadows on the rocks and boulders along the rivers worn path. Looking out, Austin was struck by the vastness of space and his smallness upon the earth.

Austin's thoughts turned inward. He accepted that his dad wasn't totally to blame. Austin couldn't avoid the truth any more than he could ignore the facts. He had become prejudiced and narrow minded where his dad was concerned.

His dad did have a softer, kinder side, unfortunately, he kept it well hidden. At times, he was a very caring person. Memory took him back to when Jordie was in kindergarten and one day the other kids had teased him because he was the shortest in the class. Jordie came home in tears and that night he turned to his dad. Tilting his head back and looking up at his dad, Jordie asked seriously, 'Will I be as big as you when I grow up?' Richard had smiled a slow smile that transformed his carved features into an expression of unbelievable tenderness. He knelt down to be eye level with his young son. 'You might even be taller,' he answered, just as seriously.

Austin came to realize that maybe the armor had tarnished over time but the hero was still inside when he was needed.

Memories made Austin smile as it took him further back to when he was Cassie's age. He remembered his dad lifting him up and placing him on his shoulders so he could be tall enough to watch the town parade. There had been time back then for his dad to share in family outings. The loss Austin felt wasn't for himself alone. When Austin was young his father often played with him. His dad no longer had time for adventures with Jordie and Cassie. When had he changed and let business always come first?

Austin's thoughts turned, now deeply engrossed in the future. It was time to forgive and move forward. Ignoring the jeering, scoffing voice in his mind, Austin pushed his fears to the back of his mind. His entire future was at this important crossroad. He could do it. He knew he could. The hardest part was accomplished. He had made his decision.

Austin found a familiar tree and sat down. Leaning against the trunk and drawing his knees up, he wrapped his arms around them. He felt unexpectedly tired, as though in the past couple of hours he'd come a long way. As though, only now, he'd come to the end of his journey. He took a long, deep breath and exhaled it slowly. Tomorrow he would go home. Austin made himself comfortable and closed his eyes. He was in no hurry to leave for he had finally found peace. Within minutes he was sound asleep.

Chapter Ten

Time passed unnoticed and soon the first glimmers of dawn were lighting the sky in the east. Beautiful shades of orange and blue were quickly stealing away the darkness when Austin awoke. How tranquil the dawning of a new day. It offered rays of hope that would gently take away the dark demons of yesterday. Sitting there, Austin took the time to put his life in perspective. He sat forward and studied the horizon. With miles of velvet forest below the rugged mountain peaks, it was easy to feel small. It was also a comfort. Life's everyday problems seemed small, too. Austin faced the day with a brighter outlook and hope shining in his smile and beating swiftly in his heart. He let out a sigh and felt a renewed determination. Tomorrow had become today.

Austin's initial sense of apprehension was fast giving way to a state of nervous excitement. He was anxious to get going but took a few more minutes to appreciate the beauty surrounding him. The birds in the trees began calling the day to each other. Even the birds sounded full of happiness and hope at the start of another day. Austin listened hard, tucking the moment, like the smells of the land, into his memory. He'd take these memories with him for later. Austin couldn't explain it, the feeling of sorrow which was interwoven with his happiness.

There were dark shadows under his eyes but they glowed with happiness. As the new day dawned, Austin understood that life was a journey. He'd simply taken a side trip that had led him off course for awhile. It was time to get back on track and be accountable for his actions. Austin played it over and over in his mind and imagined all the things he should have done. Over the last couple of days all those 'should haves' had haunted him along with hindsight and second guessing. Jake was right. Forward was the only direction he could go. It was time to be honest with himself no matter what the consequences.

Austin took a deep breath. Even if he'd left home in anger and stayed away to spite his parents, Austin now realized that it was the height of irresponsibility. Looking back, there was a lot of good he was trying to forget. In spite of all the good things that had happened to him in his life it had taken Jake to convince him of his worth. Jake had given Austin a much needed dose of confidence and courage. Austin now felt able to cope. It was important to go back home and to get back on course, this time with a purpose.

Austin looked forward to the day, having recognized that life's purpose is to move forward. Beyond the dreams, the reality. The words played in his mind. The problem with daydreaming is you skip over all the obstacles to your goals, which is a great deal easier than tackling them. It's okay to dream but dreams can't become reality without action. Austin understood at last that reality did indeed lie beyond the dreams and it was that truth from which he couldn't escape. Looking back, Austin could see this so clearly. Why hadn't he been able to see it sooner? All this time he'd been dreaming of the moment when he'd be free and it had come to him unaware. He already was free.

Austin had been at Echo Hill only a few days. It felt like years. He looked perfectly at home in his surroundings. The mountains, and Echo Hill, had brought him solace but he knew it was time to go home and make new dreams. There would be time enough to venture forward and live his dreams. Where would they take him? Austin had no idea. He had to trust that he could deal with anything, whatever it was. This time away had given him a new outlook. Austin knew he owed it to his family, even more to himself, to deal with life as it was. Austin drew a long uneven breath and pushed away the doubts and fears that had obsessed him for too long. He immediately felt an unexpected sense of well-being, glad that he was going home. An encouraging feeling of contentment encircled him. It was a feeling Austin hadn't had in a long time and he savored it.

Not a cloud in the sky; a clear day. Just like a clean page waiting to transcribe the future. This was no longer the young boy who had left home in anger with no purpose. Changes had taken place; the big changes were within. Austin knew he had grown up over the last few days and he felt pretty good about who he was. Gone was the arrogance. There was something new there now. It was mirrored in his eyes. The immediate future, he felt, would be good. The distant future was too far away to look at. Austin smiled out to the universe. He had truly found himself. He was able to forgive himself and he would take responsibility for his actions. He had already blamed his parents enough. The realization came to him that he would never be the same. He smiled at the simplicity of his newly acquired knowledge. Austin also recognized that it wouldn't be easy.

It didn't matter that his dad might never understand him. What mattered was that Austin could now accept that it was okay. Austin was no longer judging his dad's life. He could only judge his own. If he had learned nothing else, at least he had learned that for things to change he must change. It was a sad moment for Austin as he realized that his dad might never change. Perhaps his gestures were often misinterpreted. His mom was the family mentor who would always be there to help her children know the other side of their father. Austin now knew that his mom always understood and accepted this. Poor Dad. Austin hoped his dad appreciated how lucky he was to have her. His mom was a very wise woman.

Austin reached over and patted his trusty friend. "Come on, Sam, it's time to go home," Austin declared in a voice strong with newfound hope.

Jake had left the porch light burning. The sprawling ranch house was so welcoming in the early morning light. Austin was glad that the house was still. As much as he appreciated all that Jake had done for him and all that he had taught him, actually saying good-bye would be too hard. Last night had been difficult enough between Jake and Austin.

Gently closing the door, he turned the porch light off before entering the kitchen. The morning sun was streaming through the window, lighting the kitchen with a warm glow as it had that first morning. As a final gesture of thanks, Austin went over to the cupboard, found the coffee filters and measured five generous scoops of coffee into the basket. Rinsing out the glass pot, Austin had to smile. He'd actually acquired the taste for stronger coffee. Austin flipped the switch to the on position, glad that it would be ready when Jake got up. Quietly, he fixed himself a bagged lunch to take along and within minutes he was ready to go.

Austin sat down at the kitchen table to write a brief note of thanks. In this short time, he and Jake had shared some of the worst, and best, that life could offer. It wasn't every kid who found a Jake in his life; he was like a father without the edge. Jake's kindness and strength had lifted him from the depths of despair.

Once Austin started, the words spilled onto the page. "Thank you for letting me stay for a few days and for helping me work through my anger. You knew, better than me, how much I had been allowing my emotions to run my life. You took the time to really listen to me and let me say anything and everything I wanted to. Sometimes I wasn't very nice. You already know how sorry I am about that. You taught me to have the strength to deal with life as it is and move forward. You're right. I can be in control of my life anywhere. I've done a lot of thinking and it's time for me to go home. I'm heading out. Forgive me. It would have been too difficult to say good-bye in person. Besides, hitch-hiking gives you a lot of time to ponder life. I need a little more time to sort things out in my head before I face my parents. I love my parents. Yes, my dad, too. I've missed my family and it will be good to get home. A lot of what you and I talked about over the last few days has had a tremendous effect on me. I wrote this poem one afternoon by the river. You gave me the confidence to share this with you. Thanks again. Austin."

Austin pulled a crumpled piece of paper out of his jacket pocket and placed it alongside the note. He knew Jake would understand. It was time to leave but this time he wasn't running away. Austin was simply choosing another direction, one that would get him back on course.

Austin bent down and stroked Sam. "You watch out for Jake." He choked on his words. Austin rose and went to the door, Sam immediately beside him, anxious to join him on whatever new adventure this day would bring. "Not this time," Austin whispered. "Today you must stay."

Sam sat back on his haunches and like that first morning he looked up at Austin with his soft almond-shaped eyes. Like the obedient dog he was, he stayed. As Austin quietly closed the door between them, he heard Sam's whimper of farewell.

Having said good-bye to his two new friends Austin paused to appreciate the view. The mountains were green and majestic around him. He watched the sunlight shining through the trees, breathed the air so fresh and crisp. Austin savored the stillness as a gentle breeze ruffled his hair and caressed his cheeks. "No wonder you love it here, Jake. Be happy." The same words that echoed through the hills many years ago when spoken by Mr. Blackburn.

Hands in his pockets, in a poise of absolute confidence, Austin took one long last look. The view was ever the same, blue sky over beckoning mountains. Pensively, he stared straight ahead. Finally, he forced his gaze away from the mountains, the driving force that had led him here. Austin sighed. They could wait.

Taking a deep breath of morning air, he felt his chest fill with excitement. A week ago he felt he was a million miles from home. Today, it was just down the road and he was ready to take that journey home. Smiling, Austin walked down the steps. Squaring his shoulders he set forth. Today was a new beginning. No more looking back with regret. Austin would look forward to each new day and live it to the fullest. With a renewed sense of purpose and a stronger sense of his own worth, Austin stepped off the verandah and started walking down the driveway.

Jake awakened in the early hours. He could hear Sam whimpering at his door. Instinctively, he knew that Austin had gone. As he passed by the spare room Jake looked in to find that the bed was made and the clothes that Austin had borrowed over the last few days were folded and laying on the chair. "Independent as ever," muttered Jake.

As he entered the kitchen, the room was filled with the delicious aroma of fresh brewed coffee. Without thinking he grabbed two cups. Frowning, he put Austin's back. Jake poured himself a cup, sat down at the table and opened Austin's letter. He smiled as he read the letter and knew that Austin would be okay. The poem confirmed Jake's belief that Austin would follow his dreams. The knowledge of this warmed Jake's heart. Nonetheless, there was a little pang, not of pain, but of emptiness. Jake had really enjoyed the last few days, even though Austin had made him think more about what might have been. There had been a long, lonely gap in Jake's life and for the last few days a large empty void had been filled. Although it had been difficult for both of them at the beginning, a real friendship had developed between them.

Jake knew he would miss the kid.

The familiar feeling of loneliness shrouded Jake and he ached for Katherine. Austin had brought back many memories that Jake thought were buried. Although Katherine had remained a part of his everyday life, there had been a gap that couldn't be filled. Jake missed the emotions Katherine had always evoked; the depth of feeling, the anticipation, the soul-deep satisfaction that came from being with her. None of which he had allowed himself to think of for years, but all of which had surged back with the arrival of Austin. Thinking back over the last few days with Austin, Jake now realized how lonely his life had been. Austin had filled that void for awhile but he had also opened up old feelings. Jake knew he couldn't go back in time but the future looked bleak now that there was no one here to share his life with besides Sam. Unaware of the lapse of time, Jake took a drink of his cold coffee.

Jake felt lonelier than he had in years. His home, usually his sanctuary, seemed too big, too quiet. At loose ends, he wandered from room to room. The whole house rang with empty echoes. In the living room Jake stopped, sat down and lost himself for an instant in the past. He tried to image Katherine sashaying into the living room, humming while she dusted the coffee table and the mantle, stopping to enjoy the fragrance of her rose. After only minutes had passed, her memory suddenly faded. Jake's mind struggled to conjure the image of her, but it failed. She wasn't coming back. She didn't live here anymore. This was the reality of his life. He had to face it. All that was left were creaking floors and echoing hollow rooms. Jake pulled the patchwork quilt around him and drew it tight to ward off the loneliness he felt. He sat motionless, lost in memories.

Jake attempted to get on with his day. The time passed slowly as the morning drifted into afternoon and the afternoon limped into evening. Although it had been a long, lonely day it took effort to go to bed that night. Sleep was far away. Jake lay in the darkness, tired and lonely, listening to the wind wail past the window. The clock beside the bed, ticking rhythmically, showed it was only two-thirty. The long hours stretched before him. Jake knew it would be a long, lonely night. By the time proper sleep came, it was already early morning.

Chapter Eleven

As a result of a restless night, Jake overslept and the sun was well up. He awakened feeling lethargic. He'd lain awake for hours. Part of the reason was the recurring image of Austin. Jake had never felt less like getting up. Pulling himself out of bed he was determined not to let thoughts of Austin disrupt his day as they had disturbed his night. As good as his intentions were Jake realized it would be far more difficult than he hoped.

Sam was laying at the back door waiting for his buddy Austin to return. "He's not coming back, Sam." Even to his own ears his voice sounded harsh. The dog whined but he didn't leave his post beside the door. Feeling badly, Jake bent down and caressed Sam's ears. "When you showed up unexpectedly at my door you didn't belong to anybody else so I could keep you. We had to let Austin go. He has a family that loves him. You didn't."

Jake looked out the door. "He'll be okay. He should be home today if he isn't already. But it's pretty quiet around here again." Jake sighed heavily, "I miss Austin, too."

Sam continued to whimper. To prove that Austin wasn't there, Jake opened the door. After only a slight hesitation, Sam ran down the driveway. When he came back he went to sit beside Jake who was leaning against the verandah. Sam slumped into a prone position beside his master, dark eyes half closed as he panted heavily. Jake reached down and patted his head.

Unwillingly, Jake let his thoughts reflect on the last few days. He had been quite content with his life until Austin, the silent intruder, had forced his way in unannounced. Austin had yanked Jake back into the present, into reality.

That reality was that he had built a wall around himself after Katherine had died and he had been content to stay safe inside and watch the world around him. No longer could he remain locked in the past. He realized that he'd been forced to think and talk about his past more in the last couple of days than he had in years. Yes, life would've been so different if his wife and son hadn't died. The need for family had died with Katherine. Young Austin had changed that. Jake thought of the son he never saw grow up. Would he have been gentle spirited like his mother or more like Austin, proud and strong in his beliefs? Jake wondered if he'd have been a good father to the boy. Would he have had the courage to let his son make mistakes, take risks, follow a dream?

He had known the right things to say to Austin. It was much easier to look at someone else's life and tell them what to do than it was to look at your own life objectively. How easy to tell Austin to move forward even though he hadn't. He had wasted too many years alone.

What about his own life? Was he getting too caught up in his work and not making the time to enjoy life? Now that Jake thought about it, he hadn't been out for a horseback ride at all this year.

Maybe one day Austin would come back for a visit. Maybe he could invite Austin back in the summer to watch Billy compete in the Cheyenne rodeo. The thought brought a smile. Life does move forward.

Jake retreated into the house. Never, since Katherine had died, had the house appeared less inviting and he wandered from the kitchen to the living room and back again, unable to settle anywhere for long. His steps echoed hollowly through the vacant rooms. Jake tried to ignore the aching emptiness Austin had left behind but the whole house mocked him. Austin had made him acknowledge how lonely he'd been. Jake attempted to do some work. He tried to slip back into his familiar routine just like it was before Austin had intruded into his life.

All day long the hours limped desperately by. Jake couldn't muster the energy to get himself to work. He was feeling irritable and disgruntled and he wasn't used to such feelings. Jake tried to keep his mind occupied but it wouldn't cooperate. It insisted on thinking of Austin.

Jake stepped outside. Sam, too, was out of sorts, laying on the verandah, waiting. Jake called to the dog, "Let's go get the mail." They strolled down the winding lane, enjoying their leisurely walk to the mailbox. The shadow of a circling eagle flitted across the ground as Jake neared the mail box. For sheer grandeur and majestic beauty there was nothing to compare with the eagle. He glanced up at the winged predator, admiring the insolent grace of its gliding flight. Immediately, Jake's thoughts drifted to Austin, recognizing the same free spirit of the youth.

"Just bills," Jake said aloud, as he opened the mail box and rifled through the assortment of envelopes and advertisements. Together, with the daily paper, he headed back toward the house. Sam ran happily at his side. The lawns were green and lush. Maybe he would mow and fertilize later in the day. Light showers were forecast for late evening.

Inside, Jake helped himself to coffee and drank it while he skimmed through the paper. Turning the page his eyes were drawn to the article in the middle of the page. The headline, "*Tragic Death on Interstate*" leapt out at him and left him with a sick feeling. Jake read on. "*Last night at approximately 5:30 p.m., a hitch-hiker was struck and killed by a hit and run driver. The victim was a seventeen- year-old male named Austin James Smith.*" Tears could not hide the pain in Jake's eyes as they blurred his vision before falling onto the article he was reading. Silently, he wept. Austin Smith had reached his journey's end.

DREAMS

Everyone dreams but not everyone has a dream.
Those who take risks can have dreams come true.
It takes a very special person to follow his dreams
And when his dream comes true he has accomplished something.

A dreamer will look back when he is old and tired
And see that his life was all it could be.
He will look back and see that his dream came true.
He was loved.
(Austin James Smith)

Part Two

Chapter One

Jake Hanson sat alone in his truck watching mourners enter the church. Jake hadn't been here before and he wasn't sure why he was here today. He'd only known Austin Smith for a few days. Yet he felt compelled to come to the boy's funeral. He waited as long as he could before going in. Once through the door, he removed his hat and rotated it nervously between his fingers. The church was nearly full so he quickly moved to a seat off the isle near the front.

It was a strange experience. He knew nobody and nobody knew him. Jake recognized the immediate family. Austin had been very accurate in his description of them.

The father, Richard Smith, sat in the front row next to the aisle. He was a powerful looking man and his stony expression showed no emotion. The careful emptiness of expression concealed whatever he was feeling. Nothing was going to penetrate the cold mask.

The mother, Allison, was seated in the same row. Her black hair was pulled into a coil at the nape of her slender neck. She turned to say something to her husband revealing the sculptured lines of her face. Great sorrow was evident as tears flowed down her face. No evidence today of the vibrant lady Austin had so affectionately talked about.

Between both parents sat the younger sister Cassandra, a lost little soul, white-faced and wide-eyed, who held her mom's hand tightly. At six, she was too young to understand everything. It was evident that she was bewildered and frightened.

On the other side of the mother sat Austin's brother. Only twelve, Jordie looked too much like his father, rigid and emotionless. Too grown up to hold his mom's hand, he clasped his own tightly together, exercising great restraint out of respect for his brother.

Jake also knew how difficult it would be for all of them in the weeks and months to come. Nothing would ever be the same again.

Jake had come to say his own farewell to the boy and if he was being honest he hoped to learn a little more about the youth who had intruded on his life and changed it forever. His gaze moved to the memorial table. Austin's picture sat next to a beautiful urn which was engraved with an eagle against a stunning blue finish. Jake thought it most appropriate as it replicated the free spirit of Austin. He stared at the picture. It was strange seeing Austin's face again. A wave of sadness washed over Jake. A young life wasted. The boy was only seventeen. The picture had caught the natural and easy smile that Austin had flashed on more than one occasion and Jake wondered what mischievous thought had been caught by the eye of the camera. The handsome face was impressive in its strength and it showed an intangible suggestion of manhood. Jake studied everything on the table, each item telling a little of the boy's short life. A life that Jake knew so little about. His eyes lingered on a pencil sketch of a wolf obviously done by Austin. Jake knew that Austin was creative. The poem Austin had written and left behind was in his wallet. Now he knew he had been artistic as well. It came as no surprise.

There were many young people grouped together throughout the church. Just a few rows in front of him, sitting with a middle-aged woman, sat Austin's best friend. It was easy to pick him out from the colorful commentary shared by Austin when he'd stayed at Jake's home. The woman was obviously his mother for the family resemblance was striking. Jake's heart went out to this young man who would forever miss his best friend. Having glanced at the leaflet handed to him when he entered the church Jake knew that Ryan would be giving today's eulogy. Jake knew how difficult it would be for Ryan to say good-bye.

The only funeral Jake had attended since his wife's passing fifteen years earlier was his dad's five years ago. He hated funerals. So why was he here? The kid wasn't even family.

A hush fell over the room as the organ began playing "Whispering Hope." As the minister spoke Jake allowed his mind to wander back to the day he met Austin.

The boy was spirited and proud and very, very angry and had run away from home. Jake recalled the boy's angry words justifying his actions. Torment was mixed with fatigue and he was in no condition to make a logical decision. Jake had hoped by letting Austin stay for a couple of days to regain his strength that he wouldn't make a drastic life-changing decision based on anger. Jake also knew that if he'd allowed Austin to leave that first day he wouldn't have gone home, not while anger as well as pride continued to stand in his way. Austin was at a crisis point in his life and Jake had been there to help him work through it. Given time, Austin made his own decision to go home. As silently as Austin had entered Jake's life he left it.

Jake was drawn back to the present when Ryan's voice broke through his thoughts. Jake's concentration was intense as Ryan began to speak of his friend.

"Mr. and Mrs. Smith, Jordie, Cassie. I can't tell you how sorry I am about Austin. What happened to Austin was terrible. It isn't fair that we have to say good-bye to him today. It's a sad day for all of us."

Jake nodded his head in agreement for he was aware of the boy's pain. Austin had shared many stories about Ryan and Jake felt sorry for the boy.

Ryan looked out at everyone as he continued in a gentle voice, "Austin was a very special person to all of us. He was a terrific big brother. Yeah, he teased Jordie and Cassie. That's what big brothers do. But he was always there for them and the important thing is they knew it. He was a great guy who was smart, athletic, fun." Ryan smiled wistfully. "We all know he had a terrific sense of humor. Austin had it all but he remained decent. He'd probably be surprised at how many of his friends are here today but I'm not. It was because of whom he was that so many of us liked him and he never realized how important he was in all of our lives."

"My mom said that it's by chance that you meet a person. It's by choice that you become friends. Austin and I became friends the first day we met. We could do anything or nothing and have a good time," Ryan said fondly. A shadow crossed his face. "Friendship isn't always easy. A true friend is someone who knows all about you and likes you just the same. There are certain things that only friends can share." Ryan drew a deep breath before continuing. "Real friends are there for each other in good times and especially in bad times. Austin was a true friend."

Jake listened enthralled. He was overcome by the heartfelt honesty coming from the young boy as he spoke of his feelings for his friend. It was obvious that the boy was more sensitive and sincere than Jake had imagined. Austin had talked often about his friend Ryan and Jake could understand why the two had been such good friends.

Ryan's voice cracked and he took a moment to compose himself. "I loved Austin like a brother but I don't know if I ever told him." He looked out anxiously at those seated in front of him. Jake wondered if it was intentional that Ryan's gaze came to rest on Austin's dad. "Don't not say it because you think, hey, they already know. Tell them that you love them, today. Because tomorrow they may not be here. It isn't fair, but people we love most, like Austin, are sometimes taken from us too soon," the boy declared emphatically.

Jake felt the sting of tears behind his eyes. It was so true, so tragically true.

Ryan turned to the picture of his friend. Tears filled the boy's eyes and his voice broke as he continued, "I did love you, Austin. I'm sorry if I never told you. You were the brother I never had. I miss you but you'll always be with me. Memories may be all I have left. Thankfully, memories can't be taken away." With heartfelt sadness, he whispered his final farewell, "Friends forever." His eulogy complete, the tears were allowed their release and fell silently onto Ryan's pale cheeks.

Jake wished he'd been able to sit at the back of the church. He would have made his escape at this time but Jake had no choice but to wait. He shifted uncomfortably as the organist began to play. Everyone rose to their feet. All eyes were on the family.

Richard Smith stepped back and waited as his wife and children stepped into the isle. Jake watched as Allison took her daughter's hand as they started walking to the back of the church. Richard placed his hand on his son's shoulder as Jordie preceded him down the aisle. Just as Allison reached Jake's row she looked over. Jake's own face paled as he was struck by the incredible likeness to Austin. A sharp, painful jolt pierced through him. He needed desperately to get out of the church and into the fresh air.

As soon as he was outside Jake breathed deeply taking in the life-giving air after the stuffy, confined atmosphere in the church. Hat in hand, he walked directly to his vehicle. Once inside, he leaned back against the head rest and closed his eyes. There was a large lump in his throat. He thought he'd choke on it and he felt sick. God, how he hated funerals.

Jake sat for a long time in his truck before turning the key. He didn't want to go to the cemetery but he knew he needed complete closure and he had to say his final farewell to Austin. He remained in his truck until the last vehicle drove away. Jake walked slowly to the fresh grave. Bending down he placed a single rose next to the other flowers. A cool breeze had picked up and Jake dug his hands deep into his pockets as tears fell onto his cheeks. He remained lost for a long time in the deep shadows of sorrow; present intertwined with past.

Chapter Two

Allison Smith sat on the grassy area beside her son's grave, a forlorn figure whose shoulders sagged as she sat hunched over. It was a dismal summer day and no one else was about. Heavy storm clouds blocked the sun. The atmosphere around her reflected her dark mood. All the joy was gone from her life.

Being with Austin sometimes helped, but not today. She couldn't prevent his image from tormenting her, the longing to hear his voice, the need to touch him. Suddenly the emotions of the past few months overwhelmed Allison and tears spilled over and ran down her cheeks. She felt as though her whole world had spun out of control. It had been three months since her son's death and today the depression and hurt had been overtaken by anger.

During those first weeks she was numb and Richard was so supportive. She'd been dazed with shock and disbelief. She went through the motions automatically. People were always around. Everyone had been more than kind. She didn't have to be alone and she didn't have time to think. That came later. Friends weren't calling as often. Allison understood. It was easier not to call than to listen to Allison cry when they talked about things like graduation or they shared the latest gossip. Allison didn't care who was dating who this week. Their lives hadn't changed and they'd moved on. Not so for Allison. She didn't know what to do with her free hours. Her days were long and lonely. The nights were longer.

Immediately after Austin's death, she'd taken a leave and a substitute teacher had finished the school year. Jordie and Cassie went back to classes and she made sure she was home every afternoon when they came home. Richard went back to work and spent more and more evenings at his law office or locked in his den at home. Richard kept telling her that crime took no time off but she knew that it had become his escape. For Allison, there was no escape.

Now that school was out the summer lay ahead and the days were even longer. She felt forsaken and very depressed. She wasn't coping. Allison knew she needed to find the strength to take care of herself if she was to find the strength to help Jordie, Cassie and Richard. She simply didn't know how.

A biting breeze tossed her hair from side to side often covering the slightly hollowed cheeks of her pale face. Allison sat still letting the wind play over her skin and hair. She shivered but it wasn't from the cold. It was from the dark memories that haunted. If only she could dispel the torturing memories. She didn't need to remember those days for she didn't want to relive the pain. Today, there was no escape. Closing her eyes, Allison gave in to the memory. It all came rushing back, the police officer, the shocking news, the nightmare to follow.

Responding to a firm knock at the front door, Allison got up to see who was calling. They weren't expecting company and the kids were out playing with friends. Allison gasped when she opened the door. In front of her stood a uniformed police officer.

"Mrs. Smith?" the officer asked, his tone odd.

Allison's face drained of color and her eyes were wide with sudden fear. There was something terribly wrong. She was sure of it. "Why are you here?" She barely breathed. The words were a panicked whisper.

Richard, who had also heard the door was now directly behind his wife. Richard didn't give the officer a chance to reply, "Is Austin in trouble?"

"I am here about your son, Sir. May I come in?" he asked evenly.

Richard and Allison retreated into the living room and the officer stoically followed. He waited for them to sit down on the sofa before he sat in the chair across from them. Allison reached for her husband's hand and held it tight while he remained stiff and silent. How the police officer hated days like this.

Allison glanced over to Richard, her eyes wide. She was frightened and her fear showed. Every nerve in her body screamed in protest but not a sound passed her lips.

She sat motionless until Richard finally demanded to know, "Where is Austin?" His face was grave. "Has there been an accident? Is he all right?"

The officer was young. It was difficult to hide the pain he felt for this family. He spoke slowly and politely, "Your son was struck down by a hit and run driver." He had to clear his throat before continuing, "I'm sorry, your son was killed on impact."

Allison could only stare at him as he spoke, trying to focus on his words as horror lodged in her throat. He couldn't mean what he was saying. The shock hit both parents full force, stunning them with disbelief.

It was Allison who broke the silence, "No!" she screamed, shaking her head. "I don't believe you. It can't be Austin. I'm sure it's some mistake." This only happened in nightmares. It couldn't be happening to them.

The officer didn't answer. He shifted uncomfortably and watched as both parents struggled with the news.

Allison turned to her husband. Stumbling over her words, she pleaded, "It can't be true, Richard. Tell him it can't be Austin!"

"I need someone to identify the body and pick up his last effects," the officer said deliberately.

Richard nodded, too upset to trust his voice. Allison's face remained blank. She was still in a state of shock.

The officer continued, "There isn't much, simply a watch and wallet." His discomfort was apparent.

A flicker of hope lit Allison's eyes. "Maybe somebody stole his wallet. Maybe."

Richard didn't let her finish, "Honey, don't do this."

"This can't be happening," Allison cried out in despair.

Richard's face crumbled, he hung his head and dropped it into his hands. He covered his eyes but not soon enough to conceal the glisten of tears. All of a sudden it was too quiet in the room. It was like life itself stood still as both parents remained frozen in shock.

The officer had to continue. It never got easier. "Our station received a call from a Jake Hanson. He'd read about the accident and called to say that your son had spent a few days with him and that to his knowledge he was on his way home. His address and phone number are on file if you need it."

Richard recovered first. He drew himself up. "I'll go with the officer." He turned back to Allison, who was sobbing quietly. She met his gaze when he asked, "Will you be all right until I get back? Do you want me to call your Mom to come over?"

"Oh, Richard," Allison cried out in anguish as she clung to him. "How are we going to tell Jordie and Cassie that they will never see their big brother again?" Sobs racked her body and her husband held her tight. Tears continued to flow for she was helpless to stop them.

Richard gave his wife a searching look. "What do you want me to do?" he cried, confused and desperate.

She pulled herself away to wipe the tears from her face. Allison realized he was just as scared and confused as she was. He sounded like a little boy turning to his mom for an answer. With that realization came another and her natural maternal instinct took over.

Composing herself, with difficulty, she turned and put a reassuring hand on his shoulder. "You go with the officer, Richard. I'll be okay. I'll wait until you get back to call family but I can't wait to tell the kids. I think it might be easier if I tell them by myself," she added carefully. "I don't want Jordie to feel he can't cry and he wouldn't if you were here."

Allison had always taken on the parental role so naturally. It wasn't as easy for Richard so he let Allison take control.

As Richard left with the police officer Jordie rushed through the back door. "What's up? Dad do something wrong? I saw the cruiser outside." The excitement of a twelve-year-olds imagination was evident in his voice.

"No, Jordie. They just need your dad to go and help them. Can you go next door and get Cassie and bring her home?" she asked, hoping that her words didn't sound too forced.

Jordie noticed the tears in his mom's eyes. Even to Jordie, it was obvious that she'd been crying. "What's wrong, Mom?" Jordie asked, immediately anxious and concerned.

Allison was touched by her son's concern. She forced a smile to her stiff lips, "Bring Cassie home and then we'll talk." Jordie raced out the back door and Allison prayed for the strength she'd need to tell her children about Austin.

Minutes later she heard them as they came through the kitchen and she took a deep breath. Once she had both children sitting on the couch where she and Richard had sat not much earlier she knelt down in front of them. Allison felt her mouth go dry. She moistened her dry lips and knew she was trembling. "Jordie, Cassie, listen to me. Something dreadful has happened, something terrible. It's Austin." Tears again filled her eyes. Allison kept it simple. "The sad truth is Austin's not coming home." It was hard getting the words past the huge lump lodged in her throat. She swallowed hard. It didn't help. She tried again. "A car hit Austin and he died." The words were barely audible.

Both kids stared at their mother in disbelief. Cassie immediately broke out crying. Allison pulled her into her arms. Jordie sat motionless, blinking hard. His chin quivered but he refused to cry. Jordie whispered, "You're lying." For a moment he stared accusingly at his mom and then he ran to his room screaming, "This is horrible. I hate this."

Mother and daughter sat for a long time as Allison rocked her youngest child in her arms. "It's okay, baby girl, it's okay. Everything will be okay." But it wasn't. Everything was wrong. Finally, Allison suggested to Cassie, "Let's go get you ready for bed and Mommy will lie beside you until you go to sleep."

Cassie nodded her head in agreement and Allison took her daughter in her arms and carried her to her bedroom.

After Cassie finished saying her prayers she looked over at her mom with soulful eyes. "Is Austin in heaven? Will God tell him I said hi?"

Allison's broken heart shattered into smaller pieces. As she answered, "Yes," to her daughter's question, she wished it was that easy to believe.

"Do I have to wait until I go to heaven to see Austin?" her daughter asked innocently.

It was a monumental moment. "If you close your eyes right now can you see Austin?" Allison asked, with false brightness.

Cassie shut her eyes tight, squeezing out two more tears that streaked down her plump cheeks. Her little mouth turned upwards and her darling dimples were evident as she proudly declared, "I can see him."

"Well, princess. Now you know that you can see Austin anytime you want to. He just won't be here at home with us anymore but he can be with us anytime we want him," she promised seriously. That seemed to comfort Cassie for now.

Once Cassie was asleep Allison moved on to Jordie's room. Her youngest son was lying on his bed stunned and dry eyed. She knew this conversation wasn't going to be as easy. Allison sat down beside him. She gently stroked his hair.

"Is Cassie okay?" His eyes were enormous and filled with doubt. He was already worrying about his little sister the way Austin always did.

"She's sleeping. How are you doing?" Getting no response, she looked at him closely. She could see underlying anger and she braced herself. "Jordie, talk to me," she urged, drawing a long breath. "Please," she begged.

The words he flung her way were filled with hurt. "Why didn't you or Dad go after Austin when he ran away?" There was resentment in the boy's tone as he glared at her. "You could've made him come home," Jordie accused. The tears he'd been holding began to stream down his cheeks. Through the blur of her own tears she saw his grim face.

"We talked about this the day he left, Jordie," she reminded him, in a low voice. "You remember how upset he was." Allison cupped her young son's face. Anger was evident in the boy's big brown eyes. She shook her head, "Austin wouldn't have listened."

"You could've made him listen like you make Cassie and me listen," he challenged.

Allison protested, "Dad and I both thought he'd go to Ryan's until he'd cooled off. When he wasn't there I called all of his friends but none of them had seen or heard from him. We had no clue where he went so how could we find him? If only he'd phoned," she broke off.

Jordie sat up and looked at his mom with terrified eyes, desperate for some reassurance that everything would be okay. She looked away because nothing would ever be the same.

"It isn't fair. Austin's really dead. I'll never see him again." Hopeless sobs followed.

The heavy weight in the mother's heart increased. She hugged Jordie and kissed his wet face. "Jordie, we all wish it was different."

Her young son remained rigid. Allison knew he was frightened. "I'm scared too because I don't know what to do," she confided. Allison dropped a light kiss on the top of Jordie's head. "Try to get some sleep," she said softly. "I'm going to go and wait for your dad."

Chapter Three

Allison broke out of the painful memories she had not wanted to live through again. Numb and cold, she shifted her position and leaned against the headstone. Like other times, Allison talked aloud to Austin but today anger coated most of her words. "I have all these unanswered questions. I want to know what happened when you were gone. Where did you go? Why did you stay away? Why didn't you phone?" Helpless to stop herself, she cried out, "Maybe if I had some answers I wouldn't be so angry right now. No. I'm damn mad and I don't like how I feel. God wasn't fair when he took you from us." All of a sudden it was too much and Allison broke down. Leaning forward, she placed her hands over her face and wept.

An electrifying sensation shot through her body followed by a mixture of apprehension and unease. She dried her eyes. At that moment, she knew what she had to do and she had to do it alone. Obsessed by the endless questions, she knew she had to go see Jake Hanson. If she wanted to escape the nightmare that trapped her, she had to deal with all her demons. She had to know what happened. Jake Hanson might be able to tell her something, anything. While she was looking for answers maybe she would find peace.

The sun remained hidden behind gathering clouds. It had turned colder and Allison drew her sweater around her. She shivered and knew it was time to go. She hated leaving and the tears once again began their familiar flow down her cheeks. As if to echo her despair, Mother Nature released her own tears and the wind cried through the trees. Allison quickly gathered herself up and sadly headed home.

Silence echoed through the house, a silence that said no one was home. She hated coming home to an empty house. It seemed that it was always empty these days. Allison went directly to her desk. Her hands were trembling as she rummaged through the drawers. Where had she put it? Finally, she found the card from the police officer. Her pulse raced with anticipation. Three calls and two hours later she had directions to Jake Hanson's place. Now, should she make one more call? Should she call him first? No. She wanted to be face to face when she confronted the last person she knew who had seen Austin alive.

Allison was restless waiting for her husband to come home. Richard found her prowling around in the kitchen preparing supper. He sensed her anxiety.

"What's wrong?" He looked tired and Allison could see the lines of stress etched in her husband's face.

She took a deep breath. "Nothing's wrong," she lied. Then she released a heavy sigh. "Richard, I need to get away for awhile so that I can come to terms with all that has happened. If I can do that, maybe I can deal with things again at home." She didn't tell him how she intended to do this but she did know that he would never understand her going to see a stranger.

Richard's eyes widened in surprise. "I can't get away right now. You know we're due to go into court on the Chandler-Adams case."

Allison gave an exasperated groan, "Do you ever think about anything other than work?" Allison asked in a hard, flat tone. She shook her head, "Don't bother to answer that. Besides, I didn't mean us." Allison's voice was low, but there was no mistaking the edge, "I need some time to myself."

Richard seemed momentarily taken aback. "You have lots of time to yourself," he reminded her. His wife threw him an angry and challenging look.

Allison shook her head, "I need time by myself away from here. It's too sad here." She knew she was depressed and didn't have the energy to do anything. "I can't go on pretending there's nothing wrong." She was unable to keep the note of frustration out of her voice.

"Meaning?" Richard's eyes were like slithers of steel in his stern face.

Allison knew that lately she hadn't been concealing her emotions. That took effort and these days it took all of her effort just to breath. She'd been in a mood of black despair and resentment at fate for months. The resentment had taken a firm hold and her anger was evident. It wasn't like she wasn't aware of it herself. She just didn't know how to deal with it. It was the continuous feeling of spinning out of control that also continued to frighten her.

"I haven't been doing a very good job as either a mother or a wife. Can't you see that I know this?" Allison fought the tremor in her voice.

Richard heard her desperation. He tried reassuring her, "You're a terrific mother."

Allison broke in, "And a wonderful wife. Understanding and patient, all the things it takes to keep a happy home," she taunted back. Bitterness had broken into her voice as her frustration surfaced. "There is no happiness here anymore. The laughter is gone. It disappeared when Austin left. I don't like the atmosphere around here. It's so tense and quiet."

Richard tightened his lips to keep from retaliating.

Angrily, she pointed a finger at him. "I hate your calm restraint. Sometimes I wonder if you feel anything at all." Distraught, Allison began to pace. Her nerves were frayed and she wasn't sure if anything she was saying was getting through to him. Allison looked over at her husband. "I don't like myself right now. I have to get away from here," she said adamantly. Allison lowered her eyes but there was no way to hide the misery that overwhelmed her.

"What about the kids, Allison? You know I can't be home with them and they can't stay by themselves." His voice was loaded with sarcasm.

A thread of hostility was evident as she replied, "Of course I know that." Allison took a deep breath. "I talked to Mom and she suggested a holiday for the kids. My parents want to take Jordie and Cassie to Disneyland. I decided that I'd go to the cottage while they're gone." Now that she had prepared him with her idea the tense lines in her face eased.

Richard made a snorting sound of disdain. "What about baseball. Jordie will miss a lot of games. He made a commitment to his team."

Allison interrupted, "Don't be disagreeable. Some things are more important. I think the kids need time away." To which she quickly added, "We all do."

Richard hunched his shoulders. "Well, I can't believe you want to take off and be by yourself. It's not going to change anything." He sighed with impatience, "The time for grieving can only go on so long. Why can't you get over this?"

Allison was too confused to answer and glanced away. Tears stung her eyes, anger and hurt mixing together. She walked over to the window and stared out. Nothing had prepared her for the trauma of Austin's death.

When she glared back at him, Richard knew he'd phrased the remark badly. He saw the hurt building in his wife's expression. It had become all too frequent. "There's nothing wrong with what you're feeling but running away isn't the answer." His voice sounded bleak, "You can't escape the fact, Allison, no matter how much you want to. Austin is gone."

Allison flared back, her chin jutting out and her eyes furious, "You dare to accuse me of running away, yet you do the same thing under the demise of work. Since Austin died you've been working longer hours at the office. When you are home you lock yourself in your den." Allison's eyes grew stormy and anger flushed her cheeks. "This is like a nightmare that I can't wake up from. I'm entitled to grieve however I want to. This has been so hard but your lack of understanding makes it harder. These days you don't see anything that's going on. Jordie's withdrawn and sullen and Cassie's clingy and wants to be with me all the time." She chocked on her words, unable to continue.

Richard took her in her arms. She blinked in surprise. "I'm not trying to hurt you, Allison," he said more gently.

But he had. Allison pulled away, "Let's not argue about this." The potential for it was there. "We're both touchy. Let's leave it for now." Tears gathered in her eyes and she blinked them fiercely away.

Richard's look softened when he finally spoke, "How long would you be gone?" His gaze searched her expression.

Allison gave an indifferent shrug, "I don't really know." She knew she was being non- committal but she was still mentally making her plans. Allison looked away but she felt her husband watching her. "Let's talk about it after supper. I haven't said anything to the kids about Disneyland. I wanted to talk to you first. Wash up and I'll call the kids."

Supper was another quiet one. Even before Austin's death the atmosphere was often fraught with tension and conflict. Allison resented it and didn't know how much longer she could go on living like this. Cassie was the only one who chattered, unaware of the tension around the table. Jordie ate his supper quickly and remained withdrawn in the abstracted manner she'd noticed since his brother's death. He was quieter and never seemed to laugh anymore. Her son was drifting away on a sea of despair and Allison couldn't find the life-line or the strength to pull him back to shore. She was struggling not to drown in her own sorrow.

"Daddy, the tire on my bike is flat. Will you fix it?"

"I'll do it after supper, pumpkin," Richard answered automatically.

Right after supper Richard headed for the den.

"What about my bike?" Cassie asked.

He turned to Jordie. Before Allison could stop him, Richard told his son to do it.

Jordie's face hardened and his jaw set stubbornly. His steely gaze never waivered as he refused. "I'm busy. Besides, she asked you," he added insolently.

"Don't get smart." When Richard turned to Allison for support she turned away. She knew how futile such arguments could be. It had been the same with Austin and Richard.

Richard's eyes narrowed, his face was stern and unyielding. "If I tell you to do something you'll damn well do it."

A grim look hardened Jordie's features in a way that was reminiscent of Austin. "Make me," he countered, with dangerous coolness. In this mood Jordie was capable of anything and Allison didn't want another fight.

"Shut up, Jordie," she cautioned.

Rage smoldered in the young boy's eyes. "Why should I?" Jordie was being defiantly belligerent.

"Don't talk to your mother like that," Richard snapped, in a no nonsense tone. His features had contorted into their habitual expression of dissatisfaction.

When Jordie fired his mom a reckless glance he received another silencing look from her. Jordie's jaw clenched and he pushed himself away from the table. The boy missed the look of disdain from his dad but Allison noticed it.

Richard's temper flared, "Go to your room."

Jordie refused to leave the kitchen.

Allison looked at her husband with disgust. Inside her head she could hear Austin and Richard screaming the same way, the way they had the day Austin ran away. Allison's brittle control snapped. "I want you both to quit fighting. This is the very reason that Austin left."

Cassie started crying.

"Quit your bawling," Richard ordered with crisp authority.

"Don't be mad at me," Cassie gasped and ran to her mother.

"Don't frighten her with your courtroom voice, Richard," Allison said, her own anger rising. She turned back to her daughter, "He's not mad at you." She flashed Richard a dirty look before adding, "He's just mad in general."

Allison bit back another angry retort that sprang to her lips for she hated fighting in front of the kids. She had to wonder how a man who was so good at negotiating mergers for others seemed to have so much difficulty when family was factored into the equation. He'd been having trouble relating to Austin ever since Austin had grown old enough to challenge an issue. Now the same thing was happening with Jordie. She glared at her husband. "Richard, you're a damn fool. When are you going to learn?" Was he incapable of realizing how devastating the effects of their arguing could be?

Obviously, for he again belittled Jordie, "You've become as insolent as your brother."

Suddenly, and without warning, Allison burst into unstoppable tears. "I can't go on like this," she screamed. Sobbing, she ran from the room. Richard heard the bedroom door slam. Immediately after, he heard Jordie's bedroom door close with a resounding bang. This was becoming an all too familiar routine. Richard raked his hand through his hair in frustration.

Once her anger had subsided, Allison returned to the kitchen. She peered wearily out the window and saw that Richard and Cassie were out by the garage working on Cassie's bike. She started clearing the table.

A few minutes later Richard came in. "Jordie still in his room?"

"No, he left. A few of the guys are going to watch a movie at Trevor's. He promised not to be late," she added.

"He's become so defiant. Why do you let him get away with that?" Richard demanded, shaking his head in a gesture of exasperation.

"I've tried to overlook a lot of his actions lately."

Richard interrupted, "Quite making excuses for the kids, Allison. I won't condone his behavior anymore."

"Jordie needs more time. He misses his brother and he's still mad."

"In my opinion you're too soft on the kids," Richard retaliated, cold and insensitive.

Allison turned and glared at her husband. "You're too strict. You're unreasonable." Her voice rose with dismay. "That's our problem, your ideas and mine are totally different," she declared, her voice growing angrier. "It's not my fault that you get more opinionated every day."

Richard's face darkened. "Now it's all my fault and I'm the bad guy."

"Sometimes it's useless talking to you." Allison sighed heavily as she fought to keep her composure. How did she reach him? She couldn't let it go. "It might have made a difference if you'd asked Jordie to fix Cassie's bike instead of telling him to. I thought you'd have gotten smarter by now. Making demands doesn't work. It didn't with Austin. What makes you think it'll work with Jordie?"

"What's with him these days?" Richard asked, with unmistakable scorn. "He's turning out just like Austin."

"Would you rather he turns out like you, arrogant and hurtful?" she spat back. She knew she was being cruel to Richard. For once, Allison refused to apologize.

The unkind outburst by his wife drew a concerned look from Richard.

It suddenly became very quiet in the room. The silence became unnerving.

Allison was the first to speak, "I hate this constant fighting, Richard. The tension around here is killing me. I want some harmony back in my life." Tears welled in her eyes. "We've been quarrelling more and more over the kids, over work. It isn't fair for our children to grow up with constant bickering and resentment." Her eyes flashed with anger and Richard knew better than to cross her when she looked like that.

Anxious to change the subject, Richard said, "Cassie's bike is fixed. She's riding up and down the sidewalk."

Clearly hearing what he said, Allison chose to ignore him and began running water into the sink. The tension was thick and she didn't want another scene. She didn't have the energy for this. Silence dragged between them.

On the verge of further discussion, Richard thought better of it. He'd noticed the determined set of her shoulders and her continued silence spoke volumes. Uncertain about what to do, he chose to remain silent and retreated to the den.

As Allison puttered in the kitchen she continued to fume. You'd think the man would have learned by now. She was tired of the arguing. She felt her life was one continuation of torments and not one person in her family cared how she felt.

In his den, Richard picked up a file and looked at the black text not seeing the words. He frowned as he put the file back down. In frustration, he loosened his tie and unfastened the top button of his shirt. He hated it when they fought. He hated it more when she was right. Allison deserved an apology but he remained seated. He didn't understand her anymore. She used to be so easy-going and good-humored. He shifted wearily and again picked up the file.

The door opened and Allison came bursting into the room. With barely disguised impatience he swore under his breath. He didn't have time for this. He tried ignoring her with little success. Realizing she wasn't about to leave, he looked up. His face wore an expression of irritability rather than welcome.

Richard had little consideration for his wife, spending most of his time working. But there were times, like now, when she demanded his complete attention. She stood in front of him, her face grave. She was fully aware that he was busy but she was determined to speak her mind. She refused to allow him to brush her off like other times.

Richard drew a deep breath while making a dismissing gesture, "Allison, I really don't have time for any of this."

"I don't care," Allison declared, as she sat herself firmly in the chair across from him. She was hurting and he was closing her out when she needed him to comfort her and share her pain. When he didn't respond she snapped back, "You better start making time for us. Your work can't always come first."

Richard sighed with impatience. "I'm doing what I have to do."

Her reply was harsh. "You're doing what you want to do."

Richard gave his wife a direct, unsmiling glance while defending himself. "There are a lot more challenges in corporate law."

Allison pulled herself forward on her chair and placed her forearms on his desk and gave him a doubtful look. "You love it, Richard. You thrive on the challenges. Unfortunately, you've become a workaholic. You seldom give the kids any attention."

"You're too busy with the kids," he accused back.

Allison was shocked. "Someone has to be. What kind of a father have you been lately, or husband for that matter?"

175

Startled and hurt, Richard drew a deep breath before answering, "I've worked damned hard at this marriage."

"No, Richard. You've just worked damn hard."

For a moment Richard appeared too stunned to reply. "I thought you were done with this." He glared at his wife sharply.

It went unnoticed as Allison continued to fight back. Husband and wife had argued about this before. "You get so involved in your work that you forget what really matters. You're killing yourself for what?"

Richard quickly looked up, an expression of grimace on his face. "Of course I work hard. I'm doing it for you and the kids. What's wrong with that?"

"You're doing it for our family? What family? One of our children is dead because of your need for power and money. Who knows what will happen to the other two. What about me? Do I look happy?"

She turned to him. "Has it brought you happiness, Richard?" she asked soberly.

Richard hung his head and dragged his fingers through his hair. For a moment they were both silent.

Allison waved her hands in the air. "Is all of this worth the life of a child?" She continued on before he could answer. "Work has become your life."

Richard gave an exasperating shrug, his expression closed and tight, "Will you get off that already?"

Allison persisted, trying to keep her voice calm, her words rational, "Your work consists of telling other people what to do. It doesn't stop at the office. You bring it home where you continue barking orders to all of us. Where does it get you? Nowhere, that's where." Allison sat back in her chair, putting space between them.

Richard knew exactly what she meant. "I told you I handled things badly at supper. I'm sorry," he added in a low, flat voice.

She wasn't about to let up. "You want everything your way. It's simple. Follow the rules and there are no problems."

Richard defended himself, "Kids need responsibility."

"Of course they do. Lately you're expecting more and more from Jordie, just like you did with Austin and always under your conditions."

Richard was shocked at the bitterness in her voice but he was tired of his wife always making him out to be the bad guy. For a moment they were both silent. When Richard finally spoke his voice was gruff, "I fixed Cassie's bike."

"Not without a fight. You spent all of five minutes with her and none with Jordie. They both need some time with their dad. Now more than ever," Allison added accusingly. "They're missing Austin and neither one of them understands how something so terrible could happen." Her voice softened, "They need both of us. An encouraging word from you now and then would mean a lot to them. Richard, you'd better start before it's too late with them, too."

Richard's face remained stern but he didn't argue.

Knowing she had his full attention, Allison continued to choose her words with deliberation. "I'm tired of sticking up for you and trying to make you look good so the kids don't hate you. Keep it up and I won't be able to stop them." She paused to let her words sink in. Allison couldn't help how she felt and she was tired of keeping her feelings to herself.

For a moment her husband's face looked startled. He stared at her in disbelief but there was something in her eyes that said she was serious. "You never used to be like this, Allison."

Richard lifted his shoulder, turned away, and Allison had the distinct impression he was trying to hide his hurt. When he turned back, a frown darkened his features. The lines in his face seemed to deepen. Richard tried changing the subject, "I'm under a lot of pressure."

Allison was unsympathetic. Her look never wavered. "We all are. It may not seem significant to you but the pressure you've been putting on Jordie lately is just as real and just as frightening." She looked at her husband with faint anxiety. After a moment she managed more calmly, "Ease up on him, Richard. He's just a boy."

"This is really about Austin again." Richard's face was bleak.

"Maybe." Allison couldn't deny his accusation but it had become more than that. She needed to make Richard understand. "You really don't get it, do you? The kids are beginning to demand your time and if it takes on a form of rebellion at least they're getting your attention. Don't make the same mistakes with Jordie."

There was a long silence. At last Richard spoke, "You've accused me of not seeing what's going on and that I have no feelings. Well, you're wrong, Allison, and it hurts me to think that you feel that I don't give a damn about you or the kids."

Her eyes met his and she shook her head sadly, "That's not what I'm trying to do."

This time it was Allison who changed the subject. With annoying insistence, she asked, "Can Mom and Dad take the kids to Disneyland so that I can get away for a few days?"

Richard tried to hide his look of weary resignation to no avail. "I don't care. Do what you want."

"I'm doing this for us," Allison cried out in despair. Seeing the confusion on her husband's face, she added, "Time away will help all of us." Allison needed desperately for her husband to understand. "I'm trying to come to terms with everything but it's so hard."

"Running away will help?" he asked sarcastically.

Allison immediately groaned. "I'm not running away," she denied, deeply resentful.

"Well, that's how it looks to me. What's this really about?"

Allison, who had risen from her chair, paced the floor in frustration. She shook her head. "I don't know. Maybe it's about us." Her voice was low. "This isn't just about tonight. It's been happening for a long time. We're becoming more and more like strangers who go their own way and then come home to sleep under the same roof."

Richard opened his lips to speak but Allison kept on talking, "We have no friends anymore, anything we do together socially is related to your business." She turned to face her husband. "When is the last time we had friends over for a simple barbeque?"

Richard broke in sharply, "How the hell do I know. I'm a lawyer, not a social secretary. Besides, you've hardly been in the mood for entertaining since the accident."

Allison ignored the interruption. She seemed preoccupied with her thoughts. "How long has it been since you looked at me and really saw me? Or I you for that matter?" she added. "Do we even know who we are anymore?"

"What kind of nonsense are you bringing up now?"

Ignoring his question, Allison suddenly asked, "Do you love me, Richard?" Allison desperately needed Richard's calm reassurance.

The question jarred him and he looked extremely uncomfortable. He hesitated for a moment before admitting, "I don't like the woman you've become since Austin died."

In frustration, Allison pushed her thick black hair from her forehead and looked at her husband with candid blue eyes, "In all the years we've been married I've done what it takes to support you and make our life together happy. I've done everything for you and the kids. You've changed. I don't think it was for the good and I've pretended that it didn't bother me," she said, quite seriously.

"You're dwelling on insignificant things," Richard retaliated, in a voice that was tight with indignation.

Allison raised her appalled face to her husband, "Austin's life was not insignificant."

Richard threw his hands in the air, "That's not what I meant. You're the one who's changed. I don't know who you are anymore." He looked at her in despair. "You're a stranger to me who is consumed with bitterness, drowning in sorrow and angry at life. Nothing I say or do is right anymore," he added in frustration.

Allison gave him a guarded look. He had to feel what she was feeling to understand her loss and her anger. "I know that I've changed since Austin's death because everything around me has changed. His death opened my eyes to a lot of different things that I'm trying to come to terms with." She could have added, "Including my feelings for you." She didn't but she couldn't meet his eyes.

Allison went back and sat in her chair. She knew that the change in her had baffled her husband and she was aware that there were times she intentionally hurt him. She couldn't help herself because she was hurting, too.

Because she wasn't proud of her behavior Allison attempted to make amends, "We've all said and done things that have hurt. It's gotten worse. I want to stop the flow of hurt. None of us are happy anymore. I have to find a way to change that."

Richard stared at his wife. Allison sat there regarding her husband through eyes that missed nothing. Gradually the effects of their argument faded and she watched as the lawyer façade was replaced by a look of vulnerability and his shoulders hunched forward. Richard realized he really didn't have any say because her mind was made up. He had to accept that.

Richard straightened and took an audible breath, the kind Allison had come to associate over the years with the yielding of wills. All the severity left his face. Resting his arms on the desk he leaned forward. With weary resignation he finally spoke, "When would you go?"

Allison's face brightened. She moved forward in her chair, breathing more easily. "I haven't said anything to Jordie and Cassie but they would go today if we said it was okay. I suppose in a couple of days. Mom and Dad said to just let them know."

Richard gave his wife a searching look. Allison smiled recognizing that he was a man that needed details. She had to admit that she was impatient now that she had made her decision. "How about Monday, then they don't have all the week-end traffic," she suggested eagerly.

"It's summer. The roads will be busy anyway," he informed her.

She gave a nervous laugh, "Of course it is. I wasn't really thinking." This was just another sign of her confused state. Allison pleaded, "Please try to understand."

For once his tone was gentle and the frown around his mouth softened, "I'm trying."

Richard looked up at his wife and managed a reassuring smile.

Chapter Four

It was mass confusion everywhere and Allison was attempting to remain calm. All she had to do was get through the morning. In an hour they'd all be gone. Richard was leaving on a business trip and as soon as he was finished packing he'd be on his way. The timing was perfect because the kids were leaving today for Disneyland. It also eased the guilt she felt when she first told Richard that she needed to get away. He wouldn't miss her if he was gone, too. Then she had to wonder if he'd miss her even if he wasn't.

"Where is my windbreaker?" Richard yelled from their bedroom.

"In the back closet. Why? You never take it on a business trip?" She didn't wait for an answer. Allison was still looking for the kid's book bags so they could pack things to keep themselves busy during the long hours spent riding in the car. Maybe they were in the storage room in the basement.

Allison ran back upstairs as the phone was ringing. Grabbing the extension in the kitchen she breathlessly answered. A trained voice on the other end began, "Good morning. Are you the lady of the house?" Allison hung up. Telemarketing. Like she had time for any of this. There were still a few things she had to do to finish getting herself ready. She rubbed her forehead as she felt a headache coming on.

Richard and Allison passed each other in the kitchen. Richard, with his windbreaker, went into their bedroom. Allison, with the book bags, went into Cassie's room.

One look at her daughter's bed added to her frustration. "Cassie, you can only take what will fit in this bag."

Cassie looked up at her mom with big blue eyes looking for understanding. "I know, Mommy. I don't know what to take."

Unfortunately, Mom's patience was wearing thin. "Well you better decide quickly or you won't be taking anything. Grampa and Gramma will be here soon and we want to be ready." Allison counted slowly to ten as Richard called from the front door. "Kids, your dad is leaving. Come say good-bye." Getting no response, she raised her voice and yelled impatiently, "Jordie, Cassie, come on. Your dad needs to leave."

Richard wished both kids a good holiday as they hugged him good-by. He was surprised by the hug from Jordie. Maybe the time away from one another would do them all some good.

The kids took off to finish packing and Allison and Richard were left alone. Richard gave his wife a concerned look. Austin's death had been hard on all of them but especially on her. When she took a step away he grabbed her around the waist and pulled her close. He lifted her chin gently with his finger forcing her to meet his eyes.

Tears welled in her eyes. It would've been easy to turn into his arms like she used to and let him hold her close. Instead, Allison tried to pull away but Richard held her back. She watched as his jaw line hardened, his lips compressed. Allison shifted her position. Her nerves were stretched to the breaking point. She could tell by Richard's rigid position that he, too, was struggling for control. As he looked at her his expression was very sober. When Allison dropped her eyes miserably Richard released his hold and Allison moved away from him.

Richard's jaw was hard and his voice grim as he spoke, "I'll have my cell phone on if you need me."

Allison responded defiantly, "I'll have mine with me but I'm going to let the calls go to my voice mail."

"Hmm," was all her husband said. He was not smiling.

"I'm a big girl." She tried to laugh away his concern. "I can take care of myself."

Richard remained unconvinced.

Allison sighed. "Okay, I'll call when I get to the cottage if it will make you feel better," she promised indignantly as her headache intensified. This was nonsense. Was he already forgetting his promise to her that he would give her a week alone to think things out?

Richard knew he had to be content with that promise. It didn't stop him from adding, "You know I worry about you. Are you sure you'll be okay by yourself?" There was weariness in his eyes and regret in his voice.

Yes, she was certain. Allison had admitted to herself that she was looking forward to the brief escape from the demands of her family and their daily pressures. She smiled at him with effort and her reply was a little edgy, "I really need this time to myself but I promise to check my voice mail twice a day."

"It will get easier. Time heals." Richard's eyes were filled with a silent plea.

Bitterness crept into Allison's voice as she glared back at him, "Time may heal, but it leaves a scar and scars always leave their ugly mark."

Richard flashed his wife a hurt look, started to say something and then changed his mind. She sensed his withdrawal. He shook his head with frustration. Lately, nothing he said was right. He ached to reach out and pull her back but the invisible wall remained between them. Richard smiled but it didn't reach his eyes and there was something there that Allison couldn't read. Without another word he stepped past her and closed the door.

Allison leaned against the door for a moment. She knew she shouldn't have pulled away but it was too late. He was gone. Lately, everything ended in an argument and she hated it. She'd seen the effects on the kids and knew that it couldn't continue. None of them could live with the unhappiness that surrounded them and still be okay. Things had to change, and soon. The big question was how? Allison had to find the answer. Groaning inwardly, she went to help Cassie finish packing.

Cassie shrieked with joy when she heard the car pull up in front of the house. "Mommy, they're here." Allison's dad was honking persistently as he pulled into the driveway. There was such evident glee in her little daughter's voice that Allison's annoyance was erased.

"Yes, dear. I can hear them, too."

Jordie was busy picking up suitcases as the front door opened and Allison's mom walked in. "Grampa's got the trunk open." She glanced down at the pile that was still left and shook her head. "We'll put as much in the trunk as we can. Jordie, put the pillows in the back seat along with your book bags."

"The box should go in the back seat, too," Allison instructed. "I packed a lunch for all of you. There are sandwiches, a box of cookies and some fruit."

"She packed everything but the fridge itself," Jordie teased, as he picked up the last items to take out to the car. Both ladies laughed. It was almost true.

"They have their own money for souvenirs. Cassie wants to buy presents for all her friends so good luck. She knows you'll keep her wallet for her." Turning to her son, she instructed mildly, "Jordie, keep yours in your front pocket. It'll be safer there."

"I'm not a baby, Mom."

"I'm not a baby, either," declared Cassie.

"No, you're not," she assured her youngest child. "Gramma will still keep yours for you, Cassie." Allison turned to Jordie and smiled gently. "And you, young man, take care."

"Geez, Mom." He had become so grown up in the last couple of months, maybe too much. Allison missed the son who used to be so carefree and happy.

Allison's dad placed an arm around his daughter's shoulder as they walked out to the car. Allison saw her mom exchange a glance with him, their expression identical. They were worried about leaving their daughter completely alone.

"I'm going to be fine," Allison declared, a little too brightly. "Don't worry about me. Now, get going and have fun. Say hi to Mickey for me," she added.

Grampa closed the trunk and shouted, "All aboard."

Jordie grabbed both pillows and hit Cassie over the head instead of just handing her one. Never a dull moment with kids.

Allison looked at her mom and dad and shook her head and smiled. "Good luck." She knew the trip would be great for the kids. The break would be good for her.

"Love you both. Be good for Grampa and Gramma. Have fun. See you in a few weeks." She hugged them one by one. Her dad gave her a concerned smile before letting go. Allison left her mom until last. Mother and daughter smiled knowingly at each other and hugged a little longer than was necessary. "I love you, Mom. Thanks."

"I love you, too." They both wiped tears from their eyes.

"Dad and I will call in a couple of days. We'll give you a little time to yourself. You need it." She cupped her daughter's face in her hands as she dropped a light kiss on her cheek.

Allison tilted her head into her mom's comforting hand. "Call my cell phone and leave a message if you don't get me at the cottage. You do have Richard's cell number, don't you?"

"Yes dear, we have everything. Don't worry about us. Just take care of yourself."

"I will," Allison promised.

Her dad started the car and honked the horn. "Come on, let's go." Her mom quickly climbed in. Everyone waved as Grampa continued to honk excitedly as they drove away.

Allison waved as the faces narrowed and dimmed. Then they were gone and Allison was left behind in the quiet. Expecting to feel sad and depressed, she was bewildered by the feeling that surrounded her. She stood there for a few minutes to savor her sense of freedom.

Chapter Five

Allison was frustrated because it was nearly noon before she got away. Traffic had been heavy all afternoon but now it was backed right up. She could see the flagman ahead. Construction. Like she needed this. As they crawled along Allison hoped to make it through before he closed their side down. Like a child, she crossed her fingers for luck. Just then the flagman turned his sign. "Damn," Allison muttered under her breath as she felt the tension build. Impatiently, she tapped her fingers on the steering wheel as she stared out the window.

Time passed slowly. Allison massaged the back of her neck hoping to ease her throbbing headache. She noticed her furrowed brow in the small mirror above the windshield. The pale face in the mirror frowned back at her. Finally, the flagman turned his sign and the line of cars slowly began to move forward. As soon as the traffic became lighter she pressed her foot down on the accelerator. Once again, she was on her way.

The scenery was spectacular, gentle rolling hills where tumbleweeds were held captive along the fence line. In the distance the mountains were silhouetted against the backdrop of a summer sky where billowing clouds drifted endlessly. Allison barely saw the landscape. She was mentally preparing for the ordeal ahead.

An hour later, it started to rain. Allison moaned in frustration as she switched on the windshield wipers. First construction, now rain. What next? She couldn't believe her bad luck. Thankfully, the shower passed quickly. Steam lifted off the pavement and floated into the trees. A brief rainbow arced overhead and Allison smiled to herself. She wasn't about to let unforeseen circumstances get the better of her. However, she couldn't help but sigh deeply for she dreaded what lay before her. Nerves again tensed and her stomach was in knots.

Hours passed as she drove through unfamiliar terrain. She had left the rolling hills and sagebrush behind long ago and tall trees now lined both sides of the winding road. Allison struggled to control a rising sense of alarm. Had she taken a wrong turn? Tears of frustration stung her eyes. She checked the directions again.

By the time Allison recognized the turnoff she'd driven past it. She backed up and confirmed the name Hanson on the mailbox. Allison stiffened nervously and firmly gripped the wheel to keep her hands from shaking. She knew she had to get herself into a proper frame of mind before she faced Jake Hanson but a combination of guilt, fear and anger weren't making it easy. Words of silent accusation were implanted in her mind as she turned into the entrance.

The log bungalow was nestled into the hillside as if it had been there forever, situated so that it wasn't visible from the road. It was only when someone turned into the drive, through the cottonwoods, that the house was seen in full perspective. The covered wrap-around verandah was welcoming with its wicker furniture offering cozy comfort while one sat enjoying the peace and seclusion of nature's hideaway. Would she be welcome? Suddenly, doubts began to surface. Feeling the façade of bravery slipping, Allison left her car before her fears could take hold. Unexpectedly, a dog appeared from the side of the house. Allison froze momentarily with fright but the dog's expression was gentle and he wagged his tail as if greeting a familiar friend. "Some watch dog," Allison thought to herself, but her initial fear had eased as he followed her up the verandah steps. Allison knocked on the door before she could change her mind.

A stranger from the past opened the door, for Allison had an unsettling awareness that she'd seen him before. Until that moment her image had been strictly impersonal and faceless. The moment she looked into the smoky gray eyes she remembered. Allison hadn't known who he was then but she had seen him at her son's funeral and had briefly wondered who he was. Her gaze openly inspected him. She was aware of everything about him; his towering height, his broad shoulders and the penetrating eyes.

Jake wasn't really surprised to see her and his face remained expressionless as he studied her. She was more fragile than he remembered. Jake's gaze dwelt on the fine details of her face. Her skin was so pale. It looked as though it would bruise if he touched it. She had the bluest eyes he'd ever seen but there was no life in them. It was the same look he'd seen every day in the mirror for years. The look that comes of knowing that a part of your life has ended. The spark had gone out of her life, too.

"Mr. Jake Hanson?" Allison asked, her heart in her throat. As she swallowed hard he noticed the pulse beating in the hollow at the base of her slender neck.

Jake regarded her for several seconds before replying, "Yes, Allison. I'm Jake Hanson."

In front of her stood the man, who unwillingly, had become part of the most unbearable experience of her life. Color drained from her face. A tortured cry escaped, nothing else, no other sound, and Allison swayed. Jake reached out and caught her as she fainted. Sam, the dog, whimpered as he followed his master. Jake carried Allison into the living room and laid her gently on the sofa.

Allison was cradled in strong, warm arms when consciousness returned. For a moment her head swam in confusion. She attempted to get up. "Lay still." The gray eyes flashed downwards and captured Allison's gaze. Icy blue eyes glared back as she sat up.

"Are you okay?" His concerned gaze continued to search Allison's face, noting the strain and tension. Her eyes were wide and anxious and there was a revealing tremor about her lips.

Allison took a deep breath and seemed to summon some strength. "I'm sorry. I've never fainted before. It's been a very stressful day and I haven't eaten anything. I'll be fine." Aware of the stiffness in her voice she attempted to smile. "I had to come see you. The police told us that Austin had stayed here. You're my last link to Austin. I should say to his last days. I need to know what happened to my son after he left home." Sapphire blue eyes reflected the raw pain that still lived in her soul.

Jake recognized her pain. He'd come to know it years ago.

Allison faced Jake squarely. "I came for some answers."

Under the coolly delivered words he detected resentment. He was very aware of the stiffness of her posture hinting at tautly controlled anger. Jake's eyes flickered with uncertainty.

Allison's face was strained as she sat facing him.

Both of them were uneasy.

Finally, Allison spoke. "I need to know what happened while my son was here. How did he end up here? Why did he stay away so long? Why didn't Austin call us?" Her rush of words stopped as she realized that her voice betrayed her emotional turmoil. When Allison felt the hotness of unshed tears she willed herself not to cry. She laced her hands together tightly in her lap as she looked up at him. "You're the only one who can tell me."

Jake was once again struck by her incredible likeness to Austin. The only visible difference was the eyes. Austin's eyes were so dark that at times they were almost black. This lady's eyes were as blue as the deepest lake that had been frozen over. Her icy stare chilled him.

"You owe me some answers," Allison stated deliberately. She seemed deeply troubled. "Please help me before I go mad," Allison begged in desperation. The expression on her face was pure torment.

When he had difficulty meeting her gaze, Jake felt he needed a few minutes to recover. He rose and left the room without a word. Allison could hear water running in the kitchen. A couple of minutes passed before Jake returned with a glass of water. "Here, drink this," Jake said, as he handed her the glass. His intense stare forced her to drink a little water. "I'll answer all of your questions after you've had some food and a cup of tea."

"I'd prefer a strong cup of coffee if you have some," Allison admitted, her voice flat.

"That and some food." Jake's voice was firm. "I can understand you coming here, but why alone and why so late?"

Allison quickly explained, "My husband, Richard, is away. There was another conference he had to go to." She failed to elaborate, not because she didn't want to but because she honestly couldn't remember which city he was in this time. She dropped her eyes in confusion. These days her mind didn't function properly. "He's away a lot lately."

"It's too bad your husband is a workaholic. He doesn't listen very well either." Jake wasn't accusing, just making a statement but Allison caught the flash of anger in his eyes and wondered where it was coming from.

Allison was quick to add, "The kids have gone to Disneyland with my parents. I'm on my way to our cottage but I had to come here first." Her behavior became flustered. "I got away late, there was construction, it rained, I got lost."

Jake stared down at her tormented face. "I think it would be wise for you to stay the night. Emotionally, you're a wreck, physically you're exhausted. You don't need to be on the road at night." He could have added, "Or in the state you're in."

Allison had to admit that she'd given no thought to time when she set out and she didn't want to arrive at the cabin in the dark. Of course he was right but Allison didn't like the position she'd put herself in. Her face remained impassive and unyielding as she stared back at him. "I'll stay," Allison finally agreed, ungraciously. She knew it was the best thing to do.

"Give me your keys and I'll fetch your bag and put it in the guest room. If you don't mind, I'll park your car in the garage." Allison looked at him with uncertainty. "We may get hail tonight," Jake explained.

Allison took the keys from her purse and handed them to Jake, totally unconscious of the immediate trust she put in this stranger.

"The bathroom is next to the guest room if you would like to freshen up," Jake said, as he turned and left.

Allison stood up carefully and then found her way to the bathroom. She was relieved to have a few minutes to herself.

On her way back Allison stopped in the doorway to the spare room. She felt nervous tremors in her legs. Her heart started to hammer in her chest and she again felt faint. She was unaware that she'd been holding her breath and once she breathed deeply she felt better. Allison hesitated at the door, afraid to go in. She let her gaze pass over the dresser to the chair, past the window and over to the bed.

This was where her son had spent his last days. In a trance, Allison entered. She paced the room in a sad, troubled way before walking silently to the bed, unaware of the tears that slid down her cheeks. Her hand caressed the bedspread. She lowered herself listlessly onto the side of the bed and picked up one of the pillows where Austin had laid his head. Allison hugged it to her bosom as she would a child and rocked back and forth as the tears flowed. Without thinking, she laid down where her son had laid, turned her head into the pillow and cried until she fell into a deep sleep. Sleep had become her only escape.

Quietly, making no sound, Jake entered the room. Sam lay next to the bed where Allison's still body faced the door. She was asleep, curled up, a hand under her tear stained cheek. The face was pale and the cheeks were hollow. It was still a beautiful face. Her hair lay in a tangle of black silt on the pillow. Jake remembered how Austin had laid there not too long ago. Taking the blanket from the end of the bed, he gently covered her. Placing the suitcase on the empty chair he walked to the door. He stood for a moment with his hand on the doorknob. Jake sighed deeply. What was this family doing to him? Quietly, he closed the door.

Chapter Six

Branches creaked outside the window as the wind rubbed them together coaxing Allison from her precious sleep. The room had darkened. She rolled onto her back and stared at the ceiling. She was actually here. The wait was over. On the other side of the door was the person who had the answers to her recurring questions. Would they help or hurt her even more she wondered in troubled uncertainty? Either way, it was time to face her demons.

Allison straightened the bed and folded the blanket. The pillow case was still damp from her fallen tears. Undoing the zipper of her suitcase, Allison opened the lid. No need to unpack. She was only staying tonight. It wouldn't take any longer than that to get the answers to her questions. Allison removed her toiletry bag so she could brush her hair and freshen her make-up. A few strokes of blush on her cheeks and a fresh coat of lipstick brought artificial color to her face. As she surveyed her reflection her mouth twisted wryly. The image in the mirror reflected none of her inner turmoil. Sleep had eased her tense muscles but had done nothing for her nerves. Allison sighed and bracing her shoulders, she opened the door and walked out.

Allison could smell the tantalizing aroma of fresh brewed coffee.

"Feeling better?" Jake's question greeted her as she entered the kitchen.

"Not much." Her head felt slightly wooly. The paleness of her skin intensified the blue of her eyes.

Jake poured her a coffee while Allison sat down at the kitchen table. A warm breeze stirred the curtains at the open window. He placed the cup on the table in front of her and asked, "Cream and sugar?"

"Just black," she said, and Jake had a quick flashback to that first day in the kitchen with Austin. He drank his coffee black, too.

The simple meal was informal, the atmosphere was strained. Jake attempted to break the tension but he was as anxious as his guest. It didn't take him long to realize that there would be no polite small talk with this lady.

"Where do we start?" he asked. Jake sat there sipping his coffee slowly, watching her. Getting no response, Jake said, "Why don't you go first."

Setting her empty cup aside with a shaking hand, Allison took a deep breath, visibly summoning her courage. Her chin jutted out and her eyes flashed as her expression changed. Looking up at him she felt the built-up anger rise in her throat. As soon as she spoke she lost control and her verbal attack began. The dam of emotions had been released and a flood of bitter and hurtful words followed, "Do you have any idea what we went through not knowing where Austin was? We didn't know if he was safe. We knew nothing at all as we waited and waited. Every minute was an hour long; every hour seemed like a day. Every time the phone rang I prayed that it was Austin. It never was." Her voice cracked and she forced herself to hold back the tears. "Every time I heard the door open I expected it to be Austin. It never was. As a parent, I would've thought that you would've had the decency to let us know that Austin was at least safe," she flung at him.

The anger in Allison's voice startled him but if she was going to be direct, so was he. Jake gave her a brief intense look. "You have made an assumption. I have no children. I have no doubt that you have made other assumptions." Jake leaned forward, speaking very seriously. "Don't be too quick to judge without having any answers, Mrs. Smith," Jake cautioned.

Allison resented his tone. Licensed by the past, she felt she had every right to be mad. Angry blue eyes blazed into steely gray eyes. She ignored his warning. Like a mother bear she continued to attack. "His brother sat by the window every day waiting for Austin to come home. Austin never came home." Her eyes held his gaze but now anguish darkened their hue.

Her disjointed ranting continued. "I called his best friend Ryan because I thought for sure that's where Austin would go. He hadn't heard from Austin. I knew Ryan wouldn't lie so I started calling his other friends. No one had seen him or heard from him. Day after day we waited and wondered. Why didn't you make him go home?" she challenged. "Why didn't you make him phone us so we at least knew that he was safe?" Now her expression was resentful and bitter. Electric currents seemed to cross and spark as her eyes met his.

A spasm of emotion crossed Jake's face. Involuntarily, he turned away to avoid her questioning eyes. How many times had he asked himself the same questions?

There was an icy sparkle in Allison's eyes when he turned back to look at her. Indignation had brought color to her pale cheeks. Allison's gaze locked with Jakes.

Jake was compelled to defend himself. "I didn't know what to do and I didn't want to scare him off so that he left. I was on unfamiliar ground." His eyes flashed a silent warning.

Allison didn't miss it and yet she refused to back down. It was as if Jake hadn't even spoken. Her anger fueled her and the harsh words continued to pour out. "That's no excuse. What hurt most was not knowing what happened to Austin. It was like a nightmare wondering where he was and if he was safe." Her voice had continued to rise as she spoke and it was when she yelled at him that he was insensitive and cruel that he silenced her with a harsh look.

Jake's face went white as the words assaulted him. "Don't sit in judgment of me because you don't have the right."

Allison was too upset to reason with. She was too angry to listen. "If there is hell on earth, we lived it!" she spat back at him.

Darkened eyes narrowed as Jake responded with answering anger, "You can't blame me for something that wasn't my fault. It isn't fair. I'm not the reason that Austin left home."

Allison became very quiet as her guilt surfaced. Her dark lashes couldn't conceal the flash of hurt. When Allison finally spoke, her words came out in an anguished whisper. "I thought that was the worst. It wasn't. In one day our family's life was destroyed." The words had caught in her throat forcing tears to her eyes. She swallowed hard and the tears spilled over. "This is more difficult than anything you can imagine," she whispered.

A look of pain crossed Jake's face as he realized the fullness of this mother's hurt. "I do know," he whispered. Little did Allison know how well Jake Hanson understood.

The questions continued. "Why didn't he phone? Austin could have. He should have," she cried desperately. She brushed angrily at the tears with the back of her hand.

Almost painfully, Jake said, "If I could do it over again, would I have insisted he call? I don't know," he admitted honestly. "I did what I thought was best for the situation at hand."

"Well you thought wrong," Allison cried.

Jake drew a hand through his dark brown hair, "Your son was an unhappy young man, so full of anger. I knew that I couldn't push him but I needed time to learn why."

Jake refilled their cups and sat back down. He took a deep breath before continuing, "At first, Austin only shared his anger. It took him a couple of days to open up. I knew how to deal with anger but I didn't know how to deal with such hurt," Jake said, and stopped.

Allison had the feeling he was waiting for a response but she remained silent although she was fully aware that Austin had been both angry and hurt when he stormed out of their house. She gripped her coffee mug tighter as she remembered the fight that followed between her and Richard. Allison bit her lip in confusion.

It was Jake's voice that brought her back as he continued, "I felt it was more important to build trust than to dictate rules. We know how effective that can be. I had to make your son understand that if he started running from unpleasantness now he would be running for the rest of his life." Jake took her hand and held it until she looked up. "I couldn't let him do that."

Jake could read her thoughts as anger flared in the blue eyes regarding him. "I've hurt you but you started this." Jake sighed heavily and then asked, with effort, "Why didn't you or your husband go after him?"

Fighting tears of loss and guilt, she said harshly, "That's none of your business."

Jake sat still as he looked at her. He leaned forward, his eyes locked on hers. "You made it my business when you came here," he stated candidly.

In defense, Allison lashed out angrily, "Kids take everything literally and blow thing out of proportion." She paused before admitting, "I thought he just needed time to cool off."

"I suppose normally that would be the case. However, Austin was deeply hurt by the cruel things your husband said that morning. How can any father call his son a failure?"

Allison hung her head, "I knew the day he left that Austin took Richard's words the wrong way. When Richard said, 'Fine, be a failure.'"

Jake continued for her, "Austin heard, 'Fine, you're a failure'. Words can be so cutting. Sometimes the wounds take a long time to heal. Don't we say awful things, not meaning them?"

"We do," Allison confessed, anger gone.

"Anger can bring out the worst in anyone because it takes us to the high end of the emotional scale. Mix in the hurt that goes along with it and a person explodes right off the chart. In just a few seconds with a few hurtful words we can cause such hurt that it can take a lifetime to heal. Austin's hurt was so deep that he felt the unknown was better than the past." Allison detected the criticism in Jake's voice.

Not knowing how to respond she looked away. Allison couldn't ignore the truth of what he was saying. Lately, she had said things that she never dreamed she'd say out loud. It was as if her control would snap and she couldn't get it back. Allison hung her head in shame for this knowledge frightened her. Nothing was normal lately she reasoned but it didn't console her.

Jake watched her with sad eyes. After a pause Jake continued, aware of the inner turmoil stirring within his guest. When he spoke his voice had softened, "I know Austin hated it when I turned the conversations back to him but they became so revealing and I needed to find out what was causing his anger. It was a challenge to learn more about him but it became easier once some trust had been established. At one time his sulleness erupted into outright hostility. That's when it became obvious who most of his anger was directed at."

Allison looked back at him. She had come here for answers and she had to know.

Reading her mind, Jake promptly continued, "Austin felt wronged by the threats from his school and from his parents. He was deeply

200

resentful of the opinion his dad had of him. Right or wrong, that's how he felt. I know Austin was caught up in his anger. He needed time to let go of his anger regardless of who it was directed at. His thoughts were in turmoil and his emotions were out of control. He needed to sort out his troubled feelings."

Allison closed her eyes, trying to ward off the words she knew to be true.

Jake's brow drew together as he remembered. He shook his head slowly, "Your husband's a busy man and Austin felt his dad always put work first."

"Richard works long hours by choice," Allison stated in a cool voice, yet her eyes flashed. "A man has little time to parent when he's working all the time."

Jake continued, "Once Austin opened up, he told me he wondered what his dad was working on that took up all of his time. He thought if he understood his work better he might understand his dad better."

Surprise was evident on Allison's face as her eyes widened. "Austin actually said that?"

"Oh he was surprised as well when he said it because he'd never really thought about it before. It's too bad that your husband has become so absorbed in his work without leaving time for his family."

Allison seemed less angry, less rigid. However, her words remained bitter. "Richard and Austin's personalities often clashed. They were such opposites."

"That's what Austin said. He didn't like the fighting but he felt his dad was trying to control his future. No consideration was been given for what your son wanted."

Allison tried to explain, "There are so many choices for kids these days. I think it's harder for them and we forget that. Richard is so self-willed and obstinate, especially if he feels it's for your own good. Once he's made his mind up about something there's no changing it. Austin was no different. He could be just as stubborn as his dad. That's when he and Richard really fought. That was the trouble the day Austin left, the cause of it all."

Jake nodded. "I know. Austin said that he and his dad were always fighting and that it usually turned into a yelling match."

Allison added with a short, bitter laugh, "Austin hadn't mastered the art of hiding or controlling his feelings." She shook her head, "They were no longer communicating."

Frowning deeply, Jake studied Allison. "It's like I told Austin. When you live with anger everything is wrong. Anger doesn't allow you to think clearly."

Allison knew how true that was. Lately, she was having trouble controlling her own anger. "You're right," she admitted, feeling uncomfortable about her initial outburst. She looked up, her gaze direct. "It's so hard to let it go when it's continually being refueled."

Jake smiled sadly. Austin had basically said the same thing.

Jake's gray eyes had lost their steely look. "I think Austin was covering a lot of his hurt with anger. I was giving him a little time to bring his life back into focus rather than allowing it to remain clouded by that anger. I put it down to youth but I knew it wasn't just that. Austin truly felt his dad was trying to control his life." Jake's eyes grew hard. "He actually said ruin instead of control. Austin said his dad didn't approve of his choice about college."

Allison broke in, "That's putting it mildly. It was an ongoing conflict between the two of them. His dad wanted him to go to his alma mater after graduating. If not there, than at least to an elite college. It didn't matter to Richard that Austin wanted to go to our local college until he knew what he wanted to do." Allison looked up at Jake, "Why couldn't his dad see that?"

"That's what Austin kept asking." Jake sighed heavily, "I don't know, Allison. It's too bad, though. Austin wanted to live his life based on his decisions, especially about college."

Jake shook his head, "Austin was strong enough to know what he didn't want. He simply wanted time to discover what he did want. Austin had a deep inner conviction that he had every right to take control of his own life."

Allison had to ask Jake, "Why didn't you make him go home?" It was the second time she had asked him that and Jake again refused to answer, choosing to look away instead.

Allison's touch on his arm brought Jake back to the unanswered question. It compelled him to look at her and Allison saw his desperate need for understanding. Jake looked pointedly at Allison. "Each day the trust level became stronger. I wanted it to be his decision to go home."

Allison studied Jake. He was obviously sincere, if misguided.

"Your son and I talked a lot. He admitted that he was afraid to call because he didn't know what to say or what to expect from his parents. I helped him to realize that there's nothing to fear if you're honest with yourself and not afraid of the outcome. Austin was ready to call you that Sunday night. I thought he had." Allison believed Jake but didn't know why.

"I retired early and Austin went for a walk. We agreed that he would let me know his decision in the morning. I'd offered to drive him home but he was gone before I got up. Once again, your son was exerting his independence," Jake acknowledged.

Allison looked at him, her eyes dark with fatigue. Jake noticed the violet circles beneath her eyes. He smiled gently. "It's past midnight. The rest can wait until tomorrow."

Allison didn't return his smile. "Okay, but I'm not through asking you questions."

Jake even surprised himself when he unexpectedly said, "Stay a couple of days. Share your son with me a little more." His eyes darkened with deep sadness.

Allison was caught by his gaze and for the first time she realized the depth of anguish that he also carried from Austin's death. Looking at Jake's own shadowed eyes, Allison felt guilty. She'd been feeling antagonistic toward him without any consideration to the effect Austin's death had on him. She wasn't ready to forgive but her look was sympathetic. "I'd love to," Allison said truthfully, "but I can't." She looked away.

"Why not? You said your family is away. So you get to the cottage later in the week. Will it make any difference?"

Allison's shoulders sagged in confusion. It wouldn't make any difference but she knew that she was too tired to think clearly. "I'll see," was all she'd commit to.

Jake persisted, "Agree to share a couple of days with a lonely man."

Her heart was torn for his persuasiveness was hard to resist. It was sad to be lonely. "Maybe," she replied noncommittally. "There is a lot more I need to know, Jake," confessed Allison. There was a hint of desperation in her voice and a note of distress.

Jake nodded his head, "I know there is. Go to bed," he said, in his slow, deep way of speaking. Jake was suddenly very tired. It had been an emotional day for him, too. "We'll talk more in the morning. I promise."

Allison had to be content with his promise. It had been a long, exhausting day and she didn't have the energy to think. There would be time enough to sort through everything tomorrow. Suddenly, Allison was tired to the bone. Along with the fatigue, the dull pounding in her head had returned. She rose and went to her room.

Lying in bed, Allison was once again close to tears. She prayed for a dreamless sleep, undisturbed by recurring nightmares. She listened to the wind which had risen as it moaned through the trees. Like so many other nights her thoughts were of Austin. Allison allowed her mind to wander down the familiar trail of memories. She wanted to remember everything about him but she was afraid that time would make her forget more than just the pain.

Allison tossed and turned as she thought about everything she and Jake had discussed. Jake had enjoyed Austin's sense of humor and had seen the sensitive side underneath the recent granite exterior he'd often worn around his dad. Allison had sensed an admiration and genuine affection in Jake's tone whenever he'd spoken of Austin. He had spoken with such compassion and his voice had been so sad that her heart went out to him. Jake had been a victim of circumstances who had no experience to deal with an angry teenager. Yet he had unconditionally allowed Austin to stay in his home.

Allison's thoughts remained on Jake. She was furious with herself for losing her temper and judging him unfairly. He'd answered her questions openly and honestly even though his comments hurt her at times. He'd given her a great deal to think about and there were many things that Jake told her that she had to mull over in her mind. As tired as she was her mind wouldn't rest. Allison sensed that there was a lot more that transpired between this man and her son that Jake was unwilling to share and as she lay there she felt she could accept his silence. Many thoughts later, Allison curled up, closed her mind, and fell asleep.

Chapter Seven

Shafts of bright light filtered through the window and Allison lay for a moment enjoying the warmth. It was the delicious smell of coffee that finally made her rise. She was a little embarrassed when she entered the kitchen for it was already mid-morning.

Jake turned his head and his heart missed a beat. Allison stood there, her hair long and free, her cheeks pink. He felt a surge of being alive and of being glad that he was. He took a big gulp of coffee and then grinned. It had been a long time since a beautiful woman had stood in his kitchen with her hair still wet from a morning shower.

Allison returned his smile, "You shouldn't have let me sleep so late."

"You obviously needed it. Besides, it was late before you finally settled." He answered her questioning look, "You were restless for a long time." Jake smiled at her in sympathy, seeing the shadows and the puffiness around her eyes.

Allison knew she'd slept badly. It wasn't unusual. She'd been fighting the emotional upheaval in her life created by her son's departure, and now, more than ever, by his death.

"I'll get you a coffee. What would you like for breakfast?"

"Coffee's fine. I never eat breakfast."

"Here," he said, as he handed her a coffee.

"Thanks. Last night you promised to tell me more about Austin," Allison demanded, wide-eyed. Jake couldn't avoid her for she continued to stand directly in front of him.

Once again Jake was surprised by her directness. Then he smiled. Obviously, Austin got that trait from his mother. He stared into her sad eyes. They were asking him to understand. He did but he regretted that some of the facts he was about to share would cause more pain. Jake motioned for Allison to sit. Allison sat down but she was too tense to relax.

"What do you want to know?"

"Everything." The word was almost inaudible.

Jake settled himself across from his guest and he gripped his own cup in his hands. "I guess the beginning is always the best place to start," he said casually. "The first night here Austin slept in the barn and Sam and I didn't find him until the next morning. The second night he wasn't fully conscious of his surroundings."

Jake had Allison's complete attention. "What do you mean by that?"

Noting the look of pain on Allison's face Jake was quick to elaborate, "Austin got caught in a nasty storm and was looking for shelter. In his haste and his state of physical exhaustion he had fallen and had hit his head." Allison had to concentrate on what Jake was saying. "Austin told me that he'd managed to drag himself into my barn before he lost consciousness. He had a mild concussion but was fine the next day."

Allison's mind reeled as she visualized her son lying face down in the mud, scared and alone. She tried to shake off the black visions.

Jake felt bad. "I'm not trying to upset you, Allison, but you did ask."

Allison had paled at his words but she begged him to continue, "Tell me every detail you can remember while Austin was here." She mentally braced herself not knowing what else she would hear.

Jake, recognizing the need in her voice, continued to talk about Austin throughout the morning and time ticked by unnoticed. Allison listened enthralled, absorbing every word.

Jake paused when he heard a vehicle outside and peered out the window. "Well, aren't I being blessed with unexpected visitors," he said surprisingly. Jake seldom had company, especially on a week day. His brother waved from the truck as it pulled alongside the front verandah. Jake had to wonder why Matt was here. He looked again and was more surprised to see his mom with his brother.

Jake opened the porch door. Matt walked past him while his mom stopped to hug him. Mrs. Hanson was a short, slightly plump, pleasant looking woman with warm hazel eyes.

Matt wasn't as tall as his brother but he was still over the six-foot mark. Nor was he as lean. His face, angular and strong, was darkly tanned from working outdoors. There was a permanent squint to his eyes from years of looking into the sun and wind. There was also a lot more gray sprinkled through the thick hair that had been bleached by the sun to a warm honey brown. His jaw was just as pronounced and there was a definite twinkle in his eyes. "Morning, bro," Matt said in a deep, dark voice. Noticing Allison, he was instantly alert.

"Who do we have here?" he asked, as he reached into the cupboard for a mug and poured himself a coffee. Turning, with cup in hand, he leaned against the counter. Matt eyed Allison with curious speculation. His thick dark brows lifted and there was a faint smile playing on his lips as a flicker of sheer wickedness sparkled in his eyes. "Are we interrupting something?" he inquired, noticing Allison's damp hair and, thereby, jumping to his own conclusion.

Allison attempted to smile, hoping her expression gave no hint of her real feelings. Jake shot his brother an angry look.

Matt wasn't diverted. "Jake doesn't get a lot of company, especially overnight," Matt told Allison, with a teasing glance at his brother. "I'm surprised at you, Jake," he drawled, that wicked gleam still in his eyes. Feeling color flush her cheeks, Allison glanced away.

"You've got it all wrong, Matt," Jake said, scowling at his brother.

Matt happily continued, to his brother's embarrassment. "I took a chance you'd be working at home today." Matt quirked an eyebrow and his eyes twinkled. "But I can see you're busy," he continued to tease ruthlessly.

"Don't be an ass!" Jake's voice was sharp. He was not the least bit amused. Matt chuckled as he set his cup down on the counter.

Jake went to the cupboard for a coffee mug and filled it. "Allison, this rude excuse for a human is my brother, Matt." Matt feigned an affronted look. "This little lady is our mother, Edna," he said, with great affection, as he handed her the cup. Both boys dwarfed their mom.

Matt's voice was also filled with affection as he teased, "Don't be mislead by Ma's looks. She can be a tough old broad."

Their mother's eyes filled with warmth and good humor. She turned to face Allison with a ready smile. "My boys both take after their father," she declared, with an undertone of amusement. Edna Hanson went and sat down at the end of the table. "Ben was a big strong man just like my boys," she said proudly.

"This is Allison Smith." Jake turned to Matt, "You remember reading about Austin Smith, the young boy who was killed in the hit and run in April? Austin was her son. Allison arrived yesterday looking for answers to a few questions."

Feeling a little awkward, Allison smiled with an attempt at cool dignity. "It got late and I was in no state to drive." Allison was quick to add, "Jake was kind enough to offer me a bed for the night." She appeared to be composed but her nerves were now stretched tight.

The light teasing smile faded from Matt's face. "I am an ass. Sorry Allison, it's nice to meet you. We all felt bad about Austin."

Edna, too, offered an expression of condolence over Allison's recent loss.

"It's been rough," Allison admitted.

Matt turned back to Jake. Allison was grateful that he moved the subject of conversation to the reason for his visit. "I was wondering if you might have time to go with me to look at George Baldwin's horses. Billy didn't do well yesterday in the qualifying round. He feels Clint's horse is favoring a front leg. Talk around the arena is that George's horses are some of the best so Billy wants me to check them out before he gets home at the end of the week."

Jake turned to Allison. "Billy is Matt's youngest son and he participates in the rodeo circuit as a steer wrestler."

Matt placed a hand on his brother's broad shoulder. "I'd sure appreciate a second opinion, Jake."

"Why didn't you bring Double Joe with you?"

Double Joe was a crusty old native who had first worked for their dad. Although he was too old to do much work these days, Matt kept him on at the ranch. He had nowhere else to go, never did have any family of his own. The story they were told was that when he was a young man he showed up at the ranch. Hardly spoke a word but wouldn't leave. Ben Hanson figured he had run away from the nearby Arapaho tribe and wouldn't go back. When asked his name, he stuttered "Joe". He gave no other name but because he always stuttered he'd been nicknamed Double Joe.

"You know how Double Joe just up and disappears for a few days. Saw the back side of him two days ago and haven't seen him since," drawled Matt. "Mom decided to come along and visit with George's wife, Audrey." He turned back to his brother, "Can you come?"

Knowing Jake was about to refuse on her account Allison hid her disappointment. She glanced from one man to the other. "Go with your brother and give him a hand." She forced brightness into her tone as she added, "I'll be fine, Jake."

"It won't take long," Matt pleaded.

Allison twisted her hands together. "Go, we can talk when you get back," she insisted.

"Will you be okay if I leave?" Jake asked, still hesitating.

She nodded her head. "I've waited this long."

Jake flashed her an apologetic smile as he followed Matt to the door.

Matt called over his shoulder, "Ma, are you coming?"

Edna started to step forward and saw Allison's look of anguish. The young woman's pale face was etched with anxiety and her shadowed eyes revealed emotional turmoil. Her face looked haunted and she was far too thin. "This woman looks dreadful," Edna thought to herself. Without hesitation, she answered, "Tell Audrey I'll visit another time."

Matt was about to question his mom but Edna silently shook her head. "You two run along. If you don't mind, I'll stay and keep you company," she remarked casually to Allison.

Allison breathed an audible sigh of relief and smiled at the other woman gratefully.

"I've been sitting for hours in that big truck of Matt's. Allison, why don't you and I take Sam for a quiet walk while my sons go about their business?"

Allison knew a refusal would be impolite. Besides, the fresh air and exercise might do her some good.

Jake waved a finger at his mom, "Don't interfere."

Edna Hanson ignored her son's remark. "The sooner you go the sooner you're back," Jake's mom informed, tolerantly. "Get going, both of you."

She took Allison gently by the arm, "Come, let's go find Sam." Stepping outside onto the verandah, both ladies waved a farewell to the Hanson boys as they drove away from the house. Sam, who had chased after Matt's truck, was at the end of the driveway. Edna gave a whistle and the dog turned and came running back.

"Let's enjoy the sunshine and wander up through the meadow." The smells of summer soon surrounded them; fresh grass, the fragrance of wild flowers and Allison breathed in the freshness of the pure air. She took in the sights and sounds around her as Mrs. Hanson led them along. A flock of birds rose from their nesting place in the tall grass, startled by the violation of their privacy. Their birdsong lifted her spirits and Allison felt better. The gentle breeze was refreshing and drifting clouds overhead cast moving shadows across the landscape.

Sam scampered ahead as they meandered along leisurely. They started with polite small talk because they didn't know each other well enough to do anything else.

"As you can tell, I'm very close to my boys. I love them dearly but even at their age they can embarrass their mother. Sorry about Matt's behavior." Then she laughed gently as she confessed, "Unfortunately, his behavior is outrageous most of the time and he's a terrible tease."

Allison had no doubt that he was a flirt as well. The corners of her mouth creased with the faintest suggestion of a smile.

"Jake is much more quiet and pleasant. He has a great sense of humor, too. Being such a handsome and eligible man has made him a target for unattached females."

Allison could believe this. Her own heart had fluttered more than once in his presence. Her attention drifted and she wondered if he'd ever been married. She suddenly realized that she knew nothing about her host other than the fact that he had no children. She'd been so self- absorbed in her own world of grief that she'd thought of nothing else. Allison shuddered involuntarily. She had acted on impulse with no regard for the consequences of her actions. How different it could have been if there had been a Mrs. Hanson or if Jake himself hadn't been a gentleman. Allison chided herself for allowing emotion to curb her judgment.

Allison was brought back to the present as the elderly lady spoke. There was a twinkle in her warm, friendly eyes as Edna continued to talk about her sons. "They think they can bully me, but they don't."

Allison had no doubt that the little lady handled her family with a firm but loving hand. It was obvious the boys adored their mom and that they all cared a great deal about each other.

"I'm always glad when I can spend time with them but they're always so busy. Sometimes they're even too busy to call. Actually, Jake's pretty good. He usually calls me on Sunday's. Matt figures why call if there's nothing new. They don't understand that a mom just wants to hear their voices to know they're okay. Kids don't worry about parents the way parents worry about their kids." She laughed pleasantly, "It doesn't matter how old they get. They say it's different with girls. I sometimes envy the relationship I see with mothers and daughters." She looked over at Allison. "I understand you have a younger son and a daughter at home."

Allison looked at her quizzically.

"Jake told me," Edna confessed, in a kindly tone. "He said that Austin shared a lot about his family and that your son recognized your devotion to each of them."

Allison's heart warmed as the elderly woman spoke such kind words. Obviously, Austin wasn't filled with anger the whole time he was here. It came as a relief to know that Austin could talk so freely, and fondly, about all of them.

Edna chatted merrily as they walked along a well-beaten trail that lead to a clearing in the meadow. The sun was gently warming the countryside. While they were walking, Edna had picked a variety of wild flowers. Allison thought she was picking them for Jake's house. She was surprised when she saw two headstones at the far end of the meadow. Instantly, Allison was miles away remembering where she was

213

the dark day she decided to come here. In her heart she knew she'd made the right decision but she really needed more time with Jake.

Edna smiled pleasantly at Allison. "Do you mind if I take a couple of minutes?"

Allison's gaze followed the elderly woman as she walked between the headstones and laid the flowers down. Edna looked over, her expression sad. She passed a meaningful glance to Allison and informed her, "For what it's worth, Jake understands better than you think." Her expression was very serious. "Jake, too, knows the pain of losing loved ones." Before Allison could ask, Edna turned to the young mother. "Jake's wife and infant son are buried here. Katherine died in childbirth. He lost them both." She stopped and then added, painfully, "He lost the love of his life and a son he never got to know or love."

An odd chill ran down Allison's spine. "I'm sorry. I didn't know." Deep down Allison felt a twinge of shame. The air grew heavier; the sunshine seemed not so bright. Her eyes filled with tears and she looked away thinking about what had happened to Jake. For a change Allison's thoughts were on someone else's pain and not on her own. Allison sighed unhappily. She couldn't stop herself from crying out, "Why do some have to die so young?"

Edna shook her head sadly. "The best part of my son died that day, too. He couldn't cope with the intolerable pain of losing Katherine. Jake shut down the emotional part of his life. Friends tried reaching out but Jake kept pushing them away. He didn't want to be lined up with a prospective lady friend. Eventually, the invitations stopped coming and he was left alone. Everyone seemed to think that Jake was obsessed with grief. I guess he was," she admitted sadly, before continuing. "It was gradual but Jake withdrew from the world around him. No one realized it until it was too late. He appeared to be fine but he wasn't. Jake remained buried in the past. The feeling of despair over Katherine's death never really went away. Why would it? It's such a terrible loss when someone young dies unexpectedly."

Allison had to take deep breaths of the pure air as compassion pierced her brittle armor.

She thought, "A man with a tragedy."

Like her son, Edna seemed to have the uncanny ability of reading her mind. "Few of us live without tragedy. We don't ask to have our hearts broken."

"That's what happens and we're left alone to pick up the pieces." Allison was trying not to cry. The older woman could hear it in the younger woman's broken voice.

Tears sparkled in Allison's eyes and Edna reached out a warm, comforting hand to the girl. "You're never alone, my dear." Edna's own eyes were moist as she spoke, "Our past is a series of necessary lessons. Everything happens for a reason."

"Jordie and Cassie both have so much to learn," Allison said, through tight lips. Her words grew angrier, "But they were too young for this lesson. I can't handle what's happening."

"Death is a part of life, Allison." Edna Hanson usually spoke what was on her mind. "Nevertheless, no matter how bad your heart is broken, the world doesn't stop for your grief."

Allison gave the elderly woman a direct, unsmiling glance. "That's the way it is so deal with it," she muttered.

"Basically," was all the elderly woman said.

Anger flashed in the younger mother's eyes. "I know that in my head but my heart still cries for the loss of Austin. No mother should have to bury one of her children."

Edna's expression was sympathetic. "You've just gone through the worst tragedy a parent can experience."

Allison's tears spilled down before she could hold them back. She quickly brushed them away. "Life isn't fair. Austin was only seventeen. He had his whole life ahead of him. I wish things had worked out differently for all of us."

"Don't we all," agreed the older woman. "Life only goes in one direction. No one can turn back time."

"Does the hurt ever go away?" Allison whispered.

"In time. Your grief is normal but prolonged depression can be unhealthy. Most of us remember the love and cherish it and keep it locked away in our hearts. For most, that becomes enough and we recover enough to move forward, find someone else or at least become open to living again." Allison knew Edna was talking about her own son again. She took Allison's hands in her own. "Jake came to see me after your son's funeral. The last time I'd seen him like that, lost and scared, was when Katherine died. Jake didn't want those old wounds opened up. He couldn't understand why it bothered him so much."

"Why did he go to Austin's funeral?" Allison asked, after a minute.

"I believe he was saying good-bye to the son he never had," Jake's mother responded. "Jake had spent all those years grieving for the loss of his dear Katherine. Michael wasn't real to him for he had died just days after he was born. Thanks to Austin, for those few days Jake was able to experience a part of his life that he could only imagine to that point. For some reason, Jake and Austin bonded like father and son."

Allison's heart suddenly ached for Jake and she looked at his mom with big, sad eyes.

There was only a fraction of a pause before the elderly woman continued, "The spell was broken and Jake was free. Try to understand that Jake's life had been empty of deep emotion for a long time. He'd been buried in the past for so long. Austin brought my son back to life. He brought Jake back to us."

Edna whispered, her voice deep with emotion, "Allison, I'm terribly sorry for your loss and all of this horror your family has endured but I'm so grateful to your son and the brief time he spent here with mine. Life is colored by the people who pass through our lives. Austin brought Jake out of a very dark place. It's wonderful to see Jake exposed to real life again but he's vulnerable." Edna Hanson spoke lightly enough but Allison didn't miss the hidden warning behind the words. Yet Allison could understand, for she was vulnerable, too.

Edna continued, her voice becoming reflective, "In some ways you're like Katherine." Allison looked at Jake's mom in mild surprise. Edna laughed. "Not physically. She was as fair as you are dark. Katherine often reminded me of a wood nymph; full of life but a little mysterious. She was always darting about, appearing unexpectedly out of the blue and you'd be surprised and glad to see her. Like her, I can see that you are open and loving and will take on anything and everyone for your family. Probably for your beliefs, too. I'm sure Katherine would have been a good mother just like you."

Allison was taken aback by the members of this family. Both Jake, and now his mother, seemed to understand her so well. They accepted her presence here without question and didn't stand in judgment over her actions.

"Your son's death had a powerful impact on my son. However, this time Jake didn't withdraw back into the past. It would have been easier but whatever transpired between our sons during those few days left a very positive mark on Jake."

Edna pointed to the trees shading the headstones. "The weeping willow, of course, Jake planted when Katherine died. Self-explanatory, I'm sure. Jake just planted the oak. It was for Austin. It's strength is recognized even as a sapling. Jake saw the same strength in your young son." Allison's eyes misted over. Edna's eyes held Allison's sad ones. "You can see how much your son meant to mine."

The kindness in the older woman's voice and the gentle expression in her eyes comforted Allison, taking away some of the hurt caused by their conversation.

Edna looked up into the bright sky. "Do you mind if we return to the house? I could use a cool drink." It was much warmer than when they left and Allison was quick to agree.

Retracing their steps they returned to the house. They walked through the garden, up the steps of the verandah and into the kitchen. "Sit down and I'll make some lemonade." Edna reached for a glass pitcher from the cupboard as she spoke. The blinds were open, allowing sunshine to illuminate the gray-haired woman at the sink. "I thought the boys might be back by now," she commented idly.

While Jake's mom chatted away, Allison's thoughts kept going back to what Edna had shared about Jake and the loss of not only his wife but his infant son as well. They had both died so young. Guilt had now become a two-headed monster as she thought of her unkind remarks last night.

Jake's mom was pouring lemonade when they heard Matt's truck turn into the drive. Allison couldn't believe how quickly the time had passed. She wished that she'd had more time alone with Edna. It had helped to talk about more than just Austin and now she had a better understanding of the man who had been so kind to her son.

Both men were laughing as they came up the walk. Matt gave Jake a brotherly slap on the back. Allison's heart tore as she realized that Jordie would never again share such moments with his brother. It was a heart-wrenching moment.

Matt came through the door first, rubbing his hands and chuckling. His eyes, slightly amused, met hers. He winked at her and she blushed.

She wondered what Jake had told Matt about her. Not that there was much to tell.

"Pour a couple more of those, Ma," Matt said as he sat down next to Allison. He turned to her and grinned mischievously. "Did she talk your ear off?" he asked, with his easy charm.

"Behave yourself for a change," Edna scolded her eldest son. But her voice was filled with affection and her eyes warmed when she looked at him.

"How about you, Ma? Did you behave yourself while we were gone?" Jake asked, with a teasing smile. Ignoring him, she turned her back and grabbed two more glasses out of the cupboard. Matt laughed.

Allison had a feeling that conversations like this were a common occurrence.

Taking a glass of lemonade from his mom, Jake joined the other two at the table. "How are you doing?" His smile was tender.

"I'm fine," Allison assured him.

Jake's mom made sandwiches. Edna stroked her son's hair before she sat down as well. Allison turned away. The memory stabbed at her heart. It was a familiar gesture, one that Allison had done many times to Austin.

Conversation flowed freely and happiness filled the room. It felt good to hear the brothers laughing and teasing each other.

"Bring Allison and have lunch with me tomorrow," Edna invited impulsively.

"I don't know how long she's staying but I think we can talk her into one more day. How about it, Allison? Can you spare another day for the Hanson family?"

Jake sat back, his eyebrow cocked slightly. Allison knew it would appear rude if she refused. He had just worked her the same way that Austin did when he wanted her to do something. Allison laughed inwardly for it had brought her an odd sense of comfort. Without hesitating, Allison nodded. Jake smiled and received a glimmer of a smile in return.

The elderly lady was delighted. "Then it's settled." Edna was always glad to have company. She loved it best when it was her family.

Allison had liked the older lady and maybe she would learn more about the intriguing man who had tried to help her son.

"What a nice lady," Allison remarked, as Matt helped his mom into his truck.

"Yes, she is," Jake declared, as he waved to the retreating vehicle.

"Do you see her often, Jake?"

"More now," he replied somberly.

Chapter Eight

As they entered the kitchen the phone rang. Allison's heart pounded in her chest. In her confused state she'd forgotten to call Richard. Her mind had been fixated on her task at hand. She took advantage of the interruption and stepped outside with her cell phone. Her messages showed that she'd missed four calls from Richard. Allison groaned but she had to give him credit. He hadn't phoned until this morning but she felt guilty for making him worry. Yet she still hesitated.

The air had chilled. Allison closed her eyes and let the cool breeze caress her face as she tried to draw up some courage. She had to find a way to tell her husband where she was and why she was staying with a man she barely knew. Allison was reluctant to phone due to her own guilt and secrecy. Obviously, Austin had felt the same way. At that moment, she had a better understanding of Austin's actions and his reluctance to phone home and nodded thoughtfully. Youth allowed one to remain stubborn. Being more mature, Allison dialed Richard's number.

Expecting Richard to be in meetings, Allison was surprised when he answered. She had hoped to get away with leaving a message. Suddenly, Allison was nervous knowing she couldn't escape the inquisition. Nothing had gone her way since she left yesterday.

"Allison, are you okay? Do you realize how worried I've been? Why haven't you called? You said you'd phone when you got to the cottage." Richard sounded concerned and Allison was touched.

"I'm not at the cottage," Allison replied, her voice low. Her body tensed as she waited for his reaction.

"What did you say?" Richard asked, in astonishment. "Where are you?"

Allison's guilt was strong but her husband's tone put her on the defensive. "If you'd quit asking so many questions I'd tell you." She knew she had to tell Richard about the detour she had been compelled to take.

He wasn't happy when she explained the change of events, even less when she told him where she was. Allison could almost feel hostile vibrations coming through the telephone. "I really don't understand you anymore," Richard said, with exasperation.

"You could at least try," she accused back.

"What are you trying to prove?" Richard questioned, trying to keep his temper. His rising voice indicated underlying anger.

She didn't know how to make Richard understand. It increased her feeling of frustration. He had to feel what she was feeling to understand her loss and her anger.

"Why are you still there?" Richard's dry tone added to her tension.

Allison didn't answer even though she heard him clearly. Now that she had some answers to her questions she knew that she needed more time with Jake. The answers she had found only initiated more questions.

"Hello? Can you hear me?" Richard asked impatiently.

"Yes, sorry. It must be poor reception," she lied evasively. Allison looked over to the door, turned her back and lowered her voice as she spoke. "Jake, Mr. Hanson offered to let me stay because it would've been dark by the time I got to the cottage. He's a very kind and gentle man. Austin did stay with him for a few days. He promised to tell me all about Austin's time here." Insulated by distance, she found it easy to say, "I'm going to stay a couple of days."

Such impulsiveness was new to Allison and the unusual feeling of freedom was back. For some inexplicable reason she was uninhibited with this stranger. She not only felt at ease, she felt drawn to this man who'd spent the final days with her son. There was something about him that made it natural to trust and like him. Allison ignored the small warning within.

The air waves cracked with her husband's anger. "Are you serious?" he asked disbelievingly. Richard didn't wait for an answer. "Allison, what the hell has gotten into you?"

Allison sighed, wishing she hadn't made the call. "Don't be angry, Richard. I need to know how Austin spent the last days of his life. This man is the only one who can help me right now." She wanted desperately for him to understand.

"I think I have every right to be mad. On top of everything else you start lying to me. Now you're telling me you're going to stay at some stranger's house and I should just accept it like it's an everyday occurrence." The angry words were now coated in sarcasm.

Allison's reply was clipped, "I didn't lie." Leaning forward, she continued speaking, her tone very serious, "I didn't tell you because I knew you wouldn't understand. I was right."

"Allison, for God's sake," Richard yelled at her. "I want you to leave right now. You don't know a single thing about this man."

Allison resented both his tone and what it implied. "Now you're being completely unreasonable," she responded acidly. Tears were burning in her eyes.

"Me. You're the one who runs off to some stranger's house thinking that will help. How the hell do you think that will help us?" Richard demanded to know.

Allison chose to fight down a sharp retort. "I don't know. I just know it will."

"Well, if that's what you chose to believe, go ahead," her husband snorted.

Allison stiffened. "I am staying, Richard," she affirmed stubbornly.

Richard made a small sound of impatience. "I can't figure you out anymore."

"I don't want to discuss it any further," Allison added with a calmness she was far from feeling. She didn't trust herself to say more.

The anger in Richard's voice reached her loud and clear. "Fine. Be stubborn and do what you want. You will anyway." Then the phone went dead.

Disbelief trembled through Allison. Angrily, she threw her phone into her purse, drew a deep breath and wiped her hand across her brow. This call hadn't gone well. Doubts surfaced for she couldn't ignore what Richard had said. Was she indulging her own selfishness to escape? Was her attitude wrong? Was she being stubborn? What a mess her life was in she thought wearily. Nevertheless she wasn't about to give in to Richard. She needed more time.

Jake went out and joined Allison on the verandah. She was sitting in one of the wicker chairs with her feet tucked under her and simply staring out at the mountains.

"You okay? You look awfully serious."

Allison gave him a feeble smile as she ran her hands through her black silky hair. Her head ached, it had been an intense conversation and she could feel the tension at the back of her neck. She cupped her chin on one hand and expelled a heavy sigh.

"I just talked to Richard," Allison said in a controlled calm voice, devoid of the emotions she was feeling. "He's not happy that I'm here," she declared hollowly. At Jake's look of inquisitiveness, she confessed, "I didn't tell him I was coming here."

"Why didn't you tell him?" Jake asked, curiosity grabbing hold.

Her usually expressive eyes were troubled. "He says I'm running away. I'm not. I just needed some answers. Why can't Richard understand that?" The emotions of the last few months fueled the anger that Allison felt toward her husband. "I don't really think Richard cares," she said miserably. "I don't think he feels anything at all."

"Do you really mean that, Allison?"

Allison shook her head, for she knew that part of her anger was due to the guilt she felt when Richard confronted her actions. "No, but we aren't much help to each other. We've blamed ourselves, we've blamed each other." Allison's shoulders sagged. She knew she wasn't being fair but her life hadn't been fair either. "It's no good," Allison said, in defeat.

Jake put a hand on her arm as he spoke. "I need to tell you something that Austin said to me." He hesitated, making sure he had Allison's full attention, "Austin had reached the point where he acknowledged everything wasn't his dad's fault. He knew he was wrong as well."

Allison turned and anger sparked in her eyes for she hadn't missed the implication. "What makes you say that?"

Jake regarded her with level eyes. "I told you that Austin had managed to work through his anger. He was able to take a step back and look at things clearly. Once refocused he was able to put aside the blame, his prejudice and a lot of his hurt. Austin was ready to go home."

Wary and not quite believing what he said Allison looked at Jake doubtfully. "I wish I could be sure."

Sensing the agony she was in, Jake took her hands in his and pulled her gently out of the chair. "Come with me. I have something to show you. Don't look at me like that, I have proof."

She stared at him intently. What could Jake possibly show her that would erase her doubts? Allison's eyes showed a spark of interest as she asked him, "What kind of proof?" Getting no answer, she followed him into the house and was right behind him as he climbed the stairs to the loft.

Allison stared blankly at the book-lined wall as Jake walked directly to the bookcase and pulled a thin volume from the top shelf. He opened it and took out a single sheet of paper, leaving a second piece of paper that was yellowed with age remain inside. Jake handed it to Allison. She slowly unfolded the paper. Her hands shook when she recognized her son's writing and the words suddenly blurred. She quickly blinked the tears away and began to read.

"Thank you for letting me stay for a few days and for helping me work through my anger. You knew, better than me, how much I had been allowing my emotions to run my life. You took the time to really listen to me and let me say anything and everything I wanted to. Sometimes I wasn't very nice. You already know how sorry I am about that. You taught me to have the strength to deal with life as it is and move forward. You're right. I can be in control of my life anywhere. I've done a lot of thinking and it is time for me to go home. I'm heading out. Forgive me. It would have been too difficult to say good-bye in person. Besides, hitch-hiking gives you a lot of time to ponder life. I need a little more time to sort things out in my head before I face my parents. I love my family. Yes, my dad, too. I've missed my family and it will be good to get home. A lot of what you and I talked about over the last few days has had a tremendous effect on me. I wrote this poem one afternoon by the river. You gave me the confidence to share this with you. Thanks again." Austin.

Allison lifted her eyes and tears slowly melted the ice that had covered her beautiful blue eyes. "Thank you," she whispered.

Jake didn't say anything, he simply smiled sadly.

It was too much to take in all at once. Allison's gaze returned to the letter and she slowly read it again, branding each word into her memory.

Hot tears continued to flow and she began shaking. Soon her entire body was trembling from silent sobs and she couldn't stop.

Jake winced. He felt her pain as his own. The pain wasn't physical. It came from memories from the past and he knew the depth of the torment within her grieving soul. His heart ached for Allison and for the obvious pain he'd seen in her eyes. He knew all about the agony of losing someone. Jake took Allison into his arms and pulled her close, gently stroking her hair as if he were comforting a small child. He could feel her quick, short breaths, the trembling of her slender body.

Allison rested her head against his chest and clung to him. The steady beat of his heart was comforting as was the hand stroking her hair. Jake's embrace was gentle and healing. The tenderness was pure and honest. It would've been so easy to let him hold her close until the empty ache she felt inside was gone. Suddenly, Allison became very aware of the man's superior height and physical strength. The emotions that fluttered in her chest confused her. She pulled away for his nearness was affecting her senses.

"Are you going to be okay?" Jake asked gently.

Allison dropped her eyes in confusion and moved away from him, a little breathless. "I'll be all right," she stuttered.

"Keep the letter. Do you mind if I make a copy for myself?"

Nodding her head Allison excused herself and went to rinse her face. When she returned Jake was looking at the painting over his desk. Choosing to stand a few feet away, Allison watched him. She wondered what gripping memory she would take him from. Allison walked over and stood next to him. Nerves fluttered in the depth of her stomach for she was embarrassed by her emotional behavior. She was glad that Jake didn't say anything as he handed her Austin's letter. Allison smiled gratefully as she quickly folded it and put it in her pocket.

"Is that Katherine?" Allison's eyes lingered on the portrait of a vibrant young girl sitting barefoot in the meadows. Seeing the surprise on Jake's face, she explained, "Your mom told me what happened to her and your son." Allison's face softened at the obvious unhappiness in Jake's eyes and she said, her voice gentle, "I'm sorry for your loss, Jake."

Like all others, Allison was drawn to the girl's face, especially her eyes. The violet color of her irises was most unusual, quite unforgettable. "She's beautiful." There was perfection to Katherine's features that Allison could only liken to that of a spirit. What was it Jake's mom had called her? Wood nymph. Yes. Katherine Hanson had a unique spiritual essence to her.

Jake nodded. He smiled at Katherine with a faraway look and felt a longing for his wife who he had treasured and lost. Without turning, Jake spoke softly, "She was the love of my life. More than anything Katherine wanted children. We both did. Having a child would make us a real family and our lives would be so blessed." There was a yearning in the depth of the gray eyes darkened by sadness.

At times Jake's eyes glowed as he spoke and it was easy to guess how much he'd loved his wife. Allison felt a tear on her cheek and hastily wiped it away, hoping Jake hadn't noticed. For an instant Jake let his own intense pain show. "Life has a way of calling the shots and blind siding you. I'm sure Ma told you how they both died."

There was deep sympathy in Allison's eyes, a sharing of his pain. She nodded her head without speaking.

"I do understand your loss, Allison." Jake seriously added, "Getting hurt is part of life but grief can take away your life if you allow it to." Jake tried to explain, "I built a glass wall around me. Life was easier that way. I was trapped in sweet memories that locked me away from further pain. I was content to stay safe inside and watch the world around me. My life stopped on that emotional level." Jake smiled sadly, "I'm a very good builder. Nobody could get in but after awhile I forgot how to come out. I was locked in by memories and my undying love for Katherine. I didn't want changes in my life. Everything was fine the way it was. My emotions were numb and I could cope. I liked it that way. It was easy to live my life day to day." His voice trailed off again, deep in shadows of thought, of remembering.

Allison moved away from the desk and crossed to the window. She stared out unseeing as she thought over Jake's comment about building a wall around himself. Maybe everyone builds a wall in their own way, just a brick at a time to keep the hurt out. If angry words penetrate add another brick and build it higher.

Jake stood still watching his guest. By the bleak expression on Allison's face, Jake knew that her thoughts were far away. He watched her changing expressions as strong emotions tore at her soul.

Lost in her thoughts, Allison gave a start when Jake spoke. His tone took on a new intensity, "Then along came Austin, the silent intruder, who crashed through the door of my past. Never in a million years would I have thought that it would've been someone like your son that would change my life."

Jake's voice changed, it became more reflective. "Austin came into my life and turned it upside down." He gave a gravely laugh, "Austin forced his way in unannounced and left me to deal with him. He yanked me back to the present. Into reality. My thoughts were dominated by a seventeen-year-old boy. I knew Austin needed me and I had to figure out how to help him before he ran away from here, too."

When Allison looked at Jake her eyes were filled with tears. He met her gaze with a gentle smile. He was captivated by the woman in front of him. Suddenly, he found himself wanting to respond to her as a man and immediately steeled himself against the impulse.

Unaware of the disturbing effect she had on him Allison whispered, "This is so hard." The tightness in her voice gave it a husky quality.

"I know," he acknowledged. Jake understood her feelings, the helplessness and the frustration of trying to deal with that helplessness.

Thanks to Jake's mom Allison knew that he really did understand. She finally managed to say, "I can't hang on to this pain any longer. I want to let it go. It's like I don't know how to cope anymore and it scares me."

In spite of himself, Jake gently placed a hand on her shoulder. "Come with me. I think a walk will do you good."

Allison's breath quickened unexpectedly at his touch and she felt a pang of guilt at her reaction to him. She gave him a half-hearted smile, "You know I went for a walk with your mom while you were gone with Matt."

Jake's gray eyes danced. "The old girl took you for a stroll if you just went through the meadow," Jake corrected. "Let's go down to the river. Austin liked it there." Was it the mention of Austin or the boyish smile Jake flashed her that caused her heart to quicken?

Allison's gaze returned to the view. Clouds were rolling in an ever-shifting sky. "Those look like rain clouds to me."

"They're nothing," Jake drawled. "Or are you just looking for an excuse? Are you afraid to trust yourself in my company?"

Allison looked at him in surprise. There was a light-hearted teasing expression in his gray eyes that stopped her heart.

Once again, she ignored the small warning within her as she surrendered to his request.

Chapter Nine

The air had cooled since morning. Allison was glad that she'd grabbed a sweater and tied it around her shoulders before leaving the house. Sam, who'd been lying next to the steps, was quick to follow his master. Allison paused to enjoy the aromatic air of pine and spruce and inhale the scent of the wild flowers blooming nearby. How wonderful.

Jake smiled as he waited for her to catch up.

He led her down a well worn trail that offered the occasional glimpse of sparkling blue water. She placed her hand in his when they began their descent down the grass bank and he tightened his grip when she began to slip. Once safely down the embankment he released his hold. Jake sprawled out on a grassy spot and stretched out his long legs.

Allison continued down to the river's edge which was rimmed with gorgeous foliage. The sunlight danced on the crystal clear water and she squinted her eyes against the sun. Allison turned and walked along the river bank. Deep in thought, she sat down on an old log to reflect on the last couple of days. Clasping her arms about her knees, she was unaware that her son had sat on this very log. Tipping her face to the sun she let herself become absorbed into the silence. For an instant everything was still. As she withdrew to her private thoughts she thought of life without Austin. Her mind flashed back and forth over the events of the last three months. Allison was helpless against the onslaught of emotions but for a change she was able to think rationally. Something she had been unable to do since Austin had left.

Allison shivered. Putting her hands in her pockets she felt Austin's letter. She took it out, staring at the words as she read it again and again.

Allison drew great comfort from the knowledge that Austin really was on his way home and that he'd worked through his anger toward his parents, especially his dad. Bewilderment, along with relief, whirled within her.

Allison's focus turned inward. Jake had given her a great deal to think about. She wished that they had had more time this morning to talk about Austin but she had to admit that talking to Edna had helped her to look at things differently. Allison had finally been able to step outside the confinement of her emotions and realize that others, like Jake, were not only suffering but trying to come to terms with the loss of Austin. Recognizing this, Allison knew that the hurt her own family was experiencing was real to each one of them. Suddenly, she became angry with herself for allowing her grief to consume her like it had. Her family needed her now more than ever. Together, they could work through the grief and survive the pain.

Sitting motionless, Allison was soon lost in remembering. Time passed unnoticed as she listened to the rushing and splashing of the water, allowing it to wash away the bitterness and anger while taking strength from it. She silently released her emotions and a wonderful feeling of peace enveloped her. Allison found an acceptance for her decisions. Right or wrong, she had acted and reacted. Just like Austin.

Within her, the turmoil of the last few months stilled. Allison felt herself totally relaxing for the first time in days and enjoyed an unexpected sense of well-being. As she allowed herself forgiveness she felt Austin's presence beside her and she smiled sadly. She closed her eyes tightly like Cassie had done that dreadful night. Immediately, Austin's image came to mind and mentally she hugged him close and told him she loved him. Allison was still smiling when she came back to the present and the smile remained as she retraced her steps.

Jake was now flat on his back and his face was covered with his hat. Not knowing if he was sleeping or not, Allison quietly sat down next to him without saying a word.

"Peaceful, isn't it," Jake said, without moving.

The serene beauty of her surroundings had relaxed her taut nerves. "It's so quiet I'm sure I can hear the pine needles fall."

Jake sat up. "That's why I love it here."

Allison's gaze was drawn to the smooth line of his jaw and then to his mouth now curved in a warm lazy line. His smile was so pleasant it was impossible not to respond. Allison was surprised at how comfortable she was with this man.

"Austin and Sam came down here a lot. It's a great place to think." Sam, who'd been playing in the river, came over and sat between them. Just as Allison was about to pet him he shook enthusiastically, spraying them both. "Hey!" Jake protested, as he wiped his face.

Allison tried to hold back a smile but couldn't. Her eyes twinkled with amusement.

Jake's breath caught in his throat for she had the same mischievous light in her eyes he had often seen in Austin's. It was like having him here again.

Allison turned her face back to the sun. Jake was watching her, knowing her thoughts were far away. They sat for awhile in companionable silence before Allison inquired, reluctantly, "How were you able to change Austin's attitude while we continued to fail?"

Jake detected a change in Allison's voice since yesterday. She seemed less stressed. Gone was her earlier anxiety that often had been close to hysteria. Jake thought long and hard before replying. "I had no expectations of your son. There was no history between us for me to gauge his answers on. When I asked a question it wasn't like I was expecting him to say the right thing or come up with an appropriate response. Nor could I judge if he spoke honestly because I had no idea if he was telling the truth or not. I could only rely on my gut feelings."

Jake paused to let his words sink in. "I needed to know the reason behind his actions. So did Austin. If he was honest with me, and with himself, then maybe I could help him. It was up to him. This was the lesson I was trying to make your son understand when he was here. I knew it had to be done slowly or he would've run from me, too."

Allison remained silent but Jake could tell that she was listening intently to every word.

Jake's gentle voice continued, "So I started asking questions. I asked questions that he had to answer." Jake chuckled, "Your son can be quite stubborn. At first, Austin answered all of my questions with an angry shrug." Jake's breath came out in a long sigh. "A shrug is not a welcoming conversational tool but I persevered. If Austin answered with a one word response I'd ask another question until he was actually opening up. Despite his grumbling, we really began to communicate. Often, I made Austin think about what he said and why he said it."

The deep light of sincerity appeared in Jake's eyes. "I really enjoyed talking to your son. Austin never hesitated to express his opinions." A throaty laugh followed. "Austin and I had more than one spirited discussion."

Allison couldn't stop herself from responding, "I can well image. Spirited is a kind word, rather than heated."

"Oh, we had those, too, but there is a difference. When anger becomes a factor a spirited discussion can quickly become heated."

Allison stirred uncomfortably and then swung around and looked directly at Jake. She spoke defensively, "Austin often acted on impulse and didn't always think before he spoke. I could reason with him and Austin was learning the difference. But not where his dad was concerned. Richard likes everything to be organized and well-structured. So his view point is simple. Structure is the solution. Follow the rules and there are no problems. Richard and I've always given the kids responsibility." The frown around her mouth deepened, "It's just that Richard has a tendency to expect too much of the kids. It isn't much for Cassie and Jordie, small chores around the house like taking out the garbage. Lately, Richard was expecting more and more from Austin and always under his conditions. Doing something later didn't cut it."

Allison saw patient understanding on Jake's face as he commented, "Austin hated being told what to do."

"Of course." Allison's expression was one of deadly earnest. "I recognized Austin's free spirit and his proud determination. Yes, he had difficulty with routine and structure and often broke meaningless rules. Austin rebelled against the rigidity. His free spirit sought variety, flexibility and freedom. Richard couldn't understand that he wasn't losing his control if he allowed Austin to experience a little of his own. Richard couldn't see that it was an important part of growing up and being responsible. I recognized, more than Richard could, that Austin needed to test the boundaries. How else could he know if they had changed? It never occurred to Austin to simply ask. Lately, he was testing more and more. Austin wanted things to change quicker than we wanted them to."

Unconsciously, Allison lifted her chin just like Austin did when he wanted to make a point. "Austin never kowtowed to his father's power. He refused to give lip service to anyone. Austin would stand up for others and he'd stick with his beliefs even if they differed from those of others. This got him in trouble more than once, especially in school."

Jake gave a brief laugh, "Oh, I could tell that Austin was his own person. I bet he never hesitated to voice an objection which could easily lead into an argument."

"Those arguments just led to more." Allison looked anxiously at Jake. "Now Richard's starting on Jordie. I think that when Richard feels he's losing his control he tries being tougher. It didn't work, did it? Austin left."

"This was Austin's first major act of rebellion, wasn't it?"

Allison seemed preoccupied as she nodded and ran her fingertips through her raven hair. Watching her intently, Jake said, "So Austin chose to leave and exert his independence."

Allison once again nodded, deep in thought. "It isn't easy letting your children grow up. It's easier when they're little. A hug after a fight and you both felt better. When they get older the fights take on a different intensity, the digs are much more personal." Allison looked directly into Jake's eyes, "I have to be honest. Austin's self-alienation lately hurt. While I had to admire him for his belief in himself I didn't want anyone to break his spirit, especially his dad. I wanted Austin to live life with passion and a sense of adventure."

Jake interjected, "Austin needed to learn to control his emotions."

"You're right. I know that would've happened in time." Allison smiled wistfully, before adding, "And with effort."

"I told him that one day when we here by the river. He had to learn to control his emotions instead of continuing to allow his emotions control him. Unfortunately, Austin doubted himself." Jake went on, his voice heavy with the memory of those first days. "He needed time to find his inner belief again. Austin was desperately looking for his concept of freedom."

Jake looked to the mountains. "He was sure it was out there somewhere and he was off to find it. I tried explaining to him that true freedom had to do with the human spirit. It is the freedom to be who we really are, to be ourselves and express ourselves. I tried to make Austin understand that. You can only do that when you believe in yourself.

Only you can be responsible for every choice you make. For things to change, you must change."

Allison looked away as many of Jake's words struck a raw nerve.

Jake tipped his cowboy hat back and looked at her with his cool, steady eyes. There was something very intense in his expression. At last he spoke, "I truly believe that your son understood what I was saying, Allison. Austin came a long way in those few days."

Jake could see that their conversation had affected her. Once again they sat in silence lost in intertwined memories until Allison turned to Jake. Her eyes looked serene as she spoke freely, "Austin should've been valedictorian of his graduating class." This was the first time that Allison had talked openly about Austin with positive enthusiasm.

"I know, he told me." Jake smiled. "Austin definitely had a cockiness about him but he wasn't bragging. I was very appreciative of his intelligence," he declared affectionately. "We spent hours upstairs in the loft. He was quite intrigued by my work." Jake laughed, "Austin asked a lot of questions."

"Austin was so sure of himself," Allison acknowledged. "It often bordered on the arrogant. I could recognize it for what it was, youth more than anything. I knew time would erase some of that arrogance and replace it with more understanding. Richard couldn't see it the same way. To him, Austin was being belligerent. Austin's quick wit was often amusing and I loved the fact that he could laugh at himself." Allison smiled reflectively.

It took Jake's breath away for a moment. She was so beautiful when her smile reached her eyes.

Allison continued to talk about her child and Jake listened. Jake detected less anger in her tone. She looked more relaxed now than at any other time since she had arrived and once or twice she even laughed. Her face was softer and her eyes had come to life. The warmth of her smile was overwhelming and it held his gaze. It was like sunshine had returned to Jake's life. His eyes traveled over her face and he studied her for what seemed a long time.

"Do I have something on my face?" Allison asked, a little uncomfortable. The glint in Jake's eyes made her pulse beat faster.

Jake reached over and touched her cheek. "Every once in a while you say or do something and I see Austin again."

Allison was more aware of him than she would've liked to have been. It was rather disturbing because it was a pleasant sensation. She laughed nervously, "Austin could be so infuriating. Whew, talk about stubborn when his mind was made up." The smile faded from Allison's eyes. "I miss all the things that drove me crazy. Isn't that stupid? Now that he's gone I'd give anything to..." She couldn't continue as her voice broke. Allison gazed forward for a moment before asking, "Why do bad things have to happen?"

Jake offered no response for it was one of those questions that everyone was striving to answer but couldn't. Instead he took her hand and squeezed it gently. It brought comfort.

Tears glistened in her eyes. "I miss him so much, Jake."

Jake looked back at her with grave, quiet eyes. "I've missed him, too." Jake's voice deepened with emotion, "I can't believe how much. Austin's presence haunted me. My other memories, once so vivid, seemed to fade after he left."

"I've done a lot of introspective thinking since I met Austin." Jake shifted his position. "So many emotions that had been buried came back due to Austin. They weren't happy ones. All those feelings that kept me from moving on with my life were released. And questions, many questions like "What if?" Austin made me think about the son I never had. After Austin left, I imagined my son growing up. It's natural I suppose but I'd never done that before." Jake turned to Allison as he admitted, "You're easy to talk to. I haven't talked to anyone like this since Katherine."

Allison understood, for she had opened up to Jake about Austin in ways that she couldn't with Richard. For the second time since her arrival, she could understand why Austin had chosen to stay with this stranger instead of coming home. Jake had a way of making a point without accusation and you knew he understood the reason for your actions.

Jake's voice deepened with emotion, "At first it was hard to visualize my son. Did he look more like me or like Katherine?"

Allison smiled thoughtfully as she visualized a little boy running through the meadows without a care in the world, a faithful dog by his side.

Jake threw her a warm glance as he grinned wickedly. "I decided he looked like me," he declared, wanting to make her laugh.

Allison did laugh.

Jake went on casually, with satisfaction, "Do you know how easy it was to envision him like Austin, proud and strong in his beliefs?" Jake's look changed and he became serious for a moment. "I also wondered if I would've had the courage to let my son make mistakes, take risks and follow a dream."

It seemed that every conversation led back to Austin and they talked for a long time. Allison spoke lightly enough but Jake could tell how difficult it was for her at times.

"I'm glad that you can talk about Austin. It helps."

"It has helped me and, yes, some days are better than others."

"It's dangerous to repress things. Maybe if I'd talked more about Katherine in the past I wouldn't have stayed locked up until now," Jake confessed. "I lost a lot of my life, too."

"I'm sorry, Jake," Allison murmured apologetically.

Allison knew that Jake spoke from experience when he said, "That's life. It takes time, but time does heal."

Allison remained quiet. Her eyes darkened for a moment. These were the same words spoken by Richard the day he left to which she had reacted so cruelly. Yet, she knew Jake was right. They all needed time; herself, Richard, Jordie and Cassie. In their own time they would all heal.

Her thoughts were interrupted by a rumble of thunder. The wind had come up as time had passed and the suspicious clouds that had gathered in the distance now circled overhead.

"I do believe I underestimated those clouds. We're in for a storm for sure. We'll be lucky to make it back to the house without getting wet." His words were no sooner out and Allison felt rain drops. She was about to say something but Jake interrupted her before a sound came out, "Don't you dare say 'I told you so'."

Involuntarily, Allison smiled. "We're going to get wet, aren't we?"

Jake nodded and it was followed by a boyish grin.

Allison laughed at him as she untied her sweater and put it on. All of a sudden the clouds opened up and the rain poured down relentlessly.

"Oh, oh. We're in for it now." Jake quickly pulled Allison to her feet.

Within minutes they were soaked and so was the ground underfoot. As Allison slipped on the wet grass Jake grabbed her hand firmly in his and they took off running. With her free hand she tried to keep her hair out of her eyes while Jake firmly held on to his Stetson to keep it from blowing away. As they fought the gusts of wind, the rain pelted them. Wet and laughing like children they ran back to the house.

Chapter Ten

Jake and Allison paused on the verandah to catch their breath and watch the sky. Lightning flashed as thunder rolled. "It's going to be quite the storm before it's done," Jake predicted, as he opened the side door. He rested his hand lightly on Allison's back as they stepped inside. Nothing happened when he flipped the light switch. "Powers out," Jake declared. "I'll get some candles."

They entered the kitchen and Jake walked over and lit a candle that he'd used on other occasions. "I know I have other candles. I have to think where they are. Living alone, this one is always enough. Oh, here we go," Jake exclaimed, as he opened a drawer and found a box of tapered candles. A variety of candle holders were there as well. Jake lit another candle and handed it to Allison. "Go change into something dry and then you can help me in the kitchen. I'll get the fire going in the fireplace. It'll keep the house warm and offer us more light. How does a picnic by the fireplace sound?"

"Romantic," Allison thought immediately and she blushed. She couldn't help it for she recalled how it felt to be in his arms. "Cozy," she replied instead.

After changing into a fleece jogging suit, Allison returned to the living room. She had to smile to herself. There was a blanket spread in front of the hearth and Jake had tossed some cushions on the floor. Night had settled in and the flames dancing in the fireplace cast shadows on the walls. Jake was lighting the candles in the holders he'd set on the mantle. He, too, had changed into dry jeans and a fleece sweatshirt.

Jake turned as soon as he heard Allison. "We'll be warmer if we're close to the fire," he said quickly. He was amazed that he could keep his voice even. Allison was a beautiful woman in any light and doubts or not, he was attracted to her.

"Come and help me find something to eat."

Allison followed Jake back to the kitchen.

He opened the fridge and handed her cheese and a ring of sausage. "Here, you can cut."

"Do you have a cutting board?" She laughed at his blank look. Allison checked in obvious drawers and soon found what she needed. Grabbing the box of crackers she added them to the plate. Jake, meanwhile had his hands full with wine and goblets. Together, they carried everything out to the living room. Jake plunked his lean frame down on the blanket and Allison followed suit. The atmosphere was very romantic with the flickering candlelight and the roaring fire. Jake opened the bottle of wine with a resounding pop.

Allison giggled for she was a little nervous. She tilted her head upward and inquired lightly, "Tell me more about Katherine." Surely that would be a safe subject.

Jake was happy to comply with her request. "She was a lot like you. Spontaneous, quick to show her emotions, gentle, full of love. There was something special about her. Everybody said so." Jake kept the conversation flowing as he shared many of his happy memories. Things remembered, many things. However, the memories brought with them a stab of longing.

Talking about Katherine had relaxed his guest and Allison often smiled or laughed at his stories. Jake still mourned his wife, still ached for Katherine. "I've missed her. I feel so empty. I can get through the days because I keep myself busy. It's the long nights when there is no one around and there is nothing but the silence and my thoughts.

Those are the worst times." For Jake, loneliness had become a constant companion.

Jake spoke of suppers alone in a silent house. Allison thought of the lively meals and the constant beehive of activity right up until bedtime that had been so characteristic until recently. Jake described the loneliness of lying in an empty bed. Allison thought of the many nights that one or the other of the kids had shared the bed with her and Richard because they weren't feeling well or they were afraid. Cassie hated thunderstorms just like her mom.

It wasn't long until Allison was drawn in and sharing stories of her own. As she talked, Jake could hear the warmth in her voice and occasionally her anecdotes were filled with a touch of amusement that was oddly appealing. At times her look turned serious and there was vulnerability in her voice. Jake and Allison talked for a long time unaware of the storm around them. They both opened up and recounted events from their past. Perhaps it was the atmosphere surrounding them that allowed them to share such confidences.

Allison watched Jake in the shadows as he refilled their wine glasses. Taking a sip, she watched Jake make another tower of crackers, sausage and cheese. First bite and the tower crumbled, bringing a spontaneous laugh from Allison. He quickly joined in and the throaty sound of it worked on Allison's senses. She was surprised at how much she liked this man.

Allison's eyes glowed softly, "I haven't laughed like this for a long time. I realize now that's one of the things I've missed. Lately, there's no laughter in our house. Austin always made me laugh. He had a great sense of humor and he was a terrible tease."

Jake smiled in response. "You have a beautiful laugh. That was one of the things that attracted me to Katherine. She laughed freely as a child does and even clapped her hands. Funny, I haven't thought of that for years," Jake said absently. "There are a lot of things that I haven't thought about for years."

Allison looked up and was lost in the mesmerism of his gray eyes. She found herself unbearably close to Jake and very much aware of his powerful masculinity.

Jake's tone changed, taking on a serious note, "I don't know if it was because Katherine was so young when she died that it was easy to keep her on the pedestal I placed her on." Sadness veiled his eyes. "When you live alone it's easy to fall back on memories, especially when you remember only the good and forget the bad as you dream about what might have been. In a fantasy world there are no fights, no hurdles and no real pain. Just loneliness," he confessed.

A shadow crossed Allison's face. She remembered when her and Richard's feelings for each other were that deep. Lately, there was a growing estrangement between them. She'd become more and more dissatisfied. For a moment Allison hated Richard for that, too.

Jake's voice cut into her drifting thoughts. "Life is about give and take and you move forward in your lives together. Of course our marriage wouldn't have been perfect. Anyone who says theirs is is lying because one person is doing all the giving and the other one is always taking," he commented wisely.

That was another of their problems Allison thought unhappily as she closed her eyes. "Life can quickly erase ones dreams with reality," Allison interjected bitterly.

"Life can also reward you with far more than you ever dreamed of if you're open to receiving it. You can stay locked in the past and swear to yourself that you'll never care that much for anyone else because you know you could never live through that sort of pain again. When we love we open ourselves up to getting hurt."

Not knowing how to respond, Allison remained silent. She was aware of how lonely the man beside her was and found herself asking, "What you went through, it still hurts doesn't it?"

Time had dulled the sharp pain. "It doesn't hurt as much anymore," Jake said, and he wasn't sure if he was admitting that to Allison or himself. He sighed heavily, "In a way, that's painful, too, because you think you're forgetting them."

Jake's gaze was direct. "Austin's death could easily have allowed me to repeat the past and re-build my walls but then his journey into my life would've been wasted. There was a reason God wove our paths together, even though it was for a very short time. It's easier to tell someone what to do than it is to look at your own life objectively." He shook his head, "It was easy to tell Austin to move forward even though I hadn't done that myself. My pain was in the past and I wanted to keep it there. Life will always cause us pain but we have to go on living."

Pain was something Allison understood for she had lived with it ever since that dreadful day. It was as familiar to her as the air she breathed. "Does everyone build a wall around themselves to keep from getting hurt?"

"No. Some run away."

"Like Austin," Allison said painfully.

"Yes, like Austin." To which Jake also added, "And you."

"I'm not running away," Allison denied quickly, but not quite meeting Jake's gaze. "I can't deal with my life right now." Anguish tore through her, "It hurts too much." Tears stung Allison's eyes and she looked away, staring at the fire. "My life is so mixed up. I feel as helpless as Austin must have."

Jake tried to lighten the mood. "I took such pleasure in Austin's company. I enjoyed his strong beliefs, his active mind and his quick humor. I was just beginning to see the whole of your son. Our time together was too short."

Jake's eyes were downcast as if he were trying to hide the humor in them. He shook his head and then smiled mischievously. "Allison, you'd be surprised at what we talked about. Or should I call you, Your Highness?" Jake leaned forward, regarding her with open amusement.

Allison couldn't help but smile. "He told you about the costume trunk and dressing up."

"He sure did," Jake admitted with pleasure. Jake shared the pirate story and it wasn't long and they were both laughing. "You inspired your son to be creative and encouraged him to explore his imagination."

Allison smiled in remembrance, "I love being the evil Queen. It's much more fun than being just mom," she admitted brightly. "It allows me to say a few things that a mother should never say to her children."

Jake sobered first. "I can't see you as being evil."

"Lately, I feel that the only role I can play is the Queen of Tears and nobody wants to play with me anymore." Allison tried to smile but the effort was feeble.

"It impressed Austin that you worked full-time, yet you were so good at keeping your family and home-life stable."

"I stayed home until all of the kids were in school. It's not always easy being a working mom." Allison looked up at Jake. "Sometimes I wonder if it would've made a difference. You can't always be there for the kids if you're working." Guilt was again beginning to surface.

Jake noticed the shadow of doubt in her eyes. "Austin thought you were the best."

"He never told me," Allison said, a small regretful smile on her lips.

"Boys don't say those kinds of things to their mother."

Both were relaxed as they sat gazing at the dancing flames. Casually, Jake said, "I'll tell you something else Austin said? He said, 'The good part of me comes from my mom.' You made him understand the importance of family and friends."

At the mention of friends Allison thought of Ryan. "His friend Ryan really misses Austin. They loved each other like brothers."

"Ryan gave a beautiful eulogy," Jake acknowledged sincerely.

"He did, didn't he? Ryan and Austin had a bond that nothing could shatter. They were surprisingly alike considering their different upbringing." Allison expanded, "Ryan grew up the hard way, with an underprivileged childhood. He hungered for approval and affection but instead had been given harsh discipline. Because Ryan had no self-esteem he was always so self-critical. I think that's why he always appeared to be tense and nervous. Richard misread Ryan and judged him unfairly. The poor boy was embarrassed of so many things; his shabby clothes, being poor, his drunken dad. I never said a word if I saw Ryan wearing some of Austin's clothes and I know a lot of times Austin paid for both of them if they went to a movie."

"Ryan tended to exaggerate their differences but it never mattered to Austin." A note of pride became evident in Allison's voice. "Austin looked beyond those things and saw Ryan for who he was, his friend."

Jake responded solemnly, "It takes time before youth can differentiate between who they are and who they think they are."

Allison agreed. "I know. It's great to see the transformation when they discover this. That's one of the joys of having children. Kids are your roller coaster ride in life. They can bring you your highest highs and your lowest lows. A new day can bring a new phase and every new phase in life creates issues. Unfortunately, I don't think that kids see beyond themselves. They don't realize that this part of their life is new to us as parents and we don't always have the answers or know what to do. It's not like they come with a manual or you get to practice first." Allison's voice took on a more serious tone. "Austin thought his life was tough but it really wasn't. Life had been gentle with him. It was Ryan who had it rough growing up."

"How is Ryan handling all of this?"

"He's lost without his best friend. Ryan still comes over and we talk about Austin and how everything has changed. Ryan didn't graduate either. I'm glad he's going back to school. Like Austin, Ryan's a very intelligent boy and if he remains focused he can be successful in whatever he chooses to do. We talk about that, too. He's undecided but Ryan knows that he wants to work with young children. He has a way with them. Sometimes when Ryan comes over he and Jordie disappear for hours and then Jordie's better for a few days."

"It's not just Austin's death that Ryan has had to deal with. Ryan's dad died right after Austin. Frank Miller was a know-it-all who always drove after drinking. One drunken binge too many and he killed himself. Thankfully, he didn't kill someone else. The family didn't need to deal with something like that. They've already dealt with enough over the years."

"I'm sorry."

"Don't be." Allison's voice took on a sharpness Jake hadn't heard before, "You didn't know him and the family is actually better off without him. Ryan deserves a better life than he's had. His dad was mean and now Ryan doesn't have to worry about his mom getting beaten up anymore." Immediately, the compassion returned to her voice. "Ryan's a good kid but he went through a tough time and really tested Austin's friendship."

"I know. Austin valued their strong friendship. He told me about the day that he was stabbed trying to rescue Ryan from a gang. It sounded like both Austin and Ryan learned a great deal from that experience."

"Austin had a need for adventure. Fortunately, it didn't always get him in trouble. Austin was spontaneous and lived for today with little

248

thought for tomorrow. There was usually a twinkle in his eye and an easy smile on his face."

Jake nodded, "Austin did have a most engaging smile. He shared that wicked grin of his more than once."

Jake listened as Allison talked about her son's childhood. Jake envisioned him as a little boy but soon it was images of Katherine and Michael that drifted through his mind.

"Austin enjoyed life. His quick wit was often entertaining but it also got him in trouble more than once. Unfortunately, for Austin, his dad often regarded some of his wit as being disrespectful." Allison broke out in a smile that erased her tiredness. "I rather enjoyed his humor." The edge of her mouth gave a wanton look, "Even the odd time when it was directed at his dad."

"Don't you mean especially when it was directed at his dad?" Jake bantered back. There was a lighthearted expression in his gray eyes that stopped her heart. Jake was teasing her and Allison was enjoying it.

She could feel the heat rising to her face. Allison reached for her wine glass and drained it. She began twisting her empty glass between her fingertips nervously.

"Would you like some more wine?"

Allison smiled and the warm glow of the firelight made her eyes sparkle like stars in a velvet sky. She looked exquisite. Allison shook her head for she could already feel the effects of the wine, "Oh, no. That was delicious but I don't need any more."

"I didn't ask you if you needed more," Jake said, with a charming smile of his own.

"You're hopeless."

"I'll go see what I have," Jake said, as he pulled his long frame up.

Allison shivered for the burning wood had been reduced to cinders. Jake grabbed the quilt off the loveseat and wrapped it around her shoulders. He threw a couple of logs into the glowing coals before heading into the kitchen. The candle's flame flickered as it guided him.

"Do you want the "Blackberry Merlot" or would you like to try "Island Mist Tropical Fruits"?" Jake called from the kitchen.

"The fruity one sounds nice." Allison pulled the quilt tighter as she stared pensively at the flames that once again began to wrap around the logs. The wind howled and the rain continued to pound against the windows.

Mesmerized by the fire, she allowed her mind to wander and she smiled at memories of happier times with Richard. Her thoughts drifted off to the first time she saw Richard and the wonder of their falling in love. A college friend had dragged her to a university debate and Richard was solidly defending his views. He was brilliant and intense. Richard was strong in his beliefs and Allison had admired his skill in addressing the crowd and keeping their attention. She had tagged along with her friend when he went to speak to Richard. They all went out for coffee and continued the debate. After her friend left she and Richard had stayed and talked for hours. They quickly found they had a lot in common and Richard seemed to respect her opinion even when it disagreed with his. Soon they were spending all of their free time together and it wasn't long until Allison discovered the gentleness beneath the forceful exterior he presented to others. Together they shared their dreams. Richard talked about his goals; Allison talked of the children she wanted. In their early years he was so protective and she felt safe. Now, Allison felt controlled instead.

"I really don't like electrical storms," she confessed to Jake when he returned. When the lightning from outside lit up the living room she asked, nervously, "How long do you think the power will be out?"

"It depends on how wide the blackout is and how quickly they can find the source of trouble. Don't be afraid, Allison. You're safe."

"Just like Austin was once he found his way here."

"You were far away when I came in. What were you thinking about?" Jake asked, as he filled both of their wine glasses.

A faint tremor of excitement went through her as Jake's fingers touched her hand when she took the glass from him. "Richard and the kids, but mostly Richard."

"What's Richard really like? What made you fall in love with him?"

Allison looked up and flashed Jake a smile. "Unlike you, it wasn't love at first sight."

Something very comfortable passed between them again. Jake had experienced the same feeling down by the river once Allison had finally relaxed. It was almost like they had known each other for a long time. Austin had intertwined their lives before they had ever met.

Jake was fascinated by the lady beside him and wanted to know everything about her. She had intoxicated him with her beauty and charm. He wanted to drink in every word spoken from her luscious red lips.

Unaware of Jakes thoughts she continued to talk freely. It was warm friendly conversation. "Our early years together were tough. We were both just starting out in our careers so money was tight. Richard is very independent and proud. He wouldn't accept any financial help from my parents and his parents couldn't afford to offer any. We made the rounds of garage sales and thrift stores on week-ends. It was exciting and fun to get things that were ours even if they weren't new. They were new to us and things like that didn't matter in the beginning. We struggled but we were happy." It felt good to talk about old times.

Allison sighed, "I think they were the best years. Now, I have all the material things I need, and many I don't. In that way, I want for nothing. They're more important to Richard for they show our status in life. To everyone it looks like we have it all."

Allison reminisced about the years when they had been happier and the arrival of Austin that made them a family. Jake remained enchanted by the sound of her voice but he was also envious of the family life that Allison had. From the mists of memory Jake recalled the night Katherine told him that she was pregnant. So much sorrow from so much happiness.

Allison's voice broke through his thoughts. "When we decided to start our family Richard went into private practice. His reputation in the city grew, well earned by his triumphant performances." The joy left her eyes. "He became so intense about his work. Richard wanted more and he thought that corporate law would offer him more of a challenge. A few years ago he closed his practice and joined a large law firm in the city. Richard has since become a partner and is recognized as a very formidable attorney. His shrewdness in business and his commitment to hard work have been recognized."

Allison's fingers tightened on the slender stem of her glass. She looked up and confided to Jake, "I wouldn't want to face Richard in a cross-examination even if I had nothing to hide. He terrifies the kids at times."

Jake recalled the image of Richard at the funeral, remembering the steel control that he seemed to have over his feelings, and had to agree. So much control that Jake had wondered if the man felt anything deeply.

Allison admitted, "Richard is judicious and professionally clever. Too often he continues the role at home." She found herself admitting, "Richard has emotional and physical needs just like other men but he doesn't let them govern his life like his business does." Allison was ashamed by her outburst. It was unlike her to speak about their personal relationship.

"It doesn't sound like a very pleasant atmosphere to live in."

"It's not so bad," Allison lied loyally. She had said it lightly but with an undertone of regret. One look at Jake's face and she knew he didn't believe her. "Richard obsesses over making more money. He's afraid we won't have enough for our family and for retirement."

"Was he always like that?" Jake asked, as he again refilled both of their glasses.

Allison nodded her head but immediately rose to her husband's defense. "His dad was a hard worker but earned just enough to support a family. There was no money for extras. I respect Richard for being responsible and caring about the future of our family. Too bad he's spending too much time on our financial and his business future. He forgets that we need him to be here in the present as well. I need a husband, the kids need their father. Richard doesn't know how to enjoy what we already have. I don't think he really realizes what we do have."

"It sounds like your husband has buried himself in his work."

"He did that long before Austin's accident." Bitterness had returned to Allison's voice. "I want him to share a part in all of our lives." She looked up at Jake, "Is that asking too much?"

"Of course not."

Allison took a deep breath, and continued, "Richard has forgotten why he's working so hard in the first place. If he isn't careful, he'll be all alone with his money."

Jake frowned as a shadow of pain crossed his eyes. "Why can't some men understand that their family is the richest gift that they can be blessed with?" As the firelight outlined Jake's rugged profile, he looked sad and lonely. Allison's heart went out to him.

Allison's throat grew all tight and chocked. "I'm sorry, Jake. I keep forgetting your loss. I don't mean to be insensitive." A tear escaped as her eyes brimmed with tears.

When another tear dropped to her cheek, Jake gently brushed it away. Allison had brought with her memories of feelings that Jake thought were dead. It seemed that the members of the Smith family, first Austin and now Allison, had an alarming habit of knocking down his barriers. Jake was watching her with an absent, thoughtful expression on his face. "Austin said I would like you," Jake said unexpectedly.

Allison felt surprised and even a touch of pleasure at his words but she carefully concealed it by glancing away. She held herself still yet she was fully away of Jake's eyes upon her profile and his look took her breath away when she looked back. Jake was watching her with an intensity that made her very aware of the intimacy of the moment. For an instant the air seemed to crackle, charged by a tension that seemed to flash between them.

Dormant feelings stirred inside Jake and tonight, with Allison, it was a wonderful experience after so many years. Jake's pupils darkened with a glimmer of longing as he looked at Allison with memories in his eyes. Once again he was alive to the feelings aroused by a woman. His eyes were now smoldering and intense as he made a slow search of Allison's face. She was so beautiful. Silky hair, as black as a raven's wing, caressed her shoulders inviting a man to run his fingers through it. Her ivory skin, so soft, so touchable. Red-lipped mouth, so inviting and eyes that expressed her every thought as she gazed into the darkening smoke of his own eyes. At that moment there was no doubt in his mind. There was a definite chemistry that flowed between them.

Recognizing it as well, Allison lowered her head. Her silky hair draped down, framing her face. She felt a combination of emotions, one after another. Allison closed her eyes and gave way to feelings that filled her with a lot of conflicting emotions. A wild flush of color warmed her cheeks and she knew it wasn't due to the fire. Allison didn't know what to think. She only knew that the man beside her was a remarkably disturbing man.

Jake suspected that the over-bright eyes and the flushed cheeks indicated inner turmoil. He was acutely aware of Allison's femininity and with it she was waking buried feelings and he ached again for a woman. Time had caused Katherine to become a blurred memory, a shadowy presence in his past. Passions that he had long denied existence ignited as quickly as the wood in the fireplace. As much as Allison had stirred the embers of emotion, he knew that together they couldn't play with fire.

As swift as the moment of desire for Jake had come it fled. Allison knew that the need was not completely due to the man beside her. The burning desire within came from the longing for physical contact, something she'd been missing from Richard. How long had it been since they made love? Too long, if she had to wonder. Allison shuddered as she yearned for something she dared not give in to.

The atmosphere was tense and time stood still as they sat close enough to touch, and didn't.

"I'm tired," Allison said suddenly.

Jake's gray eyes stared into hers. A vulnerability glimmered in Allison's eyes that were as vividly blue as the Wyoming sky on a clear summer day. Jake's voice was definitely mocking when he asked, "Still running away, Allison?"

Allison shifted to an upright position. An ember of anger flamed in her as their eyes locked. "Both you and Richard keep accusing me of running away. I'm not running away."

"Go to bed. This has been a long day for both of us."

Allison took a candle and left the room in a wave of tiredness and emotionally confused.

Jake sat for a long time in his chair, Sam at his feet. Mysterious shadows played on the walls. His thoughts were now about Austin's mother. He regretted his abruptness with Allison. Jake knew she was dealing with a lot just like Austin had when he was here. But he also had his own feelings to deal with. He now felt the need for a woman in his life. Austin may have been the person to bring him out of the past but it was Allison Smith who made him want to look to the future. It was as if she'd touched his very soul. This lady had a warmth that seemed to engulf him. Anguish within stabbed at his fragile soul for Jake knew that she, too, would leave and once again he'd be alone. He also knew that he no longer wanted to be alone. The rain continued and flashes of lightning occasionally illuminate the room. Jake knew that in time they would both weather their own personal storms.

Once in bed Allison knew that sleep would not allow her an easy escape from her life. She'd come here for answers but they had created more questions. Questions she now had to answer for herself. What was she doing here alone in a stranger's bed wakeful and miserable? What about her recent actions and her own feelings? Anxiety took hold as she thought about Richard. They had grown apart arguing about everything and nothing? He didn't listen any more. Why couldn't he be more like Jake? There were a lot of contrasts between the two men and she was once again comparing him unfavorably with Jake.

Common sense told her to leave in the morning. Jake would have to pass her apologies on to his mom. Allison knew if she stayed she ran the risk of giving way to the feelings which had surfaced from Jake's compassion and caring. She could no longer deny her attraction to him. There was an aura of power that surrounded him yet he'd revealed a sensitive and caring side that touched her. It all made Jake Hanson a very exciting man. She knew that she had no right to be thinking of him. The fact remained, she was married. Yet Allison wondered if

Jake was thinking of her as he lay alone in his bed in the next room. "Don't be foolish," she told herself as she punched the pillow she had fluffed earlier. It was ridiculous to allow her imagination to run wild with thoughts of a stranger. Yet she was drawn to him. Her name on his lips was like a gentle caress. He was attentive and complimentary. It was flattering.

Allison's mental thoughts tumbled out as she blamed Richard because he had changed. Or was it she who had changed? She mentally shook her head. In truth, they had both changed. They had grown apart. Their lives were no longer parallel. Was the distance between them too great? Allison couldn't ignore the small voice inside her. Conflicting thoughts continued to bounce around in her head, negative thoughts that began to overshadow common sense. Had too many things been said in anger that couldn't be forgotten or forgiven? Deep unhappy thoughts caused her to toss and turn as she contemplated an endless future without Richard. Allison lay there feeling empty and wondering. Questions and new feelings continued to frighten her and play with her emotions. They bounced back and forth like the lightning outside her window.

Heavy thoughts, no longer of Austin, were disturbing her. She thought, now, of her other children. On top of everything else, what would leaving Richard do to her children? It hurt too much to even think of it. In her heart she knew the answer. When you have kids you're forced to think of them first. Must she live her life for her children? They grow up. They leave. They make their own lives. Was the sacrifice too great to stay? Children are resilient. They were young enough to adjust and heal. With that thought came another, a revealing thought that brought comfort. For if she believed that her children would heal in time, she knew that she would too. She and Richard had once been so happy. They could be happy again. She felt her love for her family pulling her back. The storm outside grew quieter; the rain now a gentle patter against the window. Allison pleaded for sleep to take her and in time it did.

Chapter Eleven

It was early when Allison awoke. Stretching, she listened for sounds of activity. All was quiet. Allison wondered where Jake was. On her way through the kitchen she grabbed a coffee.

Opening the door, the day greeted her bright and clear. Allison watched the sky lighten in the east. A new day was unfolding, peaceful and hushed. The world around her was freshly washed from the rain and a moist, earthy scent still hung in the air.

Allison noticed Jake walking up the drive. She stood quietly watching him. He had a natural, graceful stride which drew attention to the full length of his body. She saw the play of muscles as her gaze flickered across his chest and shoulders. There was an impression of masculinity in every move he made. Jake looked up, smiled and waved. Her heart quickened in a most alarming way and she was furious with herself.

"Good morning, sleepy head. It's another beautiful day," Jake commented idly, as he walked up the steps. He noticed that the shadows under her eyes weren't as dark this morning and the afternoon outdoors yesterday had given her a little more color. She was definitely looking better.

"Yes, it is." She felt happy. It was too lovely a day not to. Allison didn't want to consider the possibility that the man in front of her might have something to do with it. Her resolution of last night was instantly tossed aside as she asked, "What time did you want to leave?"

"It's over an hour drive but if we could go a bit earlier I can make a quick stop at the jobsite. I need to go over a few details with my foreman. If I can do it today it will free up my time for a couple of days." A shadow crossed Jake's eyes for the site he was going to was where the school was being built. He and Austin had spent a lot of time going over the shop drawings. It was during that time that the trust was first established. Austin had revealed a lot of hidden information as he opened up to Jake. "How long before you can be ready?"

"Give me ten minutes." Allison laughed softly at his look of doubt.

"I'll go get my truck and bring it around front." Jake couldn't resist teasing her, "It may not be a coach, Your Highness, but it will get us there."

Allison was surprised at the warm feeling his light teasing caused. "Idiot," she fired back, as she ran into the house leaving no time to wonder if she would regret what she had done. Allison went back into the bedroom and brushed her hair, letting it hang loose about her shoulders instead of tying it up like she often did. A touch of lipstick and she was ready. Taking an extra minute Allison studied her reflection. Her cheeks glowed, there was a new sparkle in her eyes and the lady in the mirror smiled back at her.

After a quick stop at the jobsite they headed south on the freeway. The endless sky was forget-me-not blue and thin wisps of clouds danced across the sky. Allison settled back against the cushions and before long they were chatting away like old friends. The miles flew by.

Unexpectedly, the words, "Pack up your troubles in an old kit bag and smile, smile, smile," popped into her head. Smile she did for she was feeling young and free and very happy.

Jake quirked an eyebrow and his eyes were deeply amused. "Penny for your thoughts or are they worth more when they make you smile?" His own teasing smile was evident.

Allison laughed and shared her thoughts.

As they drove along, Allison enjoyed the scenery of the countryside. Wheat fields were abundant and spread out for miles. Their golden shafts shone in the sunlight as they waved back and forth. Large herds of cattle grazed in low lying pastures. In the distance the majestic mountains stood unyielding against the horizon. Allison felt miles away from her own world and enjoyed the change.

A comfortable silence fell between them. Allison didn't know where Jake's thoughts were but her own were on last night. Through the veil of long lashes she stole a glance at his rugged profile. Jake drove with a relaxed ease with one hand on the steering wheel. Her original one-dimensional image of him had dissolved as she'd glimpsed facets of his real personality. Her eyes slid appreciatively across the taut power of his shoulders and down his strong arms. There was no denying that Jake had a strong physical attractiveness and the aura of power was more than well-developed muscles. Allison had to admit to herself that she found his strong dark looks dangerously enticing. Or was it more a case of another man igniting the desire she had wanted to feel from her husband? It had disturbed her yesterday; it disturbed her even more today. The nagging thought persisted. Allison refused to dwell on her feelings for that could put her in another traumatic state of mind. She wanted to enjoy today.

Jake glanced across at her briefly, smiled and returned his attention to his driving. He had the most disarming smile. Allison smiled back. Was she attracted to him? Stupid question. Last night she found herself liking him very much. Suddenly the cab of the truck felt very confining. Why was nothing simple anymore?

Allison rested her head against the seat back and tried to relax. Instead, she found herself going over the previous day's events and her own reaction to them. Sighing, Allison turned to gaze out the window. She was relieved when Jake announced that they were almost there.

Within minutes he was signaling to turn off the main highway. The small town was busy as locals walked down the sidewalks, peering occasionally into shop windows. Two retired farmers sat on a bench chatting away. It wasn't long before the residential streets were tree-lined and each home sat on a large lot. Jake turned into a front drive and Allison gazed at the beautifully landscaped yard with appreciation. Mature fir trees that offered privacy from the neighbours shaded the freshly mowed lawn. The front verandah was most welcoming as bright red geraniums filled hanging planters in both corners.

"It's charming," declared Allison.

"Wait until you see the back yard. Mom loves to garden. She'll want to show it to you after lunch. It's her pride and joy and it's beautiful this time of year."

Jake lightly kept his hand on Allison's elbow as they walked up the steps. Mrs. Hanson opened the door before they reached it.

"Morning, Ma."

"Morning yourself, Jake," she answered back. She greeted Allison just as warmly. "Welcome, my dear."

Allison liked Jake's mom and she smiled back. "It's a beautiful day, isn't it?"

Edna took a deep breath, enjoying the fragrance of the nearby geraniums. "The weather has been incredible. It sure changed quickly last night. Did you get showers, too?"

Jake's big voice boomed, "We had more than showers. It was quite the storm. The power was out for hours." The memory of the night before brought a flush to Allison's cheeks that did not go unnoticed by Jake's mother. Edna gave them both a swift look and frowned as she looked at Jake anxiously. He was too busy talking to notice as he commented, "The rain will green everything up again."

The smell of fresh baked buns welcomed them when they stepped into the kitchen. "Mm, sure smells good in here. Been cooking up a storm this morning?" Jake turned to Allison, "Ma's a great cook. Her potato salad is the best you'll find anywhere."

Edna put Allison at ease by including her in the preparation of the meal. The kitchen was cozy and cheerful and Allison felt an instant sense of comfort fill her as they worked together. Jake's mom had an easy way about her and Allison found herself relaxing. Jake sat down at the table and watched them as they dished up the food.

Lunch was informal and pleasant. It was a lovely meal; potato salad, moist pink ham, sliced cucumbers and tomatoes from the garden and, of course, fresh buns. Jake heaped his plate full and ate heartily. When it was gone he buttered another bun and threw in some ham. Allison watched him, as did his mother. Jake looked up just as he bit into the bun. "Dessert," he mumbled, with his mouth full.

Allison looked across the kitchen table and smiled at her hostess. "That was delicious, Edna. May I help you clean up?"

She refused Allison's offer to help. "You know it's easier to clean up on your own. Let me putter while you and Jake finish your coffee."

The conversation flowed freely and Allison continued to feel at ease. It was a pleasant change from the tension that had held her in its grip for so long.

They were still sitting around the table when the phone rang. Jake, who was closest, answered it. He looked over at his mom. "Matt needs me to run out to the ranch. Billy didn't make it to the finals so he's home early. They want me to take a look at Clint's horse." He smiled apologetically to Allison, "You can come with me or stay and visit with Ma and I can pick you up on the way back."

Allison, who wasn't up to meeting more people, agreed to stay with his mother.

Edna didn't even try to hide her delight. She had liked Allison when she met her yesterday and she had a feeling that the poor dear was in need of another woman to talk to. Her voice was teasingly affectionate as she ordered her son, "Get going. We won't even miss you but don't be gone too long."

Jake laughed and grabbed his hat as he headed out the door. He was no sooner gone and Edna asked Allison if she would like to see her back yard. Repressing a smile as she recalled Jakes comment when they first arrived, Allison admitted that she'd love to.

Allison followed Edna outside. "I love my little house and my beautiful gardens. The boys can't seem to accept that I'm really happy here. They never knew, but there were times when it was lonesome at the ranch. I find I like living alone and I'm not lonely. Here, I enjoy my friends dropping in or chatting with my neighbor over the fence."

The afternoon turned sultry as the relentless sun beat down. Scarcely a hint of breeze stirred the air. It wasn't long before the ladies decided to go indoors.

"Let's go sit in the living room. Those tall trees in the front yard keep it shaded through the afternoon and the room stays nice and cool."

Like the rest of the house, everything was neat and orderly. Large over-stuffed furniture invited you to sit and visit. Allison's eyes were drawn to a tall, mahogany grandfather clock standing in the corner as it chimed out the hour.

Edna took notice. "It's one of the few things I brought with me into town. The boys were surprised that I didn't want to bring more from the ranch." She paused, and then continued, "I married their dad right after I finished school. We moved into the hired hand's house on the ranch and his parents lived up in the main house. It was small but it came furnished with the simple basics. I made the best of it. It was a temporary accommodation because the ranch would eventually pass down to Ben since he was their only child. After Ben's dad passed on, we moved up to the main house and his mom lived with us. In our day it wasn't unusual and my mother-in-law was a nice lady," Edna stated. Then she sighed, "The big house never felt like my home. Everything was his mothers. Her dishes, her furniture, her bedding. Men don't understand things like that. After her passing, I asked to buy something new so it would be ours. Ben couldn't see the point of getting something new when what we had was still good. I couldn't argue and I quit asking. I never felt that anything in the house was really mine except for little things that I got as gifts over the years. Those are the things I brought with me."

The old lady smiled reflectively, "Ben bought me the clock for our twenty-fifth wedding anniversary. I was so surprised." Jake's mom went on to explain, "Ben was a good man but he didn't give much thought to romance. When he gave it to me he said it reminded him of me. It didn't seem like much of a compliment and truthfully my feelings were a little hurt. Ben didn't notice and went right on talking. As I said, Ben wasn't very sentimental but I've treasured every word he said that day. He told me that every second he spent with me was like the continuous ticking of the clock. It was something he got used to but every once in awhile it would chime out and remind him of its presence and then it would go back to ticking. It was as familiar as it was comforting. Ben looked at me and said that just like he always needed to know what time it was, he always needed me." Edna Hanson's eyes had glistened over.

Allison smiled tenderly at the elderly lady through her own veil of tears. Edna's Ben reminded her a little of Richard. Solid as a rock and just as emotional.

"I must confess I still miss my Ben terribly at times. We all do." She quickly wiped her eyes and then giggled. "Wait until you see my bathroom. It's pink." Both ladies laughed.

"Enough about me," Edna said pleasantly. "I must be boring you." Allison shook her head, for this lady was warm and endearing.

"Sit down, dear." Jake's mom patted the seat on the sofa next to her. Allison obeyed and pulled one of the throw cushions to her and hugged it close. It was a defensive gesture that did not go unnoticed by Edna. "I'm glad Jake will be gone for awhile. Now," she declared, "we can talk freely. You still look a little pale."

Allison turned to face her hostess, unconsciously lifting her chin a little higher and forced a smile. "I'm fine," Allison lied, not wanting to admit how worn out she really felt.

"Why don't you tell me how you're really doing?" the elderly woman coaxed. "Parents know no greater joy than the birth of a baby and no greater sorrow than the death of a child."

This was a sad chapter in this young mother's life. Allison nodded in agreement and there was a huge lump in her throat. She sat still looking at her hostess but remained quiet.

Allison's eyes looked years older than her body and Edna knew it wasn't just due to the death of her son. "I may not understand everything but it might help to talk."

Allison's eyes were dull and haunted. Edna smiled at her gently. She quickly penetrated Allison's defenses when she placed her wrinkled, age-spotted hands over the younger woman's small, fine-boned hands. "Let it all out, my dear," Edna said, in a kindly voice.

Allison turned to look up into the older lady's face. "I have no right to burden you."

"When you share your burdens the load becomes lighter."

Allison could tell that the elderly woman was understanding, compassionate and caring. It was evident in the warm, brown eyes and in the aged drawn lines that life's experience had etched on her face. A loving woman, thought Allison. So caring that she was willing to allow a stranger to indulge in her own self-pity and distress. Maybe it would help to talk to her.

"Where do I start?" Allison asked blankly.

"Why don't you simply start with yourself?" Edna prompted. "I noticed you only picked at your food at lunchtime."

Allison reassured her hostess, "Your lunch was lovely, Edna. I haven't been able to eat much. I have no appetite."

"Are you sleeping at night?"

"Not since Austin left," Allison confessed. "I'm so tired. It's exhausting trying to make everyone feel better. I did try the sleeping pills my doctor gave me but I'd go into such a deep sleep and I couldn't wake from the nightmares. I don't know which are worse, the nightmares when you're asleep or the nightmare when you're awake. It's like I'm in a bad dream that plays over and over." Allison looked at the other woman. "I want this nightmare to end."

"No wonder you're physically exhausted, my child. You know that you're still suffering from symptoms of bereavement. This has been an immensely stressful time in your life and you need to recognize that it has taken a huge toll on your body."

"Austin's death turned my world upside down," Allison blurted out truthfully. "All I want to do is cry. But I don't want to cry because I'm afraid I may never stop. So, I shut myself away thinking I can shut myself away from the pain."

"Shutting yourself away, physically and emotionally, is under the circumstances, to be expected. Life won't allow you to remain shut away for long. The rest of your family needs you. Now, more than ever."

Allison shook her head violently. It was like she couldn't stop herself now that she had started. She was surprised at the words coming out of her mouth. Things she had only thought of were being spoken out loud. "Richard has his work. He's coping just fine," Allison declared, bitterness evident in every word. "I find myself resenting Richard because of his work. He goes to work and leaves me alone to cope with everything else, the kids, their questions, their anger, my own anger. How can I help my kids when I can hardly help myself? Austin's death has had a devastating effect on all of us." Her voice trailed off.

The older woman's eyes challenged Allison, "Have you had any counseling? There must be some kind of grief group in your area. They have trained professionals to help you get through a crisis like this. This has been an emotionally stressful time for you."

Allison nodded. "I started attending weekly sessions right after Austin died. Others in the group, those who had more time to heal, tried to help me but I was really struggling. Most have lost parents or spouses but no one else had lost their first born. They couldn't seem to understand. Or I couldn't. So I quite going."

"Has it helped your husband?"

"Richard refused to go." A faint note of resentment trailed through the words. "That made me angry, too." It was a relief to speak so honestly. "I don't think that sympathy and tolerance are within the realm of Richard's understanding."

"I'm sure you're wrong, dear. Grief is grief and each of us deals with it in various ways. Men have different ways of trying to console themselves. Don't judge him too harshly. Give Richard time and be there for him when he's ready for he will need you."

The conversation fueled Allison's underlying anger. "Why can't he be there for me for a change? I need him. Is that asking too much?"

Edna ignored Allison's questions. Instead, she added quickly, "You and your husband have to learn to help each other. Only then can you really help your children. They need to know that you are both there for them at all times."

Allison uttered anxiously, "Richard has difficulty deciphering his own emotions. He doesn't have a clue how to deal with the kids and we all know how emotional they can be."

Actually, both Jordie and Cassie had remained brave throughout the days that followed their brother's death. Now the anger had surfaced, especially with Jordie, and the questions had started and she didn't know what to tell them.

Allison's memory was jogged to a recent incident with her young daughter. Just last week on her way to bed Allison had looked in on Cassie to find her daughter sitting up in bed. "What's wrong with my baby?" Allison asked as she went to sit at the side of the bed.

Cassie's little chin lifted spunkily. "Austin says I'm a big girl but it's okay to cry when I'm sad. He said I shouldn't be sad because he's right here with me. He told me he'd be with me any time I need him just like always."

Tears stung Allison's eyes and her voice was gentle with concern, "When did he tell you that, sweetie?"

"Tonight. That's why I'm awake. Austin woke me up when he kissed me on the forehead like he always does. He told me to tell you he's sorry and you shouldn't be sad either. Austin said he's okay and loves us all but we knew that, didn't we, Mommy?"

Realizing that Edna was speaking again, Allison forced herself back to the present. "Cassie is pretty young to understand. At times she escapes into a fantasy world." With an attempt at a little humor, she said, "I wish Cassie would take me with her. It would be nice to escape the reality." Allison tried to laugh but it didn't ring true.

"What about Jordie?"

"Jordie, being older, understands more. He's thirteen now," Allison added. "Another tough round of teenage years ahead."

Edna smiled knowingly, "I remember my boys when they were that age. Exasperating as ever," she confirmed, with a shake of her gray head. "All kids go through a selfish streak, a time when everything is about them and life is black and white. They have their own ideas at that age. They think their parents are fools who don't understand what they're feeling."

Allison nodded her head in agreement. "Jordie also has a lot of anger he's dealing with. He blames us both. I haven't been able to reach him since Austin died. He's become withdrawn and sulky. Jordie was always so carefree and lively."

Edna sighed. "Children, especially young teens like Jordie, have enough difficulty coping with all of the normal struggles of growing up."

"Why won't he talk to me?" Allison asked suddenly.

"I'm sure Jordie's having trouble expressing his grief and he might even feel that he can't talk to you because he doesn't want to upset you more. Kids need time to work through their emotions, too. What grieving children and even adults need most is support and understanding. Give your kids a chance to share their feelings and worries."

"I've tried to get Jordie to talk. He simply answers in monosyllables."

"Keep trying."

"I don't know what to say anymore," Allison added desperately.

"Even if the words come out wrong, Jordie will know that you care enough to listen. It won't happen overnight. The kids may keep coming back with more questions once they digest answers from earlier questions. Be clear and keep it simple but make sure they understand."

"How can I make them understand when I don't understand?" Allison asked painfully.

Edna was lost for an adequate reply. The loss of a child went beyond her personal knowledge. The older woman's heart ached for this young mother who was suffering in her grief and horror. "You're loving and caring. Life is harder for those with a sensitive soul."

"It's like I am full of anger every single day. I feel like screaming and shouting at someone, anyone just to release it. I'm mad at God for his cruelty. I'm mad at Austin for dying. And I'm mad at myself because I don't know what to do any more."

Edna gazed kindly on the young woman's face, feeling the fear and pain that this mother had to have experienced. "I know this is terrible for you and there's nothing wrong with what you're feeling. Your feelings are normal. You are going to be all right. You all will."

Jake's mom was so sincere in her concern that Allison opened right up. The anger faded from her face, intense sadness darkened the blue of her eyes as another confession came. With a moan of despair Allison admitted how guilty she felt. Head bent, she confessed to her hostess, "Do you know that the last words I spoke to my son were spoken in anger." The grieving mother's voice broke as she added, "If I could just tell him I'm sorry."

Having unburdened her soul to her hostess, Allison now found it easier to share her deepest feelings. "I hoped that coming here to see Jake would help me."

"How?" Jake's mom asked curiously.

"I needed some answers. All that the police could tell us was that Austin was coming home. I needed to know what happened while he was gone. Your son was my last hope."

"That was a brave decision to make considering you didn't know what you'd find out."

"I'm not brave, Edna. I was desperate and I prayed that in some way Jake might help me. I didn't know how but as soon as the idea came to me it was like a bolt of lightning shot through me and I had no choice but to come." Allison floundered hopelessly, "I wasn't coping."

Edna said compassionately, "No one understands another person's grief. Grief is normal but prolonged depression is unhealthy."

"That's what Jake told me," Allison answered mournfully. "He told me that when Katherine died he remained locked in the past. Life hurt too much. Because of that he watched life pass him by. One day passed into another day and all he had in his personal life was old memories. I don't want to end up like Jake did," Allison added softly, but with conviction.

Allison smiled sadly and Edna knew that her son had opened up and shared a lot more with this woman than she had realized. An odd expression came into Edna's eyes caused by concern for her son and his deep compassion for the mother of Austin. "Fear and loneliness can be very dangerous feelings. They can quickly play with emotions that cause people to do what they normally wouldn't."

The more the two mothers talked, the more Allison opened up.

It allowed Edna to feel that she could ask, "Have you gone through Austin's things yet?"

Allison immediately shrank from the question. A silence fell between them. Edna waited for an answer to her intended question. This too needed to be talked about.

The pain was once again evident when Allison confessed, "I haven't touched Austin's room. There's seventeen years worth of memories everywhere. A life-time of watching our son grow up to be a man. Now it's ended. Every time I step into his room I'm flooded with images of Austin and within minutes I feel like my world is closing in around me. It actually hurts to breath." Allison turned her head away, not wanting the other lady to see the tears swimming in her eyes.

"It would've been better to have disposed of Austin's things right after his death. You start the healing process when you accept and let go." The elderly woman's voice was gentle in its reproof.

"How can I?" Allison's voice was short. "How do I let go?" the grieving mother demanded to know. "That's all I have now. That's all that's left of Austin. I don't want to let him go. I want my son back." Allison met Edna's gaze with defiance. She turned away for a moment and then with a small gesture of resignation she turned back to the elderly lady who had lived through her own personal grief over the years. In a calmer voice, Allison continued, for she knew that this, too, had to be faced to find peace. "I kept telling myself I didn't have time or it was too soon. I haven't had the emotional strength to do it." A shiver went through her as truth reared its ugly head. Allison choked over her next words, for they were words she had never spoken. "It would mean admitting to myself that Austin is dead and he's not coming home."

Edna spoke softly, "Austin's not coming home, Allison. Your life has changed drastically but it doesn't mean that it's over."

Tears sprang into Allison's eyes.

"I'm sorry if I've offended you by what I've said," Edna said sincerely.

Allison shook her head, "You haven't. I know you're right." She looked into the older woman's eyes. "I don't know what to do with all of his stuff. He has boxes filled with junk. For whatever the reason, it was important to him. How can I throw away his memories?" Allison cried in anguish.

"What you're really wondering is will it mean that you're throwing away your own memories?" Edna's eyes were tender, full of understanding.

Allison's shoulders sagged forward as she nodded. Only a mother could understand.

"The sooner you deal with his things the better for all concerned. Give Cassie and Jordie things of Austin's that would be important to them. Box the rest up for now. Don't keep Austin's room like a shrine. That's unhealthy for all of you."

Allison agreed to this, promising herself she would do this when she got back home. As hard as it would be she knew that the time had come. The kids would still be gone. She would be alone to confront her fears and tears. Allison asked, her voice so low that Mrs. Hanson had to strain to hear, "Do you forget them?"

"Never!" Edna quickly answered. Something in the woman's unquestioning certainty reached the grieving mother. "Something or someone will say or do something that reminds you of them and that memory is so vivid it could have happened yesterday. For that brief moment they're right there with you and you treasure the gift you just received. Cherish the memories they create and rejoice in them rather than remain fixated on the fact that they are missed."

Allison merely nodded and withdrew.

Edna watched several expressions transform the young mother's face. "You will always have your memories. Our loved ones aren't here with us but they are always in our hearts."

Allison wanted so badly to believe her. She shut her eyes but it only made the mental pictures clearer as vivid memories moved through her mind, back to the past, skipping over the present and on to the future with the realization that the future with Austin was never to be.

Tears sparkled in Allison's eyes and Edna reached out a warm, comforting hand to the younger woman. "You don't have to forget how much a loved one means to you in order to move on," Edna told her wisely.

All of a sudden it was too much and Allison broke down. Sobs strangled her and she couldn't catch her breath. Tears flowed unchecked down her cheeks.

Edna took the grieving mother into her arms as she blinked back her own tears. Allison clung to her like a drowning person clinging to a life preserver. Allison felt safe and protected and wished she could stay like this forever.

That's how Jake found them. Without a word, he turned and left the pair alone. They didn't need him right now. Neither of them heard the door close quietly behind him as he left.

It was a relief to let the pain drain from her but Allison was embarrassed by her emotional outburst. "I'm ashamed. I've never behaved like this. My behavior is no better than that of a child throwing a temper tantrum. I'm sorry."

As old eyes looked into young eyes they saw so much and guessed much more. Poor child. Edna smiled kindly. "Maybe it's time you did. Perhaps you need to do it more often. It can be very effective."

Allison smiled in spite of herself. "It does seem to help," she confessed, through her tears. "Maybe I should have one at home. I'm sure Richard would be so pleased." Their eyes met and both women started to laugh.

Edna leaned over and offered Allison a tissue as she wiped her own eyes. "This may be the worst thing that has ever happened to you or maybe not." She took both of Allison's hands and held them in her own. "Life can be so complicated, with twists and turns that can change one's life in an instant. However, life goes on and so must you."

"I'm trying," Allison muttered. She dried her face and blew her nose.

Edna spoke with conviction, "You can keep going long after you think you can't."

Allison, on the other hand, wasn't so sure. "Oh, Edna. I hope you're right. Sometimes I feel like I'm in a bottomless pit and I can't get out because there's no one there to help me."

Edna smiled encouragingly, "I told you, Allison. You're never alone. Imagine you're in a dark tunnel instead," she suggested. "As you work through your different feelings you'll work your way toward the light."

"The light at the end of the tunnel," Allison quoted solemnly.

"Yes, my dear. Get through today and maybe tomorrow will be better."

A lull fell before Allison admitted, "Some days are better than others."

"You will get through this."

Allison nodded her head, "I know. It's so hard right now because it still hurts so much."

"Sadness and pain exist for all of us. We have to learn to balance them with the wonderful things around us."

Allison's face remained closed.

Edna explained, "One can get great joy from the little things in life if we take the time to observe them. Just this morning as I lay in bed I listened to the birds chirping in my backyard. It wasn't just the birdsong that I was thankful for. It was the fact that I have my hearing to listen to the whisper of the wind at night and the joy of hearing my grandchildren laugh."

Allison smiled slightly as if looking into herself. She was. She remembered how often young mothers complained about getting up at night with their newborns. She'd been grateful that hers had strong lungs and healthy appetites. Funny the things you forget, and odder yet the things you remember.

Edna patted Allison's hand, "I'll make us a cup of tea, or would you prefer coffee?"

"Tea would be nice," answered Allison, as they both stood.

"Why don't you freshen up while I put the kettle on," Edna suggested.

Allison was grateful for the thoughtful gesture. "Thank you. I'll go check out your pink bathroom." Allison could hear Edna's pleasant laughter as she went to compose herself.

When Allison returned, Edna was at the stove and a tray had been set with a china tea set. The kettle began to whistle as the water came to the boil. "I'm surprised that Jake isn't back yet," Edna said, with motherly concern. "Even grown-up children can cause you heartache. You always worry about them, about something happening to them. You laugh at your foolishness but you still go on worrying until they're home safe."

"And sometimes, like Austin, they don't come home." The words caught in Allison's throat and she began to pace. "I miss him so much." Her voice broke, "If I could just see his mischievous smile or hear him laugh. I miss his quick kiss on my cheek. I want to hug him close and tell him I'm sorry. I want to tell him 'I love you' one more time. I wish," Allison broke off, stopped by the futility of the phrase. She stared at Jake's mom through sudden tears. "I think that's where a lot of my anger is coming from. I'm angry and upset because I didn't get to say good-bye." It was a profound moment for Allison. She felt a shiver run down her spine. "Nothing is ever going to be the same again, is it?"

Edna looked at Allison through her own tears. Her heart went out to the young mother as she admitted, "No, it's not."

"I hear the door open and I still expect it to be Austin. It's so hard to admit that he's really gone and never coming back." Unknowingly, Allison had moved toward the light. This was the first time she had spoken these words with acceptance.

"I don't mean to hurt you with what I say," Edna declared, looking genuinely contrite.

"I know, Edna. I'm still trying to come to terms with the reality of my loss."

Edna put a reassuring hand on Allison's shoulder. "Come sit down. Tea's ready."

Edna placed the tray on the table and sat down across from Allison. "I enjoy using my good china. It seldom got used at the ranch. Can't you just see the Hanson men trying to fit their large fingers into the handle of these cups?"

Allison smiled, "It's a challenge raising boys, isn't it?"

"Matt and Jake are very different by nature but they were both strong-willed boys. Like brothers do, they fought over everything growing up. Matt endlessly teased his younger brother and Jake didn't always take kindly to it. Then the fight would be on again. Scolding seldom worked. Ben would stoically say, 'Boys will be boys. They'll work it out.' Jake was always a quieter boy, a little stubborn, but always reasonable. He had his limits and there were times when Matt pushed him too far. Matt sported a black eye more than once but they never told on each other." Edna laughed. "They worked it out all right. Husbands often think they know what's best. Truth is, they often don't think."

Allison had to laugh, too. "Oh, Edna. You have such a wonderful way of saying things."

Obviously, it was a lot different having two boys closer in age. It appeared that the Hanson brothers had a much more physical relationship than her boys.

Edna continued, with a fond smile, "Now, as you can see, they're the best of friends." Allison felt herself relaxing as Edna continued sharing stories about her two boys. "Matt was always the one to get into trouble. He liked to dance with the devil. Still does. If Jake came home late, Matt came home later. Both boys have their dad's dark good looks. Jake was always more shy and reserved, whereas, Matt was always a heart-breaker. All the girls fell for him, except his wife Gail." Edna allowed a chuckle to escape. "This was new to Matt and he fell over himself trying to impress her to no avail. He chased her and chased her until she caught him."

Both women laughed at that. It felt so good to laugh. There hadn't been much laughter in Allison's life since Austin had died.

Allison sat fascinated listening to Edna's recollections of her sons younger days. She shared a lot of stories about Jake and Matt and Allison was an avid listener. They sat talking and laughing about their children, one proud mother to another.

"Matt was always my challenge. He got expelled his senior year. He and his buddies got caught drinking under age. That wasn't the biggest problem. It was at the Spring Fling dance at school so of course the authorities wanted to set an example. It took a lot of persuading from Ben to convince the principal to let Matt back in. Poor Jake, he had to follow in Matt's deep footprints. There were times that Jake was judged unfairly. Sometimes Jake got even, both with Matt and with the school. These were also the times as parents that Ben and I simply looked the other way."

Allison smiled knowingly and allowed her mind to wander. General rules fit the norm. As a teacher she knew how challenging students could be but as a mother she knew that the school wasn't always right.

"Would you like more tea?" Edna asked, interrupting Allison's thoughts and drawing her back to the present.

"I'm sorry," she said. "I guess I drifted away. I'd love more tea."

"Every child is different. I don't think it matters if it's boys or girls. They will all challenge us at some time in their lives." Edna sighed, "There were times I was just grateful to get through the day without a new challenge."

Allison smiled and her face was alive. "Austin was a force to be reckoned with from the day he was born. After weeks of waiting, he decided to arrive on a beautiful Saturday afternoon. He was two weeks late and a precedent was set. Austin was late for everything. Time meant nothing but that was okay because, according to him, nothing started until he got there."

Jake's mom threw her head back and laughed. "There is some truth to that."

Allison laughed as well.

Edna noticed the change in her expression as Allison's eyes misted over. They weren't sad tears. They were simply a mother's tears.

"I remember when they handed Austin to me for the first time and I held my baby close. He lay there wailing in my arms with his little hand in a fist ready to take on the world." Remembering this, she smiled. "Austin made us a family."

"Family is important. You still have your family."

Yes she did, Allison admitted to herself. She missed her family. She missed her home. Cassie, Jordie and Richard needed her and she needed them. She needed to lie in Richard's arms until she fell asleep. She needed to hear her children's chatter, and yes, hear their squabbling. She needed to get back to her life and everything that went along with it. When she returned to them they would learn to cope. For just a little longer she needed this time for Austin. She still needed time with this family.

When Jake entered the kitchen he was surprised to see the two women laughing at the kitchen table. He looked closely at Allison, concern showing on his face. "She looks as fragile as Ma's good china," he thought to himself, although she did look more at ease than when he'd left. Grabbing a mug, he poured himself a cup of tea and joined them. Mother and son exchanged a long silent glance and Jake felt better when Allison smiled at him as he sat down.

Edna got up and started getting things out of the fridge.

"Ma. What are you doing? We just ate a huge lunch."

"That was hours ago. I won't fuss but it's long past lunch. It won't hurt you to spare your mom a little more time," she teased affectionately.

Jake remained silent as he shook his head, for he knew better.

If this was a case of no fuss, Allison wondered what to expect if her hostess did fuss. Edna's light meal was a feast. There was left over ham, pickles, buns, and a homemade apple pie which she'd popped into the oven to heat while they ate.

After supper, they chatted a while longer, then Jake announced, "We should be going."

Jake's mom quickly got up from the table. "Wait a minute. I've packed a few things for you to take home with you." Allison smiled inwardly because if "a few things" meant anything like "no fuss" Jake would literally have his arms full.

This was obviously a regular occurrence because Jake didn't hesitate to ask, "Can I have some of your homemade jam?"

"I've already put in a peach and a strawberry. Remember to keep the jars. And bring them back," she scolded.

They all walked out to the verandah and talked for a few more minutes. Jake's strong arms encircled his mom and he kissed her cheek. "Thanks for the food hamper. I'll bring it back when it needs to be restocked." It was nice to see the mutual love between mother and son as Edna affectionately slapped her son's arm.

Another memory for Allison. How often had she and Austin bantered back and forth affectionately? Yesterday, Allison would've turned away, for the memory would have been too hurtful. Today, she smiled as she enjoyed her own memory of Austin's familiar kiss.

"I'm so grateful to you. Thank you for everything that we talked about and for listening. You've helped me a lot. I think I'll be able to help my family more when I get home." The common bond of motherhood had allowed the two of them to be open and honest.

Allison had vented, released her anger, shared her guilt and wept. The older woman had sat and listened, consoled, counseled and wept. Both women smiled in understanding.

Edna leaned over and kissed the young woman's cheek. "Call me when you're back home, my dear."

Allison's eyes expressed her appreciation. "I will," she promised. Hugging the wise and caring woman, Allison added, "Thanks, again, for everything."

Jake waved to his mom as he turned down the street.

Edna waved back, her face still and thoughtful. She'd noticed the exchange of looks earlier, the quick glances between Jake and Allison. Jake's eyes had often lingered on Allison's face while the two ladies talked. Both were vulnerable and she prayed they would be wise. If not, it would mean hurt for Jake and hurt for Allison. Fate could be such a powerful force.

As they drove down the street, Jake waved to a neighbor out in the yard. "This is a great community. Ma's very happy here. I think she was glad to get off the ranch."

Allison surveyed him with deliberation. "How about you? Do you miss the ranch?"

"Sure I do." Jake's voice was expressive as he added, "I was lucky to have grown up where I did. Every season creates its own work on a ranch. No one was ever idle. Dad included us in everything and we learned everyday values working side by side. Matt loves the ranch as much as Dad did. It's his life. His eldest son, Glen, is the same way."

Curiosity made her ask, "Then why did you leave?"

Jake responded patiently, "I love building more and my dad understood that. The ranch is still home to all of us. Mom goes out often to spend time with Gail. They do a lot of canning. You know, women things."

Allison didn't miss the twinkle in his eye and knew Jake was teasing her again. "Your mom's a great lady. She spoils you."

"That's what mothers do best," Jake nodded, with satisfaction. "They never stop mothering." There was no mistaking the admiration and respect in his voice.

Allison leaned back and closed her eyes. She soon lost herself in the droning hum of the engine. She was grateful for her time with Jake's mom. Allison realized that, like herself, Edna had similar experiences, good and bad, in her years as a mother. The difference, though, was that Mrs. Hanson had time to heal and the experience to understand.

Chapter Twelve

Allison had been very subdued on the ride home for it had been another emotional day. She was glad when they turned into the drive.

"It's such a pleasant evening. I think I'd like to sit outside for awhile before going in," she said, as they walked up the verandah steps.

"Do you want to be alone or do you mind my company?"

Allison smiled up at him. It wasn't solitude she was looking for. She'd felt alone for too long already. "I'd enjoy your company. We really haven't had much time to talk today. Could you give me a little time alone though? I need to make a couple of calls."

Jake went into the house to allow Allison her privacy. He sank into his familiar chair in the living room and waited.

Allison paced back and forth across the verandah, for once finding little comfort in the view. The air was still and hushed and fine shafts of sunlight filtered through the clouds. Allison took a deep breath of the crisp mountain air. Resting her arms on the railing, Allison looked out, allowing the beauty of her surroundings to dispel the sense of anxiety that disturbed her. She took another deep breath. This one for courage to face the task ahead.

Grabbing her cell phone, Allison curled up in the chair. There were two important calls she had to make. She made the easy one first and spent the next twenty minutes talking to Cassie and Jordie and then her mom. Avoiding certain questions and redirecting conversation she was able to keep her whereabouts unknown. Allison smiled once they were disconnected. The kids sounded great and they were having a wonderful time. Now for the next call. She could no longer postpone her call to

Richard. Allison knew that she'd been avoiding Richard while she thought about her life. Her life with Richard and the kids and her life without Austin.

Richard's voice broke into her train of thoughts. "Allison? It's about time you called. I've been worried about you."

Allison recognized the concern in his voice. She felt guilty, but relieved. She wondered if his concern would change to anger when he found out she was still at Jake's?

"Why haven't you returned my calls? Where are you? Are you at the cottage now?"

"I haven't left for the cottage yet," Allison confessed.

"You're still there?" She could hear the frown of surprise in his voice. "I can't believe you stayed."

Hoping to distract him, Allison quickly asked, "How is your conference going?"

There was a long pause. "There was no conference. I just needed to get away."

Allison let out the stunned breath she was holding. "You lied to me?"

Richard's tone became defensive, "I did, but you're no better. If you care to recall you didn't tell me where you were going either," he retaliated.

Allison couldn't keep the dispirited tone from her voice. "You didn't understand why I had to, did you?"

"You're right." Sarcasm was evident in her husband's voice. "I'll never understand how some stranger is going to fix things."

Her husband's words rekindled Allison's anger. "You don't know what I'm feeling. I keep thinking that Austin will walk through our kitchen door. You don't know the emptiness inside of me. The agony, the endless quiet, the waiting even though I know Austin's never coming back." Her voice broke and she couldn't continue.

"I do understand," Richard said quietly.

The glint of anger remained in her eyes. Allison struggled to speak through the tears in her voice, "No, you don't."

"Yes, I do. Better than you think. I've tried moving on the only way I could. It was easy to cope during the days because my work was so demanding."

"Is that why you kept taking on more and more work?" Allison asked accusingly. "I thought it was just habit."

"Partly," Richard answered truthfully. "Unfortunately, it isn't working."

Allison didn't know what to think. This was so out of character for her husband. "Where have you been?" She was anxious to know.

"I went home. Not our home," he quickly explained. "Home to where I grew up. It seemed like a good place to start." Richard's tone became serious, "I was trying to find out where I got lost from there to here. I know I lost a lot on the way and I was hoping if I went back I could remember some of the important things or find them on my way back."

"Did you?" Allison asked, when he paused in his telling.

Allison heard him take a deep breath and expel it loudly. "One thing I did find out was that I need you. I need you so bad right now it hurts."

The pain in her husband's voice cut through her anger, she hadn't known that he felt this way. He was adept at concealing his real feelings. Tears welled in her eyes but she didn't cry.

This conversation wasn't at all what she'd expected. There had been something else in Richard's voice that she hadn't heard before, a tiny flicker of anxiety that bordered on fear. She closed her eyes attempting to focus her thoughts.

"Do you remember when we met?" Richard asked unexpectedly. "You were charming and flirtatious. You weren't my type but you seemed to show up wherever I went. There was a directness about you that you never tried to disguise."

Allison smiled as she recalled the early sparks that had ignited their relationship. "You had inspired me with your quick intelligence, your strong beliefs and your quiet charm. I wanted to know all about you."

"That must be why you were always running into me on campus."

It was refreshing to hear the light teasing note in his voice. "You mean our chance encounters? I had to get your attention one way or the other."

Allison's heart warmed a little as Richard continued, "You grabbed my attention with your sense of humor and kept it when you'd tease me when I became too serious."

Allison especially remembered how quickly their love for each other had surfaced and blossomed. "You'd hold me in your arms and we'd talk about our fears and our dreams." A faint smile edged her mouth.

"Your hopes and dreams became mine but then my dreams changed." His comment made a painful smile come and go on Allison's face. "I've confronted the truth about myself and I didn't like what I saw, what you've seen for a long time. Look, I've made a lot of mistakes. I should never have allowed business to become my whole life."

"A man has little time to think or worry or be involved with his family when he's working all the time," Allison reminded him, knowing she was being cruel.

Richard continued without acknowledging her accusation. "I allowed it to consume me and I was unaware. I know you tried to tell me but I wouldn't listen. I've finally seen it for myself. I got caught up in the climb to the top. The sense of power was overwhelming. It had a firm hold, and yes, I enjoyed it." It was a truth he had to admit.

Richard's voice cracked as he struggled with his words and his emotions. "Unfortunately, you have to pay a price to get where you are and it's not always what you expected. You can lose the most precious things you have and not know they're gone until it's too late." This was the hardest thing he had ever admitted.

Allison had never heard him speak so openly before. Involuntarily, she nodded her head, unable to speak. His confessions tore at her already fragile soul.

Richard swallowed hard, "I know I've neglected to leave time for any of you. It was a drastic mistake, a mistake that colors everything."

"Yes, it was," Allison retorted coldly. "Making a living isn't the same as making a life."

Richard was gripped by his own kind of fear, the fear that came with guilt and desperation. "I know. My God, I was so wrong." There was a pause before he added, "Not just about this either." There was weariness in Richard's voice; moisture on Allison's lashes.

Richard wasn't finished, "I hated my own dad when he was too busy for us even though I knew why he had to work so hard. I swore I'd never be like him." Richard's anguish tore from within. "How did it happen, Allison? When did I turn into my dad?"

Allison broke in when he faltered, "Richard, I don't want to hurt you but I've tried to tell you. Over and over. The truth is you wouldn't listen." They both knew she was right but it didn't console either one of them.

Looking back, Allison couldn't remember when things changed. They had once been so happy. When did they begin to grow apart and start arguing over everything and nothing?

"Can I tell you something else?" Richard asked sadly. "I also realized that I was a little jealous of the side of your life I don't share."

"What are you talking about?"

Richard voice was deadly serious, "The kids don't need me. They have you." This statement pierced Allison's heart like an arrow.

"Don't be ridiculous," Allison stammered. "They need both of us, just in different ways and at different times. As Jordie gets older he'll turn to you more and more. Austin tried but you were too busy and you kept pushing him away. You've missed a lot," she pointed out.

"I know," Richard admitted earnestly. How sad he sounded. Allison's heart went out to him. "More than anything else, I do love you and the kids. I always have." The sincerity was evident in his voice.

"Life isn't always easy," Allison said emphatically. "Nor is love. Love has its limits."

Although he was afraid of the answer, Richard had to ask, "What's become of our love?"

Allison stared silently off into the distance. There was no response because she didn't know what to say.

"I love you, Allison. You have to believe that. I'm trying to tell you how much you matter. I will always love you. Please tell me it isn't too late," Richard begged unhappily. "I'm not really as bad as you like to think, you know."

Allison was angry but not because of Richard. She was still lashing out at her husband when he was trying desperately to reach out to her. She'd only been trying to help make him understand. Had she been expecting too much of Richard?

Richard broke the sad silence, "In all the years we've been married that was the one constant. I thought you knew how much I love you and I didn't need to tell you. I'm sorry. I should've told you every day." His voice was almost inaudible as it trailed off. Richard knew that they were both thinking the same thing. "I should've told Austin." Desperation was evident in his voice, "I can't change overnight, Allison. But with your help I know I can."

"I hope you mean it," she cried. Suddenly Allison felt sorry for him and the ice around her heart began to melt. "We need to share everything, Richard."

"I'm sorry that I've disappointed you. I do love you, Ali." Richard's endearment made a painful smile come and go on Allison's face. He hadn't called her that in months. She struggled for control as tears misted her eyes. She gazed at the horizon, conscious of the lump in her throat that came with the knowledge of how much he truly loved her.

Allison could image him raking his fingers through his hair. It was a habit of his when the conversation became too personal. She smiled to herself.

Richard wasn't finished, "I understand better than you think. I've been going through it, too. It isn't until you face a major catastrophe in your life that you face up to your own inadequacies."

That hadn't occurred to Allison until now. Maybe Richard was right.

"If I could say or do anything to make it all right I would. This is something that will not go away. It's something that will not change."

"You're right about that," Allison said dryly.

"I've thought a lot about a few of the hurtful things you said recently. This has been just as hard on me," Richard said, miserably unhappy. "I loved him too, Allison. I haven't forgotten what Austin meant to both of us."

"Did you ever tell him that?"

Richard's reaction was immediately defensive, "How do I know." He then sighed heavily. "Probably not. I assumed he knew," he added, as an afterthought.

"A big assumption, Richard." Allison's tone was not one of accusation. Rather, it was one of guilt. "We forget to tell each other how we feel when it comes to love. Yet how quick we are to tell someone that they're bad or wrong. I don't just mean you, Richard. Unfortunately, we all do it."

"Do other fathers and sons go along without talking about their feelings and assuming that everything is fine because they think the other person should know how they feel?"

"I don't know. I do know that you and Austin should've talked more. There was a lot about our son you didn't know."

"I didn't take the time to find out," Richard admitted sadly. Allison heard the despair in her husband's voice and her heart ached for him. Such a sad lesson to learn.

"It took a tragedy to open my eyes to what I've missed. It was from that reality that I couldn't escape." Allison had never considered that Richard had his own demons he was dealing with. "I failed where Austin was concerned. His death wasn't my fault and it wasn't yours either. It was a freak accident."

Allison heard his voice through a haze of thoughts. Richard was right and she knew that she had to accept the facts. She swallowed the lump in her throat, "I know. We've been down that road. We've blamed ourselves enough. Some things will have to change at home."

"I need you to help me so I don't make the same mistakes with Jordie and Cassie. Come home so we can talk," Richard begged.

Allison was aware of the struggle going on within him. She, too, was struggling. "I don't know what I feel right now, Richard." Her voice trailed off in defeat. Allison was trying to be as honest as Richard had been. Maybe before this she knew but right now her emotions had affected her rationalization. She smiled cynically. Maybe it was her sanity that was unstable. Silently, Allison questioned herself. Was it familiarity that was keeping them together? Or was it the past that really did cement two people together for life? Allison wrestled with her own confusion.

"Whatever lays ahead we'll get through it together," Richard vowed. Allison could hear the determination in his voice. Through her sadness Richard's words had warmed her heart.

She fought back the tears and at last was able to admit, "I can't run away like Austin."

Richard's voice was husky and slightly unsteady. "Are you still going to the cabin?" Allison heard the silent plea in his voice.

"No. It's time to come home. There's a lot that we have to talk about."

"Then I'll see you tomorrow?" The regret in his voice was replaced by relief.

"Yes, I'll see you tomorrow. Good night, Richard."

She heard him say, "I love you, Allison," and the phone went dead.

The expression on Allison's face was heartrending and introspective. Suddenly the tears came, all the tears that hadn't found their release. She cried for Richard, who needed understanding. She cried for Jordie and Cassie, who had to deal with hard life lessons at too young an age. She cried for those who still suffered deeply at the loss of Austin. Finally, she cried for herself for all of the same reasons. Allison sobbed her rage and her grief out loud to exercise her demons as she allowed the emptiness to wash over her.

Jake had heard Allison making her calls. The words were muffled but Jake knew when she began talking to Richard. Her tone had become much more serious and there were longer pauses in her conversation. Jake also heard her cries from the verandah but he couldn't go to her. His throat tightened and he closed his eyes to prevent his own tears from falling. Jake did not move as the shadows closed in around him.

Allison cried until there were no more tears left. Dry-eyed and completely spent, she smiled knowingly and admitted to herself that she needed her family as much as they needed her. She wanted to go home.

Chapter Thirteen

Jake stood silently at the door and watched Allison as she sat on the top step staring out at the mountains. It was a familiar pose for Austin, too, had spent time gazing out at the same mountains while he was trying to understand his life. Jake remained silent as he gave Allison the time she needed to sort out her tangled emotions and the events of the past few days.

The stunning summer sunset continued to highlight the sky. Allison was unaware of the passing of time for her mind was elsewhere. She was trying to absorb her conversation with Richard. It had been years since he'd been so open and revealing. Like her, he'd been masking his unhappiness and his pain was as real as her own. She hadn't realized the depth of Richard's feelings for all of them, including Austin. With that, her thoughts again turned to Austin's death. She knew that nobody was to blame. It had been a tragic accident. Paling, she admitted this to herself and with that came the knowledge that she had a lot to share with Richard. Unconsciously, Allison's hand went into her pocket and she touched Austin's letter. Fragmented thoughts drifted through her mind. 'He thought you were the best… He loved his family, even his dad… He wasn't mad any more…. He was coming home.' Austin was coming home. It was these last words that echoed over and over in her mind.

Lost in deep thoughts, Allison was unaware of Jake until he sat next to her and put his hand on hers. "You okay?"

Allison looked up and met his gaze and their eyes held. "I will be."

"I know you will. I'm sure Austin got his strength of character from you. There are certain values that can only be acquired by being exposed to them all your life. You raised him well. You gave him a solid foundation. You had a fine son. Jordie and Cassie will be fine, too."

"It's been quite a day. Your mom helped me to see a lot of things differently," Allison confessed. "I have a feeling that you helped Austin the same way." She gave Jake a questioning look. "Why do you think Austin ended up here?"

Jake's eyes were on her, a reflective quality in their gray depths. "I don't know, but I thank God that he did. When we were up in the loft I told you that Austin needed me. I guess I needed Austin, too."

They looked at each other in the faint light and smiled.

Allison's smile faded. "I've been angry at everyone. My whole world was torn apart. I needed time to think things out."

"So did Austin."

"I do know that now, Jake." Allison's voice was sad. "You offered my son a gift of hospitality and friendship when he needed it. Here you are having rescued another Smith from despair. You gave me the time I needed just like you did with Austin." A flicker of gratitude remained in her eyes.

Together, they watched the lingering sunset as it painted the distant mountains with shades of purple. The night air was scented with the fragrance of pine as it drifted in the air. Serenity surrounded them and they sat still enjoying the peace it brought with it.

It was Allison who broke the silence as she shared her thoughts. "I think being here changed Austin," surmised Allison.

Jake shook his head. "Places don't change people. People change themselves. Being here had a positive influence on Austin. Once he settled down I was able to help him put things into perspective and I could see the changes happening each day. The time here helped Austin to see things differently and he was able to develop a renewed sense of worth."

"It's helped me, too."

She became aware of the fact that Jake had become very silent. Sam came and laid his head on Allison's knee. She gently stroked his ears. Allison leaned back and closed her eyes, just for a minute. When she opened them Jake was studying her intently. Jake knew her time with him was over. He also knew he would miss her. It was a solemn moment.

Jake rose and leaned against the verandah post. Allison began to sense that his silence was due to more than her leaving. He turned and looked down at her, his expression painful. A muscle twitched in his jaw. Allison's eyes widened as she looked at him searchingly.

When Jake finally spoke Allison could hear the anguish in his voice, "I've a confession to make." His face was set, his eyes were grim. "I was being selfish. I'd come to realize that I was letting your son be mine for those few days. I knew Austin had unconsciously decided to go home sooner." Jake almost seemed to be talking to himself and his voice trailed off, "Maybe if I'd pushed him."

Allison rose and went to stand next to him. Her eyes studied Jake's tormented face.

Jake continued, "I could have, no, I should've driven him home."

Allison pressed her fingers to his lips in an effort to silence him. "Don't go there, Jake. You couldn't know what would happen."

"I tell myself that," Jake said, in a low voice. "Still I keep wondering."

"Jake, listen to yourself. You sound like I did when I arrived. You know Austin. He did what he wanted to when he wanted to."

Jake had to smile at what she said. "Fierce pride and proud spirit," he confirmed.

Allison nodded, "Austin made his own decisions. He was coming home and I thank you for that. Knowing that will help all of us."

Allison gently lifted Jake's head. "Fate took my son. It wasn't your fault anymore than it was my fault or Richard's fault. Nobody can be responsible for the choices others make."

Great sorrow was evident in Jake's eyes when he looked at her. Allison gently placed her hand on his shoulder. "There were so many times I questioned my own decisions. That's why I came here. There were never any easy answers. There still aren't but I have fewer questions. We all question our decisions from time to time. Wouldn't it be nice to go through life with no doubts and no regrets? To do that I think a person would have to live a very shallow life."

Jake had to agree. "Life doesn't work that way. Ma used to say, 'Some things happen for no reason. That's just life. We can't continue to ask why and we have to keep on living'." Allison was relieved to hear the change in his voice. His tone had returned to normal.

Jake took Allison's chin in his hand. "That's what Austin would have wanted." Their eyes met and held.

"Austin was lucky that you cared enough to want to help him."

"Your son taught me more than I taught him. He taught me to live again. Austin also made me think more about how things might have been. He made me reflect a lot on my own life. As I told you, there had been a long, lonely gap in my life and your son filled a large void. It wasn't until he left that I realized how lonely I've been and now I'm aware of how lonely I am. My home seems too big, too empty." Jake shook his head, "I'm no longer content with my life."

The wind had come up. It played with Allison's hair. Jake raised his hand to remove a stray strand from her face. "Your hair is like satin," he said, as his smoky eyes studied her face.

Jake had liked the many different feelings that Allison excited in him; admiration, frustration, sympathy, understanding, desire - the last of which left him with a longing for someone to share his life with. With the women he'd known in his professional and personal life, Jake had enjoyed both friendship and camaraderie. There were many women over the years who would've accepted more, but Jake wouldn't accept less. Since Katherine, he'd never been tempted to live with another woman. Until now.

Jake took a step forward. Allison didn't move as Jake leaned toward her, his lips only a breath away. His nearness shook her. Allison tried to look away but her eyes had a will of their own. Jake's eyes darkened with desire.

"Don't," Allison pleaded. Yet he saw the fire in her eyes.

Jake gently lifted her face. Allison heard the faint sound of her own intake of breath. Her pulse accelerated wildly as Jake moved his face closer and she felt the light touch of his lips on hers. They were soft and incredibly warm. Allison closed her eyes and yielded to his kiss.

They were caught in the moment, no memories from the past, no thought for the future. Allison's senses stirred; a purely physical reaction that she couldn't control. As Jake held her in his arms it was easy to forget that she was committed to someone else.

"Oh, Allison," Jake cried, holding her tight. His husky voice revealed so much. Allison remained in Jake's arms aware that she needed caring arms around her as much as Jake needed Katherine. As much as Jake wanted her to be Katherine it would never be. Allison opened her eyes breaking the spell.

Jake felt her pull away. "I'm not going to apologize."

"There's no need to. It isn't me you wanted in your arms. Your need was for Katherine, not for me." Allison realized that her own feelings were what she wanted from Richard, not from Jake.

A mournful smile touched Jake's lips. "Perhaps it is for you. Since Austin left I've been letting go of Katherine. I want more in my life,

Allison. I want to love again. I need to live again. You've brightened a dark corner of my life and chased the shadows away."

"You are a wonderful man. I'm sure you'll find that happiness again but it can't be with me. Austin was your rescuer and, to you, I'm an extension of Austin. He opened a door and you went through it. I think you're afraid that if I go you may return to your 'glass world'. It won't happen, Jake."

Allison paused, struggling to find the right words for she didn't want to hurt this man. He'd been so kind to both her and her son. Her words were gentle when she spoke, "Just like Katherine, Austin will always be a part of your life. Austin will always be with me. Our common thread is Austin. That thread has intertwined our lives and brought us to this day but it is only a single thread. With the threads of my family I've woven something wonderful and I can't forget that. Just like Austin, I want to go home, too."

The sun was settling behind the horizon and the crimson lights were quickly fading. When the final curtain of black cloaked the countryside Allison knew the end had come. Her journey here was over. It was time to go home. "Jake, I'm leaving in the morning."

"I know." There was a sinking feeling in Jake's chest. It shouldn't matter to him on such short acquaintance but Jake knew he'd miss Allison the same way he'd missed Austin. Life was much more complicated when you lived in the real world.

Allison attempted to lighten the moment. "You've been most hospitable, kind sir, but I cannot impose on you any longer."

Jake bowed before answering, "It has been my pleasure, Your Highness." To which he added, "You are a remarkable lady, Allison Smith."

The stars sparkled brightly as the silvery moon hung in the velvet sky. It was a spectacular sight and Allison gazed in wonder. One star shone a little brighter than the others and she thought of Austin. Her sadness wasn't as intense as it had been when she'd left home and she knew that her days would become a little brighter in time. Allison continued to look out at the universe with renewed hope for tomorrow.

In time, she turned to Jake and said, "It's been another emotional day. Would you mind if I retire for the night?"

"Good night, Allison," he said softly. Jake leaned his head back and stared at the stars. He looked so forlorn. Allison moved indoors, leaving Jake alone with his thoughts.

In the guest room Allison undressed and climbed into bed. Images flashed through her mind. Allison tried to hold on to them as her thoughts chased one another. Back and forth, present to past, Austin to Katherine, Jake to Richard. She sighed as her thoughts stayed on Richard. It wasn't too late for them. Their flames of love may have been reduced to embers, but it was still there and it was worth rekindling. She knew she couldn't do it alone and now Allison knew she wouldn't have to. Richard could change. It was what she wanted more than anything. New questions darted through her mind. Had she really been so caught up with the children that Richard felt neglected? Was that part of the reason that he'd turned to work? Maybe she needed to change, too. Was that the truth of her reality? Allison smiled sadly. What had she always told Austin? The truth lies somewhere in the middle. Life is never just about you. Since being here, the pain had eased and with it some of her resentment had vanished. She'd been torn by her emotions for too long. Richard and life was not as black as it had seemed. Their whole family had to accept and adjust to the changes in their lives and learn from the experience. And move forward, toward the light, she promised.

Lying there, Allison wished that she could see into the future. Immediately, she questioned her wish. Had she know that she would have Austin for such a short time could she have loved him the same way or allowed him to live his life with wild abandonment? She knew the world was full of dangers. Would she have been over protective and smothered him with her own fears? Allison smiled. She wouldn't have. Austin wouldn't have accepted it and she wouldn't do it now with Jordie and Cassie. As a mother, she'd protect them in every way she could but she had to recognize that she wouldn't always be able to keep them safe. All she could do was let them know that they were loved and that both she and Richard would protect them the best they could. Life is a gift and the gift you pass on to your children is to teach them to become independent and to live each day to the fullness it allows.

She understood that the gift of life is today with only the hope of tomorrow. Now she knew she could cope with any tomorrow. The black sorrow was behind her. There would be other shadows in the years to come. She prayed that nothing would be as terrible as Austin's death. Their family, as it was, would never be the same. Their happiness had been shattered but they were still a family. If they held on to each other they would survive.

Chapter Fourteen

Early the next morning, Allison wandered onto the verandah and leaned against the railing. Last night she had lain to rest many of her demons and today she experienced an overwhelming feeling of confidence that everything would be okay.

The world around her was beginning to waken. God's color of the day was orange and he'd painted light brush strokes generously across the sky. The sky was alive and so was she. She was inspired by the beauty of this fresh new day brimming with promise. The sun filtered through the clouds and the birds in the treetops nearby sang out their morning song. Allison let her mind remain completely blank. She thought of nothing, she worried about nothing.

Allison didn't hear Jake join her but she was very aware of his gentle touch when he placed his strong hand on her shoulder. She turned and took the mug of coffee he handed her.

Neither spoke as they watched the sky grow bright. They were at peace with the stillness around them and the hope that a new day brings.

The time here had allowed Allison to emerge from the living darkness. Being here had wiped out the sadness that had engulfed her. Jake had given her the opportunity to pull her thoughts together once she had found the answers she was seeking.

Allison combed her hair with her fingers feeling the breeze play with it and cool her. She started to speak, her voice filled with emotion, "Jake, thank you."

Jake quickly interrupted, "No need for thanks. We've all benefited from our time together. Let's remember the good and let go of the bad." Jake was watching her with a thoughtful expression on his face. "It was my fate to meet you. You, and your son, have reminded me of all the adventures that life has to offer and the love that goes along with living life." Then he smiled that slow smile she'd come to expect.

Allison took a big drink of her coffee, which chocked her on the way down. She blamed the sudden tears in her eyes to that. "I'm glad you liked Austin."

"Who wouldn't? He was charming, powerful and intelligent." Jake quirked an eyebrow, "So different from the youth I first met. He may have still been a boy but he revealed a sense of decency and honesty that showed what kind of a man he'd be."

Allison's heart filled with pride and she didn't trust herself to speak.

"Your son was ready to try again, a little more mature and with a stronger sense of self- worth." Jake smiled, "As independent as ever and all the better for his experience."

Allison shook her head slowly, a strange little smile on her lips. "Austin was like that. He lived each day with a wonderful sense of adventure."

There was never a doubt in Jake's mind. "He challenged you once or twice?"

"Once or twice? Every new phase of his life brought new challenges. Maybe it was because he was my first but I believe Austin would've tried my patience even if he wasn't. It was never dull around our house."

Jake laughed just imagining their hectic home life.

"My heart still hurts when I think about Austin. Maybe it always will." Allison's voice caught, "It helps knowing that he was happy in the end. That knowledge will make a difference to all of us." The words she spoke could not alleviate the sense of loss she felt but the bitterness had left her voice. "Just knowing this lets me know that I can cope when I get back home."

Allison's jaw jutted out, a habit Jake now recognized and found endearing. Her mind was set. "I've accepted what's happened. I can now get on with my life. I will be happy again. Just as there are different kinds of happiness, there are different kinds of love."

Old feelings had been reawakened by both Austin and Allison and Jake had to speak his thoughts, "Love means leaving yourself open to all kinds of pain."

Allison knew he was referring to Richard. She rose to his defense. "So does life but life also rewards you in so many ways. Like all of us, Richard has his good points. I've portrayed him unfairly the last few days. He's a good man. Financially, we couldn't ask for a better supporter."

"What about emotionally, Allison?"

The question surprised her. "Why do you ask?"

"Are you willing to settle for being content? You seem to have little in common."

"We have the kids and that's a bond that nothing can break."

"I'll give you that. But you both have your own interests. His time is spent on work and yours is spent on the kids."

Allison gave way to the feelings she had to admit to. "I've been doing a lot of thinking while I've been here and not just about Austin," she confessed. "It's easy to remain negative about past mistakes and unhappiness. Easier, too, to stay behind that protective invisible wall."

Jake understood what she meant. "The wall is gone, Allison. I'm no longer bound by the past."

"But I am, Jake. I didn't realize how high the wall was between Richard and me. You can't see it when you're up close. It's not until you step back and look at the whole picture that you can see everything. Maybe it's not too late to tear my wall down. I have the tools," Allison stated simply. "Love, understanding and patience, to mention only a few. I can see how much we have. I need to help Richard see beyond the material. He and I need to be grateful for each other. Our family needs to be aware of our blessings and not let them fade into the background."

Allison smiled softly but Jake's face remained somber. So was his voice when he spoke, "Richard needs to connect with your kids on an emotional level and recognize that he must help mold them as they grow and develop."

"He will," Allison said with confidence. "The fact that Richard took the initiative to go away by himself to think about everything was a huge step for him."

Jake rubbed his open palm down his face. "I sincerely hope that Richard recognizes the need to change."

Allison nodded her head in agreement. "Richard wants to change. It's more than that. He's ready to change and he knows he can."

"Are you sure? Do you believe he can?"

Allison desperately hoped so. "My husband deserves the chance to find out," she answered, her heart full of compassion. She was no longer angry at Richard but at fate that had taken their son away. "Maybe, like Austin, I was running away, too." She wouldn't allow herself to deny it anymore. "Austin's death was so traumatic." As Allison thought about Richard and her children all her doubts vanished. "Somehow, I feel everything will be okay."

Faith would carry her forward and time would help her to heal.

Her voice was confident as she continued, "It's time to go home and celebrate Austin's life and bring back the laughter. I'll tell our family that it's okay to cry but not to stay bitter." She smiled a smile so radiant that the hidden shadows disappeared. Allison's eyes were as clear and bright as a child's. She had been exorcised of the demons that had haunted her before she came here.

Jake was happy for Allison and grateful for her time with him. "It's been a long time since I've enjoyed myself with anyone as much as I have with you. I'm thankful for the presence of you and Austin in my life, even though it was too short a time in both cases."

Still smiling, Allison ran a caressing hand over the angled line of Jake's jaw. He caught it and pressed the tips of her fingers to his lips. "Richard doesn't know how lucky he is to have you," Jake said, with deep feeling. His eyes clouded with shameful longing.

Allison gave a shaky laugh. "Oh, yes he does. I tell him all the time," Allison teased, trying to keep it light. "I'll never forget what you did for Austin. You were exceptionally kind and you gave him so much."

Allison felt the grip of warm, sure fingers as Jake took her hands in his. Jake spoke from his heart. "It was nothing compared to what he gave me."

"I'm glad he found his way here that night." Allison looked up and their eyes locked. Her voice was gentle as she confessed, "I'm glad that I came here, too, Jake. I have so much to be grateful for. Thank you for everything. Especially for giving me peace."

Jake pulled her closer and touched his lips to her forehead. The kiss was light and gentle. It was one of the nicest kisses she'd ever received. Then the moment was gone.

Allison let out a long, slow breath. She whispered, quietly, "I really have to go."

Jake simply nodded. He stood, hands deep in his pockets, and watched her go. Their paths must part so their separate lives could continue. Jake was left with a sense of emptiness because once again someone he cared for would be gone from his life. This time it was different. This time he'd been able to say good- bye.

Chapter Fifteen

Jake Hanson was excited to be at Ryan Millers' graduation for more than one reason. It was the end of a journey for Jake.

After Allison had left, Jake spent a lot of time thinking about both her and Austin. Jake recognized how much Austin had changed his life in such a short time and how Allison had allowed him to feel again. Jake had wanted to do something significant to symbolize the importance of Austin's life. It was the recognition of Austin's dilemma that inspired Jake to reach out to help someone else, someone who was a lot like Austin.

Because both Austin and Allison had talked so often of Ryan, it seemed natural to select him as his protégée. Jake also knew how proud someone like Ryan could be, so he'd been discreet. Jake had kept an eye on the boy over the last five years. He was as proud as any parent that this young man was standing on stage at the podium ready to give his valedictorian speech on behalf of his graduating class. The transformation over the last five years was immediately apparent. When Jake had first seen Ryan at Austin's funeral he was so thin and too pale. Today, before him, stood a vibrant young man with an air of confidence ready to take on all that life would give him to face. Shoulders squared, he was ready. Jake smiled to himself as he watched the other graduates; so young, so strong, so proud and so ready to take on the world.

Jake was hoping that Allison Smith would be there as well. He scanned the audience looking for her. In the third row, next to Ryan's mother, he saw her. Jake's breath caught as he gazed at Allison's familiar face; the high cheekbones, the straight sculptured nose, her dark and gleaming hair. As she turned to say something to the woman next to her, Jake saw her ready smile and remembered her candid blue eyes. Jake continued to watch Allison and he had to confess that over the years he'd thought of her more times than he cared to admit.

As Ryan started to speak the two women reached for each other and held hands. Both were so proud of the young man in front of them. Jake sat up straight to listen.

"Distinguished guests, ladies and gentlemen, graduates. It's an honor for me to be speaking today on behalf of today's graduating class as we commemorate our achievements. Each one of us set a course and achieved our goals. Today, we celebrate our accomplishments. As you see us here today, we look grown-up and have the appearance of sophistication and confidence." Nervous laughter filled the air, accented by several boisterous cheers. "Although we may have fears about the future, we have courage and faith in our abilities. We can conquer these fears because we've prepared ourselves for the exciting experiences that beckon us. Today, we stand before you, confident that we will make a difference in the future."

The boy's face was radiant. "Our lives are changing. We are ready to advance into a world that is also changing, more quickly than ever. Characters are based on the changes that we go through and our experiences, both positive and negative, have helped us to become who we are today. We have the strength of character to be successful as we accept the challenges."

"Graduation marks an important time in our lives. As we depart from these familiar surroundings we are once again at a very important crossroad in our lives. The road that led us here was familiar in the fact that we were still in a comfortable environment, though somewhat different than high school. Today, we are at a major intersection, for we no longer will be in that environment that has been a buffer in many ways. From this day forward we stand alone as independent adults. We all have paths to choose and we're free to make our own decisions."

The tone in Ryan's voice became more serious, "Each one of us is responsible for our own lives but we must choose our path carefully for it will affect our journey. Although we may stumble along the way, we will pick ourselves up and continue on that open road that lies ahead of us. We will maneuver along the curves, work hard to make it up the hills and enjoy the ride."

For a moment Ryan hesitated. As his gaze wandered over the crowd his eyes were bright, charged with emotion. "May I please take the liberty of having a few more moments of your time?" Seriousness crept into Ryan's tone as he turned to his peers, "For most of you, this is the first major intersection you're facing in your life. Five years ago, I was at an important crossroad in mine. Actually, it was a T-intersection and I knew that the road I was on had to come to an end. The time had come for me to make a life-changing decision. When you come to a crossroad you have choices, including whether to stay on the familiar road that you're on. At a T, you can only go one way or the other. Only you can decide what direction to take and a change will happen either way. You will be accountable for a decision that may affect the rest of your life."

Ryan turned back to the guests in front of him and his voice became very somber. He paused a moment, his expression taking on a faraway look. "I didn't graduate with my high school classmates like most of the graduates here today. I flunked out in my senior year because I got into trouble and I had to go to a drug rehab centre. I'm not looking for sympathy. Like everyone, I had to deal with the consequences of my own actions. I thought I was at the lowest point in my life. I wasn't. Not long after I got out of rehab and just weeks before graduation my best friend was killed and my dad died three weeks later."

Ryan had everyone's complete attention. "One summer day I went for a drive in the country. I drove aimlessly, for I had no destination in mind. Without warning, I'd come to a T- intersection and I didn't know which way to go. It was while I was sitting there wondering what to do that I realized that I didn't know where I was going in my life either. I know I sat there for a long time. It was that day that I made a life changing decision. The very next day I contacted the principal of my high school. After a lot of begging he finally agreed to let me back into school. I was determined to graduate. I wasn't going to let the dreams that my friend Austin and I had die like everything else. Somehow, I would go to college. All I needed was a miracle."

A smile lit the boy's face as he spoke, "Miracles do happen. A lawyer contacted me and told me that I had a benefactor who'd been keeping an eye on me and based on the fact that I would be graduating with honors he had a proposition for me. I have no clue as to who this person is or why he decided to help me. This anonymous benefactor would pay for my education as long as I continued to remain in the top ten percent of my class. My tuition and rooms would be paid for, plus there would be a sizable living allowance so I wouldn't have to work during the school year so I could concentrate of my studies. The summers had to be spent doing volunteer work. As long as these rules were met, the monies would continue until I graduated from the college of my choice. As long as I met his requirement, he would honor his. Well, as you can see, I did, and so did he."

There was no questioning the sincerity in Ryan's voice as he scanned the audience. "Through the lawyer, I sent an invitation to my benefactor for today's ceremony. If you are out there, I want to personally thank you for your most generous gift and for being my miracle."

Ryan turned and once again acknowledged his classmates, removing his cap as he spoke, "Believe in miracles and know that rays of hope can shine through even on your darkest days. On closing, I want to say one more thing to you, my fellow graduates. It is our time." A cheer went up along with all the other caps. Pandemonium erupted as graduates shouted and cheered. Jubilation filled the air.

Jake moved to the isle and watched as Allison came his way. He smiled as he stood there watching her approach. She looked over. Their eyes met and held. They smiled at each other for several seconds.

Allison's heart quickened. She felt the same warmth she'd felt when she'd been at his home. For a moment it was as if the years of separation had never happened.

Time stood still as they studied each other.

To Jake, she was more beautiful than he remembered. Gone were the shadows beneath her eyes. Back was the spark of life in those expressive eyes that had always looked so sad. Today, seeing her, he rejoiced.

To Allison, he was still a very disturbing man. He stood tall, shoulders square and posture erect watching her with his steady gray eyes. His hair was still dark but his sideburns were now liberally highlighted with gray. Then Jake smiled, that slow easy smile she remembered.

It was so good to see him again. Jake, along with certain memories of Austin, were tucked away together in a very special place in her heart. A place she shared with no one else.

Allison continued to walk toward him. Jake waited. She extended her hand, which Jake readily accepted. She treasured the warmth that flowed between them. "What a delightful surprise. Why are you here?" Her crystal blue eyes were as sharp as ever and she studied him closely.

Before Jake could reply, Allison cried, "You're Ryan's benefactor aren't you? Oh, you wonderful man."

Jake lifted his shoulders in a carefree gesture, smiled and admitted nothing. Allison respected his silence but was grateful for the circumstances that had brought them together again.

"You're a very kind man, Jake Hanson," Allison said. "But I already knew that."

Jake stepped back to hold her at arm's length, his eyes smiling. "You look wonderful. How are you?"

"I'm fine. Oh, Jake, it's wonderful to see you."

"It's good to see you again, too. Mom will be glad to hear that I saw you."

"Please say hello to Edna."

"I will. She liked you."

The feeling was mutual. Jake's mom had reached out to her with her heart and her words. They had remained friends. "We call each other occasionally."

"I know, she always tells me."

They looked at each other, started to laugh and immediately hugged each other. It erased all of the charged tension between them.

Jake drew back to look at her. His gray eyes darkened. "It's been a long time. A lot of years have gone by. You really do look wonderful," he said again.

"Time doesn't stand still. It's been five years, Jake. Are you going to meet Ryan? He's often wondered about you." It struck her again how thoughtful and considerate this man was.

Jake's eyes crinkled in the bright sunlight. "I will before I leave."

"Ryan's still very special to our family. This is such a happy day for us but it's filled with a little sadness, too."

Allison could see the query in Jake's eyes so she answered before he could ask, "Richard wanted to come but he's away with Jordie. Jordie's baseball team is in the state finals. Are you ready for this?" Allison asked. "Richard manages the team."

Seeing the look of surprise on Jake's face made Allison laugh out loud. "Oh, Jake. So much has happened since Austin died. The biggest change has been with Richard. Jordie graduated this year from high school. He's going to work for Richard this summer and if he enjoys the work he'll consider going into law. Who would've guessed?" Allison smiled sadly. "Would you believe Jordie's the same age that Austin was when he died?"

For a brief moment they were both lost in the past. It was Allison who brought them back. "Sometimes I get flashes of wonder thinking about what might have been. You know what I mean."

Jake nodded.

Allison shook her head, "I refuse to allow melancholy thoughts of Austin overshadow this incredible day. We're all so proud of Ryan. Richard took Ryan under his wing when his dad died. He's become like a son to us."

"Speaking of additional family, I have a new family as well," Jake said proudly.

This wasn't news to Allison. Jake's mom had told her about the simple ceremony in her back yard but Allison merely smiled and let Jake continue. "I met a lovely lady. I actually met her at Matt's. You do remember my brother, the ass?"

Allison giggled as she nodded her head. It was so refreshing to be with Jake.

"I'd gone out to the ranch. Gail told me that Matt was in the barn with the new vet, Dale Cross. You can imagine my surprise when Dale turned out to be a woman. I think Matt and Gail set me up. Dale and I got married two years ago. I now have a fifteen-year-old step-daughter named Lacey. She's starting to go through a metamorphosis and soon this 'ugly duckling' will be a swan. Then what am I going to do when young men start flocking to my door. Got any advice for a novice father?"

"You and Dale are on your own. I've raised boys and Cassie is only eleven. She's worse than the boys ever where. These days my overly sensitive little girl is a drama queen and everything is at the extreme ends of her emotional scale. It can be trying but it can also be very entertaining. I don't dare laugh at her antics but there are times."

"You are happy, Allison. I see it in your eyes."

"I am. Your mom told me something that I've never forgotten. She said nobody can make you happy but yourself. When you're happy those around you are happy. After leaving your home, I let go of the bitterness and the anger. Once I did that, I was able to help the rest of my family. We're much closer now. We talk a lot and we listen even more."

Jake took her hand and held it in his grasp. "It was good to see you, Allison." Their hands stayed clasped.

"You too, Jake." Allison leaned forward and kissed him on his cheek. Their eyes met as they exchanged a final farewell.

As Jake watched her walk away he smiled to himself. He was finally free of the past. It was interesting, he thought, how circumstances could change life. One incident, or in this case an accident, had altered all of their lives. His. Allison's. Ryan's. The threads of Austin's life, his journey, had woven all their lives together and their paths had crossed. They'd all come a long way over the years and each and every one of them had moved beyond that dreadful day as they endured their shadowed pasts. How important to remember that there are no shadows unless the sun is shining. Right now, the sun was shining high for all of them.

About the Author

She is a wife, she is a mother. She works full-time. One day she came across a homework assignment written by her teen-age son. It was an English assignment which was not his favorite subject. Her son had created a journal format, as if the entries were made by a teenage boy who ran away from home in anger. As a mother does, she wondered if there was something in her own son's life that initiated the entries. Was he troubled? Was there underlying anger to his own parents? Those few pages had left so much unwritten but they became the catalyst for the story to follow.

She is just an average person who was inspired to write. Little did she know how exciting it would be to create characters, each one individual and different. To face the challenge of describing what she wanted someone else to see with her words. To create emotions for someone to feel. She discovered a new passion that has taken her in a new direction in her life's journey.